Praise
POR

"[A] riveting history."

—Benjamin Schneider, *Los Angeles Times*

"John King is an architectural Indiana Jones, revealing the careening drama and the struggle for consensus as to what a city should be. An account that is both authoritative and fun to read."

—Anthony Flint, author of *Wrestling with Moses*

"King draws upon a deep understanding of architectural theory and the social history of his city to deliver an informative, entertaining and engaging book."

—Spencer Fleury, *Spectrum Culture*

"King recounts, in rich journalistic detail, the numerous twists and turns of this story: politics versus economics, historic versus 'progress,' beauty versus commerce, and all the many other angles."   —Ray Bert, *Civil Engineering*

"*Portal* shows how an analysis of the rise, decline, and rebirth of one iconic building can reveal the character and history of a city."

—Josh Stephens, *Planetizen*, Planetizen's
Top Planning Books of the Year

ALSO BY JOHN KING

Cityscapes: San Francisco and Its Buildings

Cityscapes 2: Reading the Architecture of San Francisco

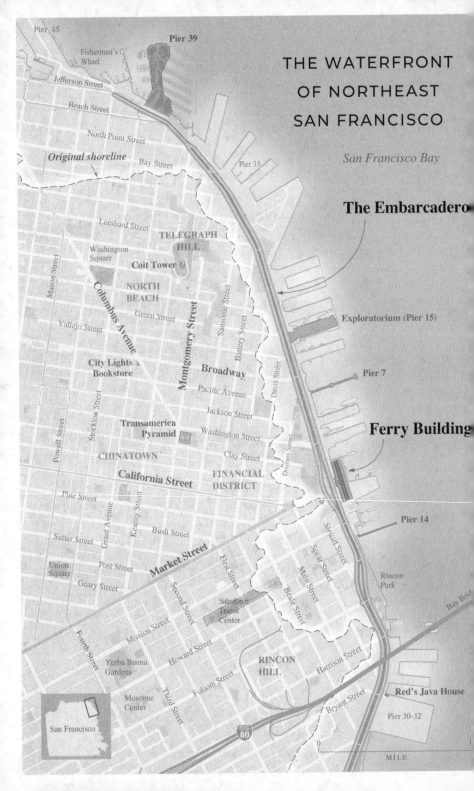

THE WATERFRONT OF NORTHEAST SAN FRANCISCO

San Francisco Bay

Pier 45

Fisherman's Wharf

Pier 39

Jefferson Street

Beach Street

North Point Street

Pier 33

Original shoreline

Bay Street

The Embarcadero

Lombard Street

TELEGRAPH HILL

Washington Square

Coit Tower

Exploratorium (Pier 15)

NORTH BEACH

Green Street

Columbus Avenue

Vallejo Street

Sansome Street

Battery Street

Pier 7

City Lights Bookstore

Montgomery Street

Broadway

Pacific Avenue

Davis Street

Ferry Building

Mason Street

Stockton Street

Jackson Street

Transamerica Pyramid

Washington Street

CHINATOWN

Clay Street

Powell Street

California Street

FINANCIAL DISTRICT

Drumm Street

Pine Street

Grant Avenue

Kearny Street

Bush Street

Pier 14

Sutter Street

Market Street

Stewart Street

Union Square

Post Street

Spear Street

Rincon Park

Geary Street

First Street

Main Street

Beale Street

Bay Brid

Market Street

Second Street

Salesforce Transit Center

Fourth Street

Mission Street

Howard Street

RINCON HILL

Harrison Street

Yerba Buena Gardens

Folsom Street

Red's Java House

Moscone Center

Third Street

Bryant Street

Pier 30-32

San Francisco

80

MILE

PORTAL

SAN FRANCISCO'S
FERRY BUILDING AND
THE REINVENTION OF
AMERICAN CITIES

JOHN KING

W. W. NORTON & COMPANY
Independent Publishers Since 1923

For information about permission to reproduce selections from this book,
write to Permissions, W. W. Norton & Company, Inc.,
500 Fifth Avenue, New York, NY 10110

For information about special discounts for bulk purchases,
please contact W. W. Norton Special Sales at
specialsales@wwnorton.com or 800-233-4830

Manufacturing by Lakside Book Company
Book design by Amanda Weiss
Production manager: Delaney Adams

ISBN 978-1-324-10523-7 pbk.

W. W. Norton & Company, Inc., 500 Fifth Avenue, New York, N.Y. 10110
www.wwnorton.com

W. W. Norton & Company Ltd., 15 Carlisle Street, London W1D 3BS

10 9 8 7 6 5 4 3 2 1

To Cynthia and Madeline,
in so many ways

CONTENTS

PORTAL

INTRODUCTION

A Trip down Market Street, 1906. *Prelinger Library & Archives.*

NO FILM OF EARLY SAN FRANCISCO IS MORE MESMERIZING THAN the twelve-minute *A Trip down Market Street*, a silent movie that was made by strapping a hand-cranked camera to the front of a cable car on April 14, 1906—just four days before the 7.9 temblor that left much of the city in ruins, leveled by earthquake and seared by flames.

Block by block, jostle by jostle, we roll forward slowly through a landscape of ghosts—not only the hatted men in dark coats and stiff bowties, or the woman in a bustled skirt boarding a cable car, or the boys darting in front of primeval automobiles, but the buildings that soon would be no more. Only one structure is obviously recognizable from the present, growing larger with each passing block: The San Francisco Ferry Building, unmistakable then as now with its steep gray clock tower above a horizontal wall of sandstone arches that terminate the view down the city's most prominent boulevard. As we draw close, a small copper-domed kiosk seems to protrude from the dignified structure; it houses the man who controls the wooden cable car turnaround where this journey comes to an end, before the vehicle is slowly rotated 180 degrees and sent back on its way.

Now imagine if that workaday apparition were to disappear and the camera continued inside, into the Ferry Building as we know it today. The layered early twentieth-century garb would give way to T-shirts and artisanal tote bags and casual business attire; the dim commotion of 1906's ticket counters and baggage storage rooms would smooth into a skylit bazaar of colorful plenty, showcasing olive oil from Sonoma County, cheese crafted in Marin, breads baked inside the building and wines from across the state. Straight ahead, one would see blue sky and blue water, the natural bay that explains why the structure originally named the Union Depot and Ferry House was put here to begin with. The film has a voyeuristic quality; unlike the viewer, these people have no idea what is to come. But it is also thrilling. It immerses us in the casual bustle of what then was the nation's tenth largest city and fifth busiest port, a prosperous commercial center along the Pacific Ocean that beckoned political and business leaders intent on expanding America's global reach. Old ways of transportation share space with the new, as cars impatiently coexist with the horse-drawn delivery wagons and slow-moving streetcars.

So much is different now, not just the landscape. San Francisco's population count hasn't kept up with cities elsewhere—today the city is only the fourth largest in its own state—but it is a true international metropolis. The city has redefined social boundaries and shaped trends in music and literature; the region's technological innovations have altered every aspect of how today's world functions. None of this is on view in those seductive twelve minutes captured nearly 120 years ago. But one thing remains: that constant at the end of Market Street, looming large in every way.

. . .

Every city has a landmark like this, a building through which one can read the larger history. The transformations that occurred around it—and how they parallel what has occurred in other American waterfront cities during the past 125 years—are the subject of this book.

Location is key to the Ferry Building's enduring relevance. The structure that opened in 1898 was deliberately placed at the point where San Francisco met the harbor, the city's reason for existence. The utilitarian wooden piers of the working port jabbed into the bay on the Ferry Building's north and south flanks. Market Street unfurled to the west toward the green hills that fold upward in the center of the city.

The purpose was functional: to provide a modern depot for ferries and their passengers arriving in San Francisco. The architectural aims were grandiose. "The tower is intended not only to mark the foot of Market Street and be the first object of interest to those coming over the bay," declared the officials in charge of the Port, "it will serve as a beacon and clock

The Ferry Building and Slips from the Bay,
San Francisco, Cal.

An early twentieth-century postcard. *Glenn Koch collection.*

tower which can be seen for many miles in every direction."
The classical look was inspired by a twelfth-century bell tower
in Seville, Spain, but the design tested the engineering limits
of the 1890s: the foundation of unreinforced concrete weighed
fifty-six thousand tons and sat atop 5,117 piles milled from
trunks of Douglas fir from Oregon that were lodged eighty
feet into soft mud below the tides. At the peak of service in
1930, forty-three ferry boats transported forty-seven million
people from five cities along the bay, creating a surge of daily
foot traffic that locals boasted was exceeded only by Charing
Cross Station in London. Equally important, the bayside depot
was "more universally accepted as a symbol of San Francisco
than any other single landmark," the federal Works Projects
Administration's guide to the region declared in 1940, serving "to identify the city in the minds of countless travelers
throughout the world." They didn't even need to see it in person. The Ferry Building adorned postcards and guidebooks,
shorthand for the city by the bay.

Yet by midcentury the symbol was in decline, its role as a transportation hub usurped by two adventurous bridges that linked San Francisco with neighboring counties to the north and east and, by extension, the nation beyond. The spans were celebrated as infrastructural triumphs, and the Golden Gate Bridge between San Francisco and Marin glowed with powerful grace. They also showed how automobiles had become synonymous with the American way of life, glorifying individual convenience over shared communal landscapes—a shift that led to such abominations as the double-deck Embarcadero Freeway that shoved across Market Street and opened in 1959, a crude barrier that severed the Ferry Building from the rest of the city until the freeway itself was demolished—by choice, not earthquake—thirty-two years later.

The decades after World War II were harrowing times for traditional cities. Diverse neighborhoods were destroyed in the name of "renewal." Handsome commercial buildings were leveled to make room for corporate high-rises, bets on the future that, too often, undermined what made their cities desirable to begin with. The Ferry Building itself was threatened with demolition but survived. Market Street wasn't as lucky, with many of its embellished masonry landmarks from the early 1900s replaced by unadorned shafts of metal and glass. The Embarcadero's hectic working waterfront grew quiet as worldwide changes in the shipping industry left piers to rot.

Amid all these pressures, and despite its forlorn isolation, the Ferry Building emerged as a new sort of civic symbol. Its endurance signaled San Franciscans' determination to protect their city's physical character from the standardized formulas of would-be urban saviors, and suggested there were other options for cities looking to reinvent themselves—an optimism justified in 2003, when the landmark came back to life.

Like the once-industrial central waterfronts of cities like New York and Boston, San Francisco's Embarcadero has been recast as a lifestyle zone. As for the Ferry Building, its renaissance of the past twenty years faces a threat from a source that nobody could have imagined when plans were drawn up in 1893. Climate change, and the rising bay tides that will accompany it, are challenging the artificial shoreline that engineers imposed before such a concept as sea level rise existed.

• • •

The saga of the Ferry Building is a story of people, as well.

Architect A. Page Brown came to San Francisco from New York in 1889 with society patrons and built an influential practice that aroused envy from his peers before he died just six years later, the victim of a freak accident involving a runaway horse. Cyril Magnin, friend to socialites and governors, led a charmed life in San Francisco as the owner of a trendsetting fashion chain but found that an urban waterfront cannot be overhauled like a clothing line. San Francisco mayor Art Agnos in 1990 staked his political future on tearing down the Embarcadero Freeway that had been damaged in an earthquake the year before—and alienated so many car-dependent voters that he was defeated when he ran for reelection.

Other people who enter the story cherished the old waterfront. They saw the building as an essential part of the city and felt it should not be sacrificed for a "new" San Francisco. Herb Caen was one, the columnist who stepped off a ferry in 1936 on his first day of work at the *San Francisco Chronicle* and was bid farewell by fans in 1997 at a public celebration held below the clock tower. In 1962, he made clear his feelings about what was at stake as city leaders sought to remake downtown's skyline: "The line, and I don't mean a mythical one, must surely be drawn at the Ferry Building," he wrote. "I can't think of a landmark I'd fight harder to save." Caen meant this in a rhetorical sense. The longshoremen who had worked those piers on either side of the Ferry Building, by contrast, endured battles along the Embarcadero that were deadly and real. They shut down the Port in a 1934 strike for more equitable hiring conditions, a ten-week struggle that exploded into violence with two union workers shot and killed by police and, days later, tanks rumbling past the contested piers.

Forty years later, not yet even in his teens, Keba Konte would visit the same area with his father around dawn to fish for crab from piers he remembers as being "in various stages of disrepair, no rails or anything," using fish heads in a net as bait. Now he owns Red Bay Coffee, which opened during the pandemic and does brisk business in a glassy Ferry Building space that faces the bay.

Back when the waterfront was at perhaps its most moribund state, Konte loved being there with his father and hardly anyone else: "You went out on a pier, you had it all to yourselves. For a kid like me it was just background, and the Ferry Building was just another boring building." Today, he's a Black business owner who can feel how having a presence in one of San Francisco's best-known landmarks gives him credibility in a society where people still are judged by the color of their skin.

"Because we're there," Konte says, referring to the Ferry Building, "as far as other people are concerned, we're qualified to be anywhere in the city. It's such an iconic location."

• • •

Ultimately, San Francisco's Ferry Building is what Konte describes, a civic icon. Not in the inflated marketing hype of

The Ferry Building, 2021. *Courtesy of Noah Berger.*

developers who slap the word on each structure they erect, or the lazy verbiage of people trying to puff up the importance of everything from burger joints to sitcoms to vintage automobiles, but something with undeniable cultural resonance.

"From the beginning, it has been the perfect expression of so many aspects of the city, shaped by different forces and different eras," says Anthea Hartig, the Elizabeth MacMillan Director of the Smithsonian's National Museum of American History in Washington, D.C.

Hartig knows the building well, having worked in San Francisco nearly fifteen years before being appointed to the Smithsonian post in 2018. She admires the architecture, plus the quality of its restoration, but in a deeper sense she's captivated by how the 125-year-old structure has remained relevant to a city that has been redefined again and again.

"It remains an icon, and it remains a beacon," Hartig says. "Even if the Ferry Building no longer serves the bulk of its original (transportation) intent, it remains the point where everything comes together."

This is a powerful role for a building to play in twenty-first-century America, where fresh fissures lace through every aspect of a society that never was truly united. Nor is the Ferry Building some egalitarian oasis, not with a caviar-centric cafe and a "luxury dog boutique" selling such fare as $10 jars of chicken meatballs for you-know-who. But it also is where affluent locals jog by people who look like they have nowhere else to go, with everyone together gazing out at the bay. Tourists are abundant, as are Bay Area residents who have been regulars at the Saturday farmers market since it opened in 2003.

By virtue of its location, the Ferry Building has always marked the intersection of the natural world and the built terrain. It's increasingly a barometer of the economy, too. Many ground-floor retail spaces emptied during the pandemic. Upstairs, along the central passage known as the grand nave with its intricate tile mosaic floor, office space is leased by high-tech tenants such as Google and Niantic, the creator of Pokémon GO.

"The Ferry Building is a hub, but also an indicator," Hartig says. "It raises the question of who is the city for, and who is allowed to partake of what it offers?"

Earlier in our conversation, she framed the question in a quite different way.

"If the Ferry Building could bear witness, can you imagine the stories it would tell?" Hartig said. "That building has been through so much."

PART I

HEYDAY

ONE

THERE WAS NO PRESSING NEED FOR A GRANDIOSE FERRY TERMI-nal in the San Francisco of 1890, particularly one topped by a sky-piercing clock tower, and nobody back then claimed otherwise. Some people on arriving ferries were here to see the exotic metropolis that in forty-five years had grown from a ramshackle hamlet of a few hundred residents into the nation's eighth largest city, but the vast majority of the riders spilling out toward Market Street were commuters en route to work from bayside cities to the east and north. They disembarked from stout vessels with wooden hulls and paddle wheels, belching smoke from dark chimney stacks. Passengers then strode briskly to cable-pulled street cars designed to ascend hills too steep for horse-drawn vehicles.

Even if someone *was* inclined to linger along the bay, there was little in the way of recreation or genteel attractions to reward their interest. This was the largest port on the West Coast, a cacophony of commerce with carriages rumbling back and forth over cobblestones and dirt, piled high with boxes and burlap sacks filled with everything from coffee beans to fresh pineapple. Some of these raw treasures had arrived from across the Pacific, perhaps Hawaii or the Philippines, others from the agricultural fields of California's central valley. Across the way from the ferries was the produce district, a haphazard terrain of narrow crowded streets.

Sights and sounds aplenty. Not a place for a casual stroll.

Nor was there anything majestic about the spot where most ferries had pulled in or departed for the past fifteen years: Ferry House, a string of sheds behind a wooden front, the one embellishment being the names of destinations served by Southern Pacific Railroad that were painted along the cornice. The railroad was the biggest tenant in the modest structure run by the Board of State Harbor Commissioners, the state agency that owned the Port: the Board had built this facility on the shoreline between Market and Clay streets in 1875 to remedy the "very inadequate accommodations" that existed prior, a polite reference to the wharves that jutted out from the muddy edge of the city wherever an operator had secured a perch. As for the structures the Ferry House would displace, the *San Francisco Chronicle* dismissed them as "a miserable lot of old tumble-down, rickety buildings," and said that with their departure "it is to be hoped the fragrance of this neighborhood will be changed for the better."

The settlement had only been given the name San Francisco in 1847. Until then it was known, to the extent that it was known at all, as Yerba Buena—Spanish for "good herb," a reference to an aromatic minty vine that grew profusely in the dunes and brush along the inconspicuous cove. Yerba Buena's setting made it surprisingly hospitable to traders or stragglers: it was close by the entrance to one of world's great natural bays, where more than five hundred square miles of water were cut off from the ocean except for a steep narrow outlet one mile wide and three miles long. Ships that did enter from the Pacific Ocean could head north and travel inland through the delta fed by what now are called the Sacramento and San Joaquin Rivers, or sail south along the marshy shoreline of a forty-mile-long peninsula that ended in shallow tidal flats.

Any captain who turned the helm starboard would soon spy Yerba Buena Cove, a scalloped lagoon nestled against broad hills that muffled the afternoon winds which otherwise would have blown sand in from the Pacific dunes. There *were* dunes to the south of the cove, some as high as ninety feet, but they formed a backdrop for the calm inlet that was just deep enough for arriving ships to pull near and unload cargo onto small boats floating above mudflats that stretched from a sandy beach near where Battery Street and Broadway are today.

The handful of mostly White traders and settlers who had drifted east from the United States in the years before 1847 weren't the first people to call the peninsula home, to be sure. Small tribal communities of Ramaytush Ohlone lived in what now is San Francisco, each with up to thirty or fifty people who moved as needed within the lands they knew, gathering fish and other sustenance during the day and returning to homes made from tule reeds. The lightweight structures might be twenty or thirty feet in diameter and ten feet high, each with an opening at the peak to allow air to circulate. There were defined boundaries between the small tribes, but their paths often crossed and intermarriage occurred.

This freedom ended when an expedition of Franciscan padres pushed into California from the Spanish Empire's Mexican colonies, reaching far enough north by 1776 to establish Mission San Francisco de Asís, which is near today's Dolores

Park and was then alongside a year-round creek that fed into the bay, Arroyo de los Dolores. The soldiers on the expedition continued farther north to erect a walled base—the Presidio of San Francisco—on a perch above the strait where the bay and ocean met. The Ramaytush Ohlone who didn't flee, and who survived the diseases brought from Europe by the invaders, were forced into fixed housing and mandatory labor to support the mission's ranching and farming operations, which extended to the south and east and are estimated to have covered more than one hundred square miles. Perhaps 1,100 men, women and children from various Ohlone tribes around the bay were living in virtual slavery at the mission when Mexico won its war of independence from Spain in 1821. The new government reduced the mission—by then known as Mission Dolores—to the status of a parish church and brought its farm and ranch operations to an end. The garrison at the Presidio was sent farther north to discourage Russian traders along the Mendocino coast from encroaching on the spacious natural harbor down the way.

Both settlements were all but empty by 1835. A few years later only eight Native Americans were recorded as living at what remained of the mission.

The year 1835 is when Mexico established its own small pueblo on Yerba Buena Cove, complete with an alcalde (mayor) and eleven electors. The lone wharf became a microscopic but official port, and the alcalde appointed a young American whaler, William Richardson, as the harbormaster—who also erected what might have been Yerba Buena's first formal "structure," a home consisting of four tent posts with a ship's sail stretched tight above them. Pretty soon he had neighbors: Yerba Buena attracted traders who saw a niche market in serving the vessels that entered the bay looking to purchase hides

and pelts, and in 1839 a Swiss ship captain-turned-surveyor
named Jean Jacques Vioget was hired to draw up a street grid
for the young pueblo, nothing fancy, eight blocks in all. Job
completed, Vioget decided to stick around and open a tav-
ern. Why not?

Life in Yerba Buena continued along these easygoing lines
until July 1846, when the USS *Portsmouth* entered the cove
and local residents learned that the United States had declared
war on Mexico that May. The ship dropped anchor, several
dozen marines and sailors went onshore to the adobe custom house that was Yerba Buena's lone substantial government building, and they raised the stars and stripes in an
appropriately laid-back changing of the guard. By the time
the Mexican-American War was over, the United States had
used it to annex five hundred thousand square miles stretching
from Texas to the Pacific Ocean, while the people living along
Yerba Buena Cove now called their hamlet San Francisco in a
nod to the old mission. They also hired a new surveyor who
extended Vioget's grid inland from the cove and plotted a
set of longer rectangular blocks diagonally to the south. The
two grids met awkwardly at what was to be a broad Market
Street, running from the bay southwest toward Twin Peaks
and the remnants of Mission Dolores and continuing from
there as far as the city needed—not that there seemed to be
any foreseeable need.

Then came the discovery of gold in 1848, 130 miles to the
east, and San Francisco exploded.

. . .

The vast protected bay was the ideal starting point for
would-be miners arriving by ship from the East Coast, Europe,
and Asia—a spot where a prospector could exit one vessel and

board a smaller one heading east through the delta to Sacramento, where the journey to the Gold Country switched to land for its final leg. With the transcontinental railroad still twenty years in the future, San Francisco became the port of call for the Gold Rush and everything happening inland. Some savvy newcomers also grasped that there were fortunes to be made servicing the gold seekers fresh off the boat, rather than risking the unknown in search of gold themselves. The first California census in 1852 recorded a population for San Francisco of 34,776. Vioget's expanding grid had come in handy, the mapped rectangles easily divided into sixths and sold off to speculators, with proceeds filling the city's coffers.

By then, Yerba Buena's benign cove was all but gone. The initial entry point for fortune hunters was a beached steamer near the shoreline at Vallejo Street, which stuck out far enough into the bay that gold seekers could climb aboard from other vessels and reach dry land via a gangplank from the steamer's deck. Hardly an ideal situation, given the passenger armada arriving from all corners of the globe, and speculators soon built at least one large wharf extending out beyond the mud flats to deeper water. The city then allowed anyone with money or resources to do the same, selling tidal lots as real estate. The new owners installed rickety wharves to reach their submerged property and erected wooden buildings on piles along them.

"The city during the first few years of congestion, instead of being developed inland . . . became largely an aquatic settlement," wrote one early historian. Nor was the settlement restricted to those sanctioned structures on nonexistent soil. As crews of passenger ships left their posts to join the gold seekers, ever-inventive San Franciscans turned more than one hundred abandoned vessels into floating storage sheds or makeshift businesses, some of them topped with shingle roofs. More than one visitor likened the bizarre and ever-morphing scene to Venice—until this strange elongation of San Francisco went up in flames in May 1851 during a blaze that destroyed twenty-two blocks of the still-compact city.

The city was rebuilt, quickly and without question—there was money to be made!—and by 1855 the waterfront had migrated as much as six blocks east of Yerba Buena's original shore. Instead of wharves, a new landscape emerged of wood-plank roadways lined with lots created by filling the shallow tidal flats with anything close at hand: ship hulls, building debris, sand carted in from the fast-diminishing dunes. These muddy acres provided an edge from which *new* wharves could extend, so that San Francisco could grow yet more.

Was this any way to build a city that would last? A consortium of seven wharf operators who had made themselves wealthy by driving piles into the bay said no. "The city front, for all purposes of commercial convenience, is being rapidly destroyed," they warned in an 1859 engineering report that described how the transplanted sand would ooze out into the bay or clog the water along docks where ships were supposed to berth. What the city needed was a stone seawall to lock a solid shoreline in place, the consortium argued. Do this, and the Port's future was assured.

Though their rationale made sense, the wharf owners hadn't commissioned the report out of civic altruism. They proposed building the seawall themselves, at their own initial expense. The city in return was expected to waive taxes on the new seawall—and to grant the consortium "the entire and exclusive right of wharfage, dockage, anchorage and tolls . . . forever." City officials were only too willing to approve the giveaway, shrugging off protests from startled residents and competing wharf operators, but the arrangement was vetoed by John Downey, California's governor at the time.

Freebooting initiatives like this—not just the audacity of the proposal but its embrace by city leaders who had already padded revenues with the sale of watery real estate—explains why the state government in 1863 decided California's busiest and best-situated port was too important to be left in local hands. That April, the state legislature approved an act transferring the waterfront to the newly created Board of State Harbor Commissioners, based in San Francisco but consisting of three members to be appointed by the governor.

The dubious state of the Board's inheritance was made clear on the eve of its first meeting, when one wharf collapsed and sent 150,000 feet of lumber into the water. Not long after this, several wharf owners went to court, saying the Port had no right to evacuate them, since they had signed their leases with the city—a time-consuming legal fight a Board-friendly historian later described as "litigation unparalleled in the annals of any other harbor in the world." Only when this was resolved in the Port's favor did commissioners begin working with engineers to devise "a permanent and effectual barrier to the encroachments of the sea."

The plan finally drawn up and approved in the 1870s mapped the future shoreline as an arc curving three miles from a fishing settlement along North Beach down to Mission Bay, another large cove that was in the process of being filled and altered with commerce in mind. The design called for each stretch of seawall to consist of a dike-like bulwark built of stones rising from a trench dredged at least twenty feet into the bay mud, rising like a stubby pyramid and capped with concrete. The mudflats trapped behind the seawall allowed the

Port to create new land for an industrial roadway—then called East Street but now the Embarcadero—that was wide enough to allow cargo to be loaded and unloaded with relative ease.

With the seawall underway, it made sense to build what became the Ferry House that opened in 1875—to serve people crossing the bay, but also to clear out older wharves so the next stretch of seawall could go in. The new location also was close to the city's emerging business district. The same Board report that bid farewell to the "very inadequate accommodations" of the prior docks emphasized that the provision of "four ferry slips and sheds . . . will afford to the traveling public superior facilities, as the ferries will connect with several of the street railroad lines."

San Francisco certainly wasn't the first ambitious metropolis to treat shallow water as future real estate. Across the continent, Boston was established on the Shawmut Peninsula in 1630 by a band of Puritans who had sailed west from England earlier that year and chose to settle on the promontory in part for self-protection: The neck of soil connecting it to the mainland was barely wide enough for a single road. Boston's population was crossing the one hundred thousand mark by the time that Yerba Buena took the name San Francisco, and filled land from flattened hills had erased any semblance of Shawmut Peninsula's original form. The cavalier abuse of tidal lands in San Francisco was also in line with the nation's self-proclaimed creed of Manifest Destiny, a term coined in 1845 on the eve of the war with Mexico. American newcomers after the Gold Rush stole thousands of acres in the city from Mexican Californians, who had been promised the right to continued property ownership in the treaty that ended the Mexican-American War. They moved onto the contested land,

The Ferry House after it opened in 1875. *Port of San Francisco.*

declared it to be their own, and then leveraged courtroom delays and confusing legal processes to outlast their victims.

· · ·

In this city that by 1870 was nearing a population of 150,000, growth spilled in all directions. New frontiers opened as soon as infrastructure or innovation allowed.

The sand dunes on the south flank of Yerba Buena Cove were a receding memory, leveled to create the land beneath the new eastern blocks of Market Street and the buildings that rose along it. Not long afterward, once-remote Mission Bay was sliced in two from north to south by the aptly named Long Bridge, a wooden structure constructed in the mid-1860s that was wide enough to hold railroad tracks and a saloon, with room left over for people to promenade on Sundays or to fish for smelt over the railings. The bridge also allowed industry to migrate a safe distance from the "older" city. Firms from sugar refineries and rope makers to steel mills settled into what then was called Potrero Point, a thick band of solid land jutting into the water. Many of the workers built small homes on the slopes of Potrero Hill directly to the west.

As for innovation, there's no better example than the saga of Andrew Hallidie—a Scottish immigrant whose story shows how for San Francisco, the Gold Rush paid dividends that had nothing to do with nuggets of ore.

Hallidie arrived at the age of sixteen in 1852 with his father after a journey that was typical for the era: they sailed from Liverpool to New York in two weeks, followed by a layover until the pair could find space on a ship jammed with gold hunters heading west by way of Panama. Father and son disembarked on one side of the isthmus, crossed to the other, and boarded a ship that touched down in Yerba Buena Cove five months after their departure from England. The father, Andrew Smith, gave up and returned to Scotland four years later. The son, who had added the surname Hallidie in honor of an uncle, stayed behind and continued his quest for riches. What he discovered wasn't gold, but his own knack for engineering, and while working at a quartz-mining mill he cobbled together a wire rope for moving cars transporting ore up and down the mountain.

"I was a passenger in the bark that carried me on in the voyage of life," Hallidie later mused, and at the age of twenty-one he realized the place for him to pull ashore was behind the lines. The young Scot moved to San Francisco and began manufacturing his wire rope, a lucrative business that by happenstance prepared him to invent the quintessential form of place-specific transportation, the cable car. The reason the city hadn't grown due west of the original cove was that the steep hills protecting it from ocean winds couldn't be easily traversed, no matter what the city's optimistic street grid might suggest. Even the slopes directly west of Montgomery Street were daunting for horses pulling carts or carriages, and that's what Hallidie later said gave him the idea.

> *I was largely induced to think over the matter from seeing the difficulty and pain the horses experienced in hauling the cars up Jackson Street, from Kearny to Stockton Street, on which street four or five horses were needed for the purpose—the driving being accompanied by the free use of the whip and voice, and occasionally by the horses falling and being dragged down the hill on their sides . . .*

Hallidie decided to take an aerial transport system he had devised for industrial mining—continuously moving cables that could transport buckets filled with ore, with a coal-fueled boiler to provide the power—and replicate it underground. He and partners purchased a city franchise to install a test run on a six-block stretch of Clay Street that rose 307 feet to the summit of what then was called California Hill. Two ditches were dug with space for a wooden turntable at either end, sand was added to improve the traction, and a looped set of thick cables three inches in diameter was laid into the ditches and attached to the wheels that would keep them taut when the need arose. The cable car itself was a variation of a horse-drawn carriage, but with grips at the bottom that latched into the cables.

On a foggy morning before dawn on August 2, 1873, Hallidie and several of his partners gathered at Clay and Jones to see if the thing would actually work. The intended driver-to-be was spooked by the 16 percent grade, so Hallidie took control, spinning a wheel to lower the grip until it latched onto the cables. The car descended, noisily but without incident, and supporters at the bottom cheered Hallidie before helping rotate the wooden turntable so that the small carriage could head back uphill.

"Had I been less familiar from experience with the problem or had I less confidence," Hallidie later wrote, "it might have been many years before the cable system would have reached the point of practical application." Instead, by 1890 there were nine cable car lines in operation. Four of them reached west to Golden Gate Park, a swath of sand dunes of about one thousand acres that had been set aside for public space in 1870, and slowly was being nurtured as a green retreat complete with playgrounds, promenades and a glassed-in conservatory devoted to tropical plants.

California Hill's upper reaches became the domain of wealthy businessmen, the most powerful being the "Big Four"—Charles Crocker, Mark Hopkins, Collis P. Huntington, and Leland Stanford, the quartet that had built the western half of the transcontinental railroad and then established companies such as Southern Pacific Railroad to dominate California's rail routes. If venerated by some people in the state, these magnates were vilified by many others as they flaunted their fortunes with ostentatious mansions atop what was soon nicknamed Nob Hill. The largest belonged to Crocker, a one-time Sacramento dry-goods merchant who led the operations in the field and was said to pack three hundred pounds on his six-foot frame. After returning to California, rich beyond imagination, he chose to build a three-story extravaganza that filled nearly an entire block. He wanted the whole block, but an undertaker with a small parcel refused to sell, so Crocker had workers erect a forty-foot-high "spite fence" on the property lines that they shared.

Both the fence and its owner were caricatures of excess in the Gilded Age—a term coined by Mark Twain as the title of his novel that was published in 1873, the same year Hallidie boarded his first cable car on Clay Street. A subsequent business initiative demonstrated the Big Four's continued lust for money and control: the quartet founded its own cable car line running up California Street, Nob Hill's main artery, with their own design so that Hallidie couldn't claim a share of the profits.

. . .

Compared to excess and westward expansion, the low-slung sheds that constituted the Ferry House soon lost whatever novelty they had possessed. A full remake of the waterfront where ferries pulled in "cannot be pushed too rapidly to please the public-minded citizen," wrote one local publication, the *Criterion*, in 1889. "The old rookeries that now stand in front of the city are its disgrace. They should be torn away with all possible speed." And what might replace them? "A structure suitable to the great growth that the city is experiencing," the *Criterion* proclaimed. "The city cannot have too many attractive edifices."

The harbor commissioners were of similar mind—eager not just to crowd in more slips and sheds, but to erect a structure with an architectural character fitting for the city struggling to move beyond its raucous past. The commission put out a contract for a more substantial seawall section at the foot of Market Street that would include a solid concrete retaining wall to provide the beginnings of a foundation for a depot that was intended to serve as nothing less than "a stately passenger depot at the gateway to the 'Metropolis of the Pacific.'"

The idea that a transportation structure could double as

a civic temple was in vogue back then, especially in prosperous growing cities that felt they had something to prove. The showcases tended to be train stations, no surprise, often with ornate masonry facades and arches that set a grand tone while hiding the structural sheds for the rail platforms. The first, Providence's Union Station, could have been a lean Gothic cathedral; Camden Station in Baltimore, which opened in the mid-1850s a few years after the one in Providence, was like some super-scaled Colonial church.

As early as 1875, the trade journal *Building News* declared that "railway termini and hotels are to the nineteenth century what monasteries and cathedrals were to the thirteenth century." A decade later, as San Francisco's no-nonsense Ferry House fell out of favor, any Bay Area resident who had visited Chicago or Detroit or Philadelphia or a dozen other eastern cities had seen what was possible. For many locals, at least those concerned with San Francisco's national image, the comparison was not flattering: "I am in favor of the new depot, because the old one is a disgrace," one trader told the *Chronicle* a few years later. "Strangers from the East who visit San Francisco laugh at its approaches, and wonder if there is such a thing as enterprise out here."

The challenge for the harbor commissioners was that such a project would be prohibitively expensive for a small state agency, which already could only add new sections to the seawall as revenues allowed. The landmark railway stations back east tended to be built by ambitious railroad empires with great resources, who conceived their stations as opportunities for self-promotion. Rather than go this route, the Board wanted to finance the new depot by selling bonds, $600,000 worth, a strategy that would require approval from California's legislature. The Board made its case by stressing not the glamor of a regal entrance to San Francisco, but the long-term economic wisdom of an approach that would guarantee "the absolute ownership and control by the state of all the water-front property," to quote the commission's biennial report from 1890. The legislature signed off the next year and put the bond measure on the November, 1892, state ballot.

. . .

As might be expected, not all corners of California were enthusiastic about steering money into a project that primarily would be for commuters in faraway San Francisco—or that a major beneficiary would be Southern Pacific, the rail giant soon to be made infamous by novelist Frank Norris as "the Octopus." Southern Pacific was the villain of choice for labor organizers and progressive politicians who viewed the monolith—or vilified it to their supporters—as a corrupting puppeteer pulling the strings of too many state officials. Even in San Jose, an agricultural community of nineteen thousand residents at the southern end of the bay, the *San Jose Herald* urged a "no" vote from "every citizen who does not believe in taxing himself for the benefit of the railroad company." This was also the broadside sounded by the *San Francisco Call*, a newspaper that characterized Southern Pacific as the force "to whom we owe the abominations in this city and state" and warned that the depot bond "would assist the plunderers to get a firmer grasp upon our throats."

The *Call* was goading its hometown rivals to punch back, and they did. The *Chronicle* in particular scoffed at such "senseless croaking": "The corporations are indifferent whether their passengers find their way through rickety sheds or a palatial depot," read one editorial. Four days later, the *Chronicle* interviewed downtown businessmen who, without exception, enthusiastically supported the bond. A recurring theme in their comments was the desire of many San Franciscans—if we can borrow a twenty-first-century term—to reposition their brand.

The new depot "should be a building that the city can be proud of," said one man, whose company sold stoves. "It should be a monument to San Francisco's progress." On election day, California voters gave their blessing to the bond measure—narrowly, by 866 votes out of the 181,726 that were cast. But a win is a win. A waterfront that had been a chaotic work in progress since the Gold Rush was now to be anchored by a structure of statuesque grandeur. Almost everyone entering the city would pass through this portal, a building designed to show the world that San Francisco was here to stay.

TWO

TWO MONTHS BEFORE THE STATEWIDE VOTE, THE BOARD OF STATE
Harbor Commissioners was confident enough about the out-
come that it selected architect Arthur Page Brown to design
what was billed as the Union Depot and Ferry House.

Just thirty-two at the time, Brown already had shown a
knack for presenting clients with buildings that were stylish and self-assured, traits that a memorable civic landmark
was expected to have. Born in upstate New York near Lake
Ontario in 1859, Brown studied architecture for a year at
Cornell University and then spent three years in the early
1880s as a draftsman in Manhattan for McKim, Mead
& White—the very epitome of polished classicism, a firm
known for the poised refinement of its buildings. The firm
drew inspiration from the past but crafted their buildings
in a way that went far beyond mimicry, repurposing classic
ideas with an assured tone that suggested the nation's culture was coming into its own. Brown's tenure predated such
McKim, Mead & White masterpieces as the Boston Public

Library or New York's majestic Pennsylvania Station, but he was on hand for the conception of the now-venerated Villard Houses on Madison Avenue, a gracious ensemble of six estates that was modeled on a Roman palazzo.

During those three years Brown absorbed not only the firm's design ethos but also the value of connections to the upper crust. He married the daughter of a New York Supreme Court justice, and his earliest independent commissions were steered his way by the widow of Chicago industrialist Cyrus Hall McCormick. A family friend of the McCormicks introduced Brown to Charles Crocker and his wife Mary during one of the couple's trips to New York. The young architect must have made an impression: when Charles Crocker died in 1888, Mary Crocker invited the twenty-eight-year-old to design the mausoleum that would hold her husband's remains.

The mausoleum's setting was the high establishment confines of Mountain View Cemetery in Oakland, and Brown conceived a somber but spectacular memorial with a terrace sixty feet in diameter from which would rise a round granite monument lined with columns and topped by a dome. The widow next hired Brown to design an "Old People's Home" in Pacific Heights as a further tribute to her late husband. Mary Crocker's death in 1889 did not bring an end to the family's patronage of Brown. The commissions were as wide-ranging as the family's financial interests, including a sprawling stone tropical fruit house in Southern California to hold the harvest from orchards belonging to the agricultural side of the business empire. The eleven-story Crocker Building, a dignified flatiron clad in granite and pressed brick with marble-swathed corridors, opened in 1891 as San Francisco's largest office building and commanded the entrance to the Financial District at Market and Montgomery streets.

The Crocker Building at Market and Montgomery streets, designed by A. Page Brown, after its 1892 opening. *San Francisco History Center, San Francisco Public Library.*

By then Brown had moved west, and he set up shop in the Crocker Building not long after it opened. There never was any shortage of business, much of it involving residences for people who moved in Crocker's circles. One early client was Southern Pacific general manager Alban Nelson Towne, who bought a Nob Hill corner parcel that Brown filled with a house where marble columns framed the entrance next to a two-story stained-glass bay window set beneath a dark wood-shingled roof. His firm also designed five enormous "cottages" in the wealthy suburb of Burlingame, part of a country club with a landscape planned by John McLaren, the superintendent of Golden Gate Park, whose ongoing transformation of that former stretch of dunes was bringing him local renown. When the country club needed a watering hole, Brown added a clubhouse meant to evoke an Elizabethan inn. Burlingame, which began as a summer home community, also is where Brown settled with his wife and three children.

• • •

There was no unifying thematic style in all these buildings, no Page Brown "look," but in the late nineteenth century that wasn't what people expected. Eclectic architecture was the rage across America, with styles from dark Gothic to mock Tudor to faux Federal all vying for attention—and this played out with intensity in San Francisco, a city where each tidal wave of growth flooded the terrain with wooden houses and commercial buildings in every conceivable veneer and historical affectation. The more money someone had, the more likely they were to show off, to the dismay of observers desirous of a more orderly cityscape. Among the most acerbic critics: Willis Polk, an architect who had worked briefly for Brown in New York and San Francisco before striking out on his own. Polk contributed occasional articles to the *Wave*, a short-lived arts and society weekly, and the pompous palaces of the nouveau riche drew his wicked ire more than once.

"The proudest boast of our modern householder is that he has all the latest conveniences and he particularly calls attention to the fact that his gables, turrets, bay-windows and filigree work are entirely original, and that nobody else has anything like them," Polk commented in one piece on the neighborhoods served by the cable car lines stretching west beyond Nob Hill and Russian Hill. "His contempt of artistic precedent is superb, and that he is successful in eliminating every feature of good architecture from his house is certain."

Besides Brown's ties to the Crockers, the new architect in town had an advantage in that his time at McKim, Mead & White taught him how to be eclectic without being crass; he

Arthur Page Brown in his Crocker Building studio, with draftsman A. C. Schwein-
furth (left). *California Historical Society.*

also had the insights gleaned from a lengthy European tour
that he took after leaving the firm. Expeditions to seek out
buildings of renown, new and old, were standard practice for
young architects of that era who could afford the journey, and
Brown put the lessons he learned to profitable use.

There were grumbles from rival architects who saw more
pretense than substance in the estates that Brown designed.
"The vogue of this gentleman is prodigious and dishearten-
ing," wrote one anonymous foe in the pages of the *Wave*, who
singled out the Towne mansion with its collage of sensations
as an example of the architect's "prominent disfigurements to
the city." Nor were his critics happy when easterner Brown
was selected in 1891 to design the California Building for the
upcoming World Columbian Exposition in Chicago, a fair on
the shores of Lake Michigan intended to dazzle the world with

its ebullient, though temporary, buildings swathed in lustrous white plaster, illuminated at night and set among lagoons and garden-like pathways.

The architectural theme of the exposition stressed the Beaux Arts style then taking hold in France, with its classical air that marked a break from the era's darker, heavier civic styles, but those built to showcase particular countries or states were encouraged to express local flavor. Brown did this by concocting an atmospheric fusion of Spanish mission and Moorish flair, stoic at the ground and effusive where it met the sky with turrets and a rounded dome. There were predictable complaints on the home front—"the thing is preposterous!" fumed a contributor to *American Architecture and Building News*—but more detached observers were impressed. Among them was a writer for the *New York Daily Tribune*, seduced by the romance of "low arches, tile roofs and picturesque domes" and how Brown "combined them in a structure which has the largeness and dignity requisite in a state building and exactly the gala appearance most appropriate to a fair." After the exposition's conclusion, the US Congress bestowed a merit award on Brown and his California Building for "use of local themes and successful composition."

• • •

It's hard to know where to allocate credit for designs like these, whether to Brown himself or to the procession of younger architects who passed through his firm, such as Polk and Bernard Maybeck—both of whom would later leave their own architectural mark on the Bay Area. On only one occasion did Brown issue an architectural manifesto of sorts: a lengthy piece for the *Chronicle* at the end of 1894 on "the possibilities of the future architecture of San Francisco."

It begins with the quintessential establishment architect staking out a position more radical than any design that his firm ever produced, bemoaning "the architectural abominations of San Francisco" and calling it "a city of possibly the most uninteresting collection of wooden structures ever erected." But why stop there? "A sweeping fire, accompanied by earthquake, would accomplish great good if we could have it without loss of life. Phoenix-like there would, perhaps, arise a city which would eclipse any American seaport."

Having staked out his position—and eerily forecasting the inferno that awaited the city in less than twelve years—the provocateur shifts to a pragmatic mode. He calls on residents and businesspeople to use substantial building materials in construction. Defer to lighter colors and tones when choosing them. Don't be afraid of buildings that look different from their predecessors, but "we should have a unity and harmony of general outline." He also tips his hat to "the attempted revival of the old mission style"—a discreet bit of self-promotion given his recent California Building.

A. Page Brown was no crusader for a particular school of architecture, and he was more inclined to craft variations on familiar themes than to forge new directions. He spent much of his time and energy navigating social circles and building his business, twin aims easily intertwined. Look at his move to Burlingame, one of the most desirable addresses on the peninsula, or how he rented space in the Crocker Building, testimony to what his office could design. But Brown had a gift, one that shouldn't be underestimated: he knew how to run a firm that could produce good buildings suited to the client's intent. In the case of San Francisco's ferry depot, this meant a structure that would function efficiently while showing that the Gold Rush city was coming of age.

We have little information on the preparations or formal research that went into the design, although in a newspaper interview after his selection Brown talked about heading east to tour recent depots such as the main terminal of the Central Railroad of New Jersey, an imposing edifice of red brick and dark arches that had opened in 1889 across from Lower Manhattan. Whatever inspirations lurked in the shadows, the design presented to the harbor commissioners and the public in January 1893 bore no relation to the Mission-Moorish mashup of the California Building, or Brown's Tudor-flavored residential work. Instead, it showed a deft transition to the grand scale required by the demands of a major transit center, anchored by an understanding that extraneous details or architectural bombast weren't needed in such a prominent, spectacular location.

The initial vision very much resembled what now exists on the waterfront, with an elongated three-story base that met the city with an arched arcade and was topped by a steep, slightly exotic clocktower. Ticket windows were to line the arcade, along with entries to the ground-floor waiting rooms and baggage storage areas, while the central bays held a pair of palatial staircases leading to the main concourse upstairs. That hall would run the length of the building below a pitched skylight, with curved trusses of steel offering lithe support. The tower above the staircases was aligned with Market Street, a stone-clad shaft complete with one large clock on each side. Slit-like windows in a subdued diagonal pattern emphasized the upward movement; above them were the clock faces and then an open four-sided pavilion with Ionic columns, followed by two circular columned tiers and, at the very top, a small rounded cupola.

. . .

Taken as a whole, the details formed an architectural composition both magisterial and inviting, imbued with a calm power that seemed preordained. And the press ate it up.

The *Chronicle* praised "the magnificent building" that "will not only be the first object to meet the eye of the passenger on the ferry steamers, but will serve as a clock tower and beacon, visible for many miles." Such prominence underscored the depot's civic role, with the paper approving of how "the fact of its being the principal point of entry into San Francisco is considered by the architect as a good reason for the erection of a monumental tower which will be a permanent architectural feature of the city." (Nor could the daily resist yet one more slap at the old Ferry House—favorably comparing Brown's proposal to "the ugly, decaying array of wooden sheds which have so long served as San Francisco's principal point of entry.")

The *Examiner*, consciously or unconsciously, tapped into the cultural message that the new depot was intended to convey:

> *"If carried out as designed the building will compare favorably with any of the great modern structures of a similar character in New York harbor and on lines of European railways, and the problem of making a monumental gateway on San Francisco's only virtual entrance, its waterway, will be solved."*

Even the *Call* had nice things to say. That paper was still no fan of the project—tucking its next-day article on page eight of the eight-page broadsheet, with a terse lead conceding,

"The San Francisco depot act has become a law. Now for the facts."—but it applauded Brown's plan for a trio of pedestrian bridges that would reach across the motley mix of pavings on two hundred-foot-wide East Street and descend into the commercial city, easing passage back and forth since "the pedestrian will have nothing to fear from cable cars and heavy trams, no sloppy, muddy cornerstones to cross, and no runaway horses to dodge."

As a further sign that Page Brown intended this to be a building of lasting importance, his formal presentation to the commissioners featured a redwood-framed watercolor rendering on a canvas twelve feet long and eight feet high—"a work of art," gushed the *Examiner*, "as creditable to the artist as the improvement will be to the city." Brown assured the commission that once the concrete foundation was in place, extending east on piles from the seawall, "It ought not to take more than a little over a year to finish the whole building and make it ready for habitation."

• • •

Monumentality and efficiency, convenience and grandeur. What more could a city want? The harbor commission was "delighted," according to the anonymous *Examiner* reporter, and "the office of the Commissioners was thronged all afternoon with admirers, and the architect and Commissioners answered questions until their tongues were tired."

Let's hope that the architect enjoyed the adulation while it lasted.

CHAPTER

———

THREE

AN EARLY SIGN THAT THINGS MIGHT NOT GO AS PLANNED CAME IN the fall of 1893, when what was to be the first and largest shipment of logs for the new depot's foundation left the harbor of Coos Bay on the coast of southern Oregon. The order was for 3,515 trunks of Douglas fir that had been cut from the forests nearby, and then floated down the Coos River and milled in the small timber town. The logs were loaded onto what the *Examiner* called a "monster raft . . . the largest cigar-shaped raft ever floated on this coast." It also was the heaviest, at least when weighed down with what the paper described as equal to 4.1 million feet of lumber.

Early efforts to tug the 625-foot-long vessel over a submerged sandbar into the open sea were unsuccessful. Once the monthly tides *were* high enough to allow the raft to clear the harbor's sandbar and depart, it encountered a storm with gale-force winds and capsized, sending the cargo of polished logs bound for San Francisco floating off into the swells, a small forest of aged timber destined for the bottom of the ocean.

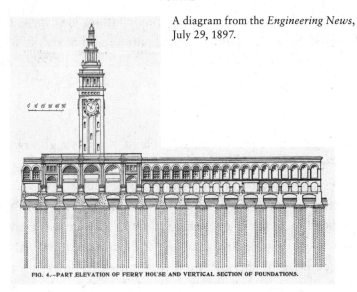

A diagram from the *Engineering News*, July 29, 1897.

FIG. 4.—PART ELEVATION OF FERRY HOUSE AND VERTICAL SECTION OF FOUNDATIONS.

The fiasco "left the contractor without material for prosecuting the work," the harbor commission said in its 1894 report. "It was necessary to procure piles from other sources, which consumed many weeks of time."

This was the first of multiple setbacks in the drawn-out construction of the ferry terminal at the foot of Market Street—some inflicted by forces of nature, others by the complexity of building a concrete foundation 670 feet long and 160 feet wide upon open water. Add to this the recurring bouts of second-guessing, investigations, and lawsuits—often stoked by political rivalries in a contentious city, and abetted by daily newspapers eager to boost sales by amplifying charges hurled at the high-visibility government project.

If the details are specific to their place and time, the saga of the building's construction is a foretaste of what happens today, again and again, with large public projects in large American cities. Timetables bog down. Setbacks are to be expected. In the long run, success or failure isn't measured by whether budgets and timelines are met. The test is what happens afterward—whether people like what they see, and whether it makes their life better as a result.

· · ·

The biggest worry throughout—at least when enough new pilings had been purchased so that construction could begin—involved the question of the foundation's stability.

After all, this massive building of stone and steel was intended to sit above open water that on average was eight to twelve feet deep—water that rose and fell with the tide above a thick layer of soft bay mud that extended down another hundred feet or so. There was clay below the mud, but bedrock was far out of reach; the seawall offered a sturdy edge to hook against but not much else. Brown's solution, later refined by Howard Holmes, the Port's chief engineer, was to design a foundation that in effect was a concrete table of immense size, with 111 fat concrete legs that tapered as they rose from the water to form vaulted arches upon which the tabletop sat. To make sure the thick platform stayed upright and even, each leg—or pier, in the technical parlance—rested on fifty to sixty tightly spaced wooden piles that were sixteen inches in diameter.

"This piece of concrete . . . is undoubtedly one of the largest, if not the largest, of its kind in the world," Holmes wrote in the harbor commission's 1896 report. "Assuming the weight of concrete to be 4,000 pds. per cu. yd., the total weight of this structure would be 112,000,000 lbs., or 56,000 net tons."

Construction crews tested the unorthodox design by driving a test pile into the mud, latching it to a nearby wharf . . . .

and balancing forty tons of iron on top of that single smooth wooden trunk for four days and nights. It held. Then the real work began. Piles were forced down twenty feet below the seawall and cut to an even length using a large circular saw. Atop the piles a watertight box would be attached, with sides extending from the piles above the waterline and the top left open. Into this box was poured the concrete that, when it hardened, formed the bottom of each thick pier. From there builders would connect the individual concrete piers with their neighbors to form the vaulted arches, and the "table" platform would go on top.

The contractor hired to build the foundation, San Francisco Bridge Co., ordered an oversized steam hammer from the East Coast to drive the piles. The machinery arrived in San Francisco and was brought to the waterfront, but "the first day it was tried, the bottom dropped out," the *Chronicle* reported. Once repairs were done, the crews on the scene discovered another hurdle—evenly cutting the tops off the logs using engine-powered circular saws was "no easy task," noted the paper, "the piles being under water."

Workers gradually got the hang of the process, and soon there were upward of 150 laborers arriving at the foot of Market Street each morning to methodically extend the arches into the bay. But as the foundation-to-be grew, several of San Francisco's half-dozen daily newspapers began sounding alarms. The concrete being poured might be shoddy. Unsafe. Badly mixed. Soon there was enough of a fuss that newly elected governor James Budd took it upon himself in February 1895 to travel southwest from Sacramento to board a small boat with three other men; they were rowed from the seawall to survey the work in progress, Budd clutching a small ax that he used to inspect what had recently been poured.

"Hatchet in hand, the Governor easily chopped out large pieces of the concrete, and his face was a study as he saw the results of his own work," the *Examiner* reported ominously. Two others in the entourage used a different tool for their "inspection": "The lightest tap of the hammer sent the nails in head deep."

The *Chronicle* missed Budd's stunt, but it happily covered grand jury hearings on the topic, such as testimony by someone who said he heard that empty cement barrels from a reputable supplier had been brought to the site by contractors and then filled with "brick dust and a small quality of cement." As much in self-defense as anything else, the Board of State Harbor Commissioners hired the heads of the civil engineering departments at the region's loftiest centers of learning, the University of California and Stanford University, to do their own study.

By June, the engineers and the grand jury had concluded their investigations—each declaring at great length that, in fact, the foundation design should ensure its stability. The concrete work was also sound, despite what the engineers criticized in some locations as "a lack of uniformity . . . due to imperfect mixing." (Budd probably inspected one of these spots, where small cavities could allow bits of the concrete to dissolve while it was still settling.)

These findings were reported with relish by newspapers that had scoffed at the apocalyptic allegations from the start. "Spite politics seem to be the cause of most of the talk against the solidity of the structure," wrote one. Another, the *Daily Evening Bulletin*, put things in context. Governor Budd was elected as part of a Democratic slate that accused its Republican opponents of being in thrall to Southern Pacific.

(Budd's predecessor, a Republican, had called in the National Guard to break up a strike against Southern Pacific. He had also appointed two of the three harbor commissioners who approved the Ferry Building contract.) "The investigation was merely a Democratic political scheme and ended in naught, because naught could possibly have come of it," the *Bulletin* smirked, taking pains to remind readers how "the *Bulletin* has all along maintained that the foundations were strong."

Even as the concrete passed muster, other skeptics challenged the safety of the wooden piles beneath the foundation.

One concern was the multitude of piles, and that "It will not be many years before the whole structure slips into the bay," one "very prominent engineer" confided in March 1893 to the *Daily Report*, yet another of the city's papers. The danger, insisted the anonymous source, was that the weight of the foundation would gradually overwhelm the submerged piles that, rather than being anchored to bedrock, were lodged into bay mud at the mercy of those ever-shifting tides: "Unless a retaining wall or embankment is built, that pressure will shove the building slowly but surely into the bay."

That was doomsday scenario #1. Doomsday scenario #2 theorized that the weight of the concrete foundation would cause those wooden piles to snap like toothpicks in the event of sudden movement. Such as an earthquake.

"A lateral movement is what the engineers say will cause the predicted trouble for the ferry building," the *Chronicle* wrote in 1895. "This, they argue, could be brought about by various causes, but principally by earthquakes." Which was hardly an idle threat in a seismically unstable city. Old-timers could still recall the upheaval in October 1868, when a tremblor with an estimated force of 7.2 on the Richter scale killed at least six people in San Francisco and caused several buildings to collapse.

These charges didn't lead to investigations, but they lingered in the air. The only test that would assuage San Franciscans' anxieties would be an actual earthquake—a test the people could neither predict nor desire.

· · ·

There were other dramas as well.

The *Call* claimed that Brown had plagiarized his tower's design from one in New York (a building by his former employer McKim, Mead & White, no less!). When the Board of State Harbor Commissioners rejected all eight initial bids to drive piles into the shallow bay and erect the concrete foundation on top, the low bidder went to court in an attempt to be awarded the contract anyway (the court said no). Governor Budd and the harbor commissioners bickered for months over the question of whether the sandstone for the building's facade should be mined in Nevada or Arizona—or pulled strictly from quarries in California, as eventually was the case.

Amid all this, Brown's practice continued to grow. In addition to numerous private mansions, he and his firm designed a quintet of speculative houses in Santa Barbara for the Crocker family, and a private club in San Jose. There was the Swedenborgian Church on Nob Hill, now a National Historic Landmark, and two bridges in Golden Gate Park. The footbridges were among several structures done by Brown for the California Midwinter Exposition, intended (unsuccessfully) by *Chronicle* publisher Michael de Young to one-up the world's fair in Chicago. Another was the fair's main exhibition

hall, the largest structure in all of California during the year
that it stood,

None of these achievements deflected the periodic attacks
against Brown that the engineering specifications for the new
depot were flawed. Or that Brown had failed to file the monthly
updates required by his contract, or that he wasn't spending
enough time monitoring the construction. During one supposed scandal, a *Call* reporter showed up at Brown's office
seeking an interview and found his prey "in the act of folding
and unfolding large sheets of drawing paper bearing the per-
spectives of ferry piers that are to be—or have been, or ought
to be." Brown responded to the reporter's sudden appearance
with a deadpan declaration that "Mr. Brown is out."

"When will you be in, Mr. Brown?" replied the equally
straight-faced reporter, who had seen him numerous times.

> *This abrupt and unexpected question seemed to*
> *amuse the architect, who had thus far played the*
> *incognito act. He dropped the plans which he held*
> *in his hands and gave his black mustache a vigorous*
> *twist on each side. After a moment's pause he said:*
> *"I will not be interviewed to-day—positively not."*

If Brown refused to offer running commentary, his foes had
no such reserve in going after an architect seen as in league
with Southern Pacific and the monied insiders of the Republican Party. Brown's most fervent opponent that year on the
commission was Edward Colnon, who had been appointed by
Governor Budd, the Democrat, and was the governor's private
secretary. Whatever the dispute, Colnon could be counted on
by reporters to fan the flames. Intending to insult the architect

Architect John Pelton's proposed revamp of A. Page Brown's design, 1895.
California Historical Society.

on one occasion, Colnon sneered that Brown "beat around the
bush and kept away from the point as much as possible" with
his "womanish" reasoning, a misogynistic barb that reporters
lapped up.

While the commissioners squabbled and the press weighed
in, the ferry building's foundation continued to grow. Rival
designs would surface periodically, including a makeover
proposed in the summer of 1895 by now-forgotten architect
John C. Pelton—a folly of orchestral bombast that included
a marble skin, an inexplicable dome, and diagonal wings
emerging from either side of a squat tower crowned with a
sculpture that in the rendering suggests nothing so much as
a supersized Roman gladiator. Colnon hailed it—"There is
art in that design"—and the *Chronicle* tipped off readers that
"Mr. Pelton is ready with his plans and prepared to step into
the shoes of architect Brown." So much for insider knowl-
edge; at its next meeting in September, the harbor commission reaffirmed that neither the design nor the architect would
be replaced.

Summer drawing to an end, Brown's job was secure. The foundation was ready to go. But the architect was not destined to see his creation take form. At home in Burlingame on October 7, 1895, Brown boarded his carriage to test ride a retired racehorse before deciding whether or not to buy the animal. As they entered the roadway near the country club, the horse broke into a gallop and Brown lost control. The steed lunged down the deep gully of a dry creek bed, pulling Brown and his cart with it.

The *Chronicle*'s account of the accident two days later was lurid.

"Brown was a frightful sight," readers were told. "He was covered in blood, and his face seemed split in two." The paper described several broken bones and confided, "It is well known among the Burlingame clubmen that Brown is an indifferent driver. In fact, he has frequently given evidence of his lack of ability to handle the reins over spirited horses." When Brown died of pleurisy of the lungs on January 21, 1896, after months of pain-wracked convalescence, the paper took a more respectful tone in describing the incident; it also acknowledged how after just seven years in San Francisco, Brown "stood in the front ranks of his profession in this city."

Notice of his death was carried in *American Architect*, a national journal, which praised Brown as "one of the leading and most progressive architects in the city" and reminded readers who had never visited the West Coast that they might know the California Building only recently dismantled in Chicago. At home, the accolades included a fond farewell to a "bright, clever, exceedingly quick-witted man" from the *Wave*—a publication that had taken its share of shots at

The Union Depot and Ferry House, 1900. *California Historical Society.*

Brown in the past, but in its tribute stressed "there can be no questioning the importance of Page Brown's participation in the local architectural renaissance."

· · ·

Brown's death didn't end the tussling over his most prominent structure, and a lawsuit over which ironmaker would forge the structural metal delayed construction yet again. But in the summer of 1898, workers readied the Union Depot and Ferry House for its debut. Not all elements of the original design had survived years of fine-tuning and cost-cutting: Overscaled bays with their two-story arches at either end of the base ended up on the cutting-room floor, reducing the length of the building from 840 to 659 feet. Brown's three pedestrian viaducts over East Street were sacrificed, too. The tower and the west-facing façade of the building were clad in gray sandstone mined at the Knowles quarry in California's Colusa County, about 125 miles north of San Francisco; the north and south facades wore skins of humble pressed brick.

Despite all this, the building was as powerfully urbane as that initial watercolor had promised. The deep arcades remained, as did the distinctive clocktower. Same for the concourse, its ceremonial aspirations conveyed by how people referred to it as the grand nave, a term more often used to describe the center of a church. As completion neared, the construction money from voters tapped out, the commissioners dipped into general funds for an extra $800 to hire the local firm Braidi & Pasquali to add an elaborate tile mosaic of the "Great Seal of the State of California," designed at the state's founding in 1849 (the expense is billed as "approaches to slips" in the Port's Harbor Improvement Fund).

The seal depicts Minerva, the Roman goddess of wisdom and war, poised alongside a grizzly bear while holding a spear in one hand and resting her other on a shield in front of sailing ships, a gold miner and the state motto, "Eureka." No mere wall ornament, the seal was centered in the floor of the nave at the point where the staircases complete their ascension through the arches from the city, into the space with its forty-two-foot-high ceiling, and walls coated in Tennessee marble.

Things were more businesslike on the ground floor, facing Market Street, where the full-length colonnade had baggage offices at either end and open-air ticket counters in between. Upstairs, off the nave, waiting rooms with flat wooden benches and modest skylights lined the eastern side of the structure along the entrances leading to the depot's ferry slips, a layout similar to the passenger gate-lined concourses we find at contemporary airports. Above the nave, the third floor held the

State Board of Trade to the south and the State Mining Bureau to the north, each with exhibit halls that travelers could visit to pass the time.

On July 13, 1898, the terminal opened, nearly six years after California voters gave it their blessing. The festivities included a band and an appearance by "soldiers of the gallant New York regiment." Southern Pacific's *Bay City* steam ferry pulled out at 12:15, crossing paths with the ferry *Piedmont* that pulled in from Oakland a few moments later. The interior prompted "expressions of delight" from visitors and dignitaries, according to the *Chronicle*, and no wonder: potted palm trees lined the nave (quite the novelty back then), where the state seal glistened beneath the peaked skylight and—no small point—the ferries emptied in one-third the time than they had at the former depot. The *Examiner* pointed out that on both the arrival and departure of the *Piedmont*, passengers "avoided the lower deck, thus attesting the popularity of the entrance through the grand nave." Page Brown's old nemesis, the *Call*, shrugged off the lack of pedestrian bridges and described the mood as festive—"Everybody was delighted with the arrangements and nothing but words in praise of the fine structure were heard on all sides."

The smoke from the political battles cleared long ago, and the legacy of what soon became known simply as the Ferry Building today bears no mark of the acrimony that clouded the building's conception—just as few people who visit Chicago's much-loved Millennium Park care that it didn't open until 2004, four years after the millennium arrived, three times over budget.

From day one, the new depot on San Francisco's waterfront fulfilled the early dreams of its boosters, that it would be more than just a building—that it would stand as a profound work of civic infrastructure connecting the city to the region and the nation, proof of urban ascendance. This larger aspect of the structure's role validated the hyperbole on the eve of completion from the Board of State Harbor Commissioners, when it issued a report meant to assure lingering skeptics that the newcomer "compares favorably with any structure dedicated to similar use, either in this country or Europe":

> *Through its magnificent corridors, arcades, and waiting-rooms will pass the tourist from abroad, with whom first impressions are the most lasting, and from the splendor surrounding the entrance leading him within the portals of the "City by the Golden Gate," will he judge of the enterprise and progressiveness of our people...*

. . .

There was one odd postscript, a coda to the controversies that preceded the depot's birth.

As construction advanced in 1897, the commissioners voted to carve an inscription commemorating their accomplishment into the cornerstone-like block of sandstone at the bottom of the southernmost column projecting from the front of the building, where the staircases led up to the grand nave. The architect hired after Brown's death to see things through, Edward R. Swain, proposed listing the harbor commissioners, engineer Holmes, Swain himself and A. Page Brown. Yet when workers had completed their task, the original designer's name was nowhere to be seen.

Local architects circulated a petition calling for Brown to be added to the pedestal. Swain sent a letter to the harbor commissioners, Colnon included, reminding them that he had recommended the same thing, only to be ignored. Given that, "I therefore ask you, gentlemen, to add the name of A. Page Brown to the inscription on the pedestal at the Union Depot and Ferry House as a tribute to his artistic capabilities in designing this stately building and as an act of justice to his memory."

The next time you visit the Ferry Building, look down at the cornerstone on the southern end of the arched grand entrance. The controversies have subsided. The architect received his due, chiseled cleanly into the stone.

CHAPTER

——

FOUR

VISITORS TO THE ST. LOUIS WORLD'S FAIR IN THE SUMMER OF 1904 had no shortage of attractions to choose from. They could stand behind a glass wall and watch butter being churned at the model creamery within the Palace of Agriculture. They could visit the Pennsylvania State building to gaze at the original Liberty Bell, that storied survivor of the American Revolution, here being guarded by policemen who had accompanied it from Philadelphia. Less rarefied pleasures lined The Pike, a mile-and-a-half-long populist promenade including an abundance of eateries and—if you were willing to pay twenty-five cents, rather than the dime required for the ostrich farm or the Temple of Mirth—a personal audience with "Beautiful Jim Key," billed in the fair's official guidebook as "an educated horse."

More civic-minded visitors had another option, a stroll along the two-block Model City not far from the fair's main entrance. This corner of the fair aimed "to illustrate the highest ideals that have been realized along particular lines by the

The San Francisco Building and its Model City neighbors at the 1904 World's Fair. *Missouri Historical Society, St. Louis, Photographs and Prints Department.*

most advanced cities in the world," according to the guide-book, the tone set in part by "buildings erected by municipalities for the accommodation of municipal exhibits." Among the cities taking part was San Francisco, which had a prime spot directly north of the exposition gates—a site where, to display its attractions, the West Coast's largest city built a seventy-five-foot-high replica of the Ferry Building.

Not the most faithful replica, to be sure; the original's long linear base was reduced to a vaguely classical rectangle, sixty feet by forty feet. The clocktower lacked a clock. The deep arcades were absent. Inside, people interested in learning about the city by the bay could study a twenty-square-foot relief map of the bay region and a huge globe "illustrating the commercial potential and advantages of our city," reported the *Examiner*. There were paintings of local wonders and photographs of local manufacturing plants, plus panoramas showing the city's growth at ten-year intervals. Some rooms were outfitted like a tycoon's study, complete with overwrought wood paneling; others held booths celebrating regional writers, California's wine trade and—perhaps a nod to Midwestern farmers who happened to stop by?—a "graphic exhibit of San Francisco's hay and grain trade."

Odd though this cameo might be in a world's fair remembered mostly for Judy Garland's 1944 movie musical *Meet Me in St. Louis*, it shows how quickly the Ferry Building came to be recognized as a defining symbol of what then was the nation's ninth largest city. "The exposition management advised the selection of the Ferry building . . . which the management very truthfully says is the best of its kind in the United States," the *Chronicle* reported when the selection was announced. And not a symbol in a nostalgic way, as cable cars are in the twenty-first century, but of progress. Innovation. "Seattle, Portland and Los Angeles are keen on the point of competing for Oriental trade and expansion for Pacific Coast manufactures and industries of all kinds, and San Francisco cannot afford to stay out of the race," the *Chronicle* wrote beforehand. The *Examiner* hailed the finished product for "illustrating and advertising the attractions of our community to the 'benighted east.'"

The role played by the Ferry Building in St. Louis was a three-dimensional, large-scale variation of its frequent appearance on postcards, book covers, and knick-knacks of all sorts. By virtue of location and design, this public depot announced the city to the world. It was a calling card, a cultural password, a one-of-a-kind landmark in a one-of-a-kind setting.

If the Eiffel Tower said Paris, and Big Ben said London, then the Ferry Building said San Francisco.

. . .

Back in real life, away from world's fair knockoffs, the distinctive structure functioned primarily as a transportation hub.
Not only did ferries arrive from seven cities along the bay,
with as many as 170 vessels pulling into and out of the slips
during commute hours, but it also was the terminus for more
than two dozen streetcar lines heading downtown from across
the city. The Ferry Building was so integral to the daily work-
ings of San Francisco—the annual passenger count grew from
four million in its first year of operation to thirty-five million people in 1910, according to the Board of State Harbor
Commissioners—that early guidebooks treated it as a launching pad more than a destination: typical was the guide published in January 1906 by the Palace Hotel's newsstand that
used a photo of the "Union Ferry Depot" as the starting point
for "Short Trips out of San Francisco," but didn't mention the
building in its "places of interest."

This same role—functional landmark rather than architectural treasure—is played by the Ferry Building in "A Trip
down Market Street" from April 14, 1906. The twelve-minute
journey travels fourteen blocks down the diagonal thorough-
fare and concludes so close to the structure that you can read
the stone where Brown's name was grudgingly added. But
the endpoint isn't why the filmmakers went to the trouble of
perching a hand-cranked movie camera at the front of a cable
car: the show is the slow survey of large urban buildings that
pauses at each corner, with an impassive clocktower in the distance, growing steadily larger.

When the journey concludes, instead of a melodramatic
pan up the eye-catching campanile, we stare at part of the
base for about fifteen seconds. An older man wearing a heavy

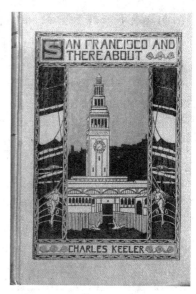

Charles Keeler's guide to "a big hustling American city." The cover illustration is by Louise Keeler, his wife.

black coat has his gray beard ruffled by a gust of wind as he stands next to the pedestal. Then we pivot as the turntable rotates counterclockwise and the cable car again faces west, down Market Street. The same view that commuters would see every morning, drama long replaced by habit.

Four years before this film, and two years before the St. Louis exposition, a handsome embossed illustration of the Ferry Building adorned the cover of *San Francisco and Thereabout*, written with an effusive flair by Charles Keeler for the California Promotion Committee. Born in Milwaukee in 1872, Keeler was raised in California and attended the university in Berkeley until he dropped out to travel the globe, writing poetry to pay his way. Upon his return, Keeler spent the following four decades straddling multiple Bay Area worlds— running Berkeley's chamber of commerce while writing radio plays and books of verse, helping to found the Sierra Club, and conceiving his own religion, the Cosmic Society, devoted to "those things that are precious in the past." His house in the Berkeley hills was designed by Bernard Maybeck, the first home by the architect who had worked briefly for Brown, a redwood-shingled structure snug on a hillside beneath a wide-spreading oak tree.

This kaleidoscope of influences, elegiac and down-to-earth, infuses *San Francisco and Thereabout.* Especially when Keeler, after several chapters of history and eight florid pages on "The Peerless Bay" ("Who shall undertake to describe this palpitating wonder of water and cloud, margined with billowy ranges?"), brings us to shore: "The great ferry boat glides into its slip and we follow the crowd off the upper deck into the magnificent nave of the Ferry Building and down the broad stone stairway to the city street." There's a brief pause to admire "the long low Ferry Building of gray Colusa stone . . . its graceful clock-tower rises above the commotion," and then Keeler describes the scene around him.

> To right and left stretches the waterfront street,
> where big docks and wharfs are lined with shipping.
> Heavy freight vans rattle and bang over the cobble-
> stones. Bells are clanging on cable cars, newsboys are
> piping the sensation of the hour; there is an under-
> tone of many voices, a scuffling of hundreds of feet
> on the cement walks, a hurrying of the crowd for first
> place on the cars.

Would such a flurry overwhelm visitors from out of town? Good! The aim here isn't simply to tout the natural setting and temperate climate, or to spin yarns of Forty-Niners and supposedly bucolic missions. There's another message: San

Francisco is "a big hustling American city" where "the wheels of the Juggernaut Progress roll along the street." The Ferry Building was the perfect spot to plunge right in—the centerpiece of one of the nation's busiest ports, with narrow piers fanning out along the waterfront on either side of the clocktower. Several piers to the north were reserved for steamers bringing produce from central California, sometimes in such abundance that excess fruits and vegetables would be dumped into the bay. To the south, freshly milled timber was being unloaded so that more buildings could rise.

Melodramatic prose aside, Keeler and the promotion committee sought to celebrate a city on the move—one that soon would all but cease to exist.

• • •

The first rupture came on April 18, 1906, at 5:12 a.m., a sway of tectonic forces rumbling along the San Andreas fault, centered near San Francisco. Twenty seconds or so later they roared into full destructive gear, tearing apart geological plates beneath California's surface as far north as Humboldt County, near the Oregon border, and south to San Juan Bautista, ninety miles down from San Francisco.

The precise location of the epicenter still isn't known, and the decades-long assumption that it was in rural Marin County has been challenged by seismologists who now place it offshore, likely west of Golden Gate Park. What is obvious is that San Francisco was no match for the forces unleashed by nature. Particularly on filled soil, disruption was cataclysmic— observers that morning recalled the surface of the city undulating, roiled by "big cracks opening and shutting . . . the street was moving in waves like the sea," to quote one patrolman on duty. He also described aftershocks where "cornices and chimneys were still dropping into the street . . . from the places where they had been loosened."

Buildings shed portions of their skin or outright collapsed; heavy machines that had been placed on the upper floors of industrial structures crashed to the ground. Yet many of the larger, newer buildings came through the temblor largely intact, damaged but not destroyed. Among them was the Ferry Building—the tower lurched back and forth so severely that several of the diagonal steel braces hidden beneath stone were pulled apart, snapping the rivets that bound them. But when the earthquake's force subsided, three full minutes after it began, the shaft remained upright, though leaning a bit to the south.

The foundation with its thicket of submerged wooden piles had done its job, just as Brown and Holmes predicted. Had a more conventional approach been taken, "there is no doubt in my mind that the Ferry Building on April 18th last would have become a thing of the past," a structural engineer wrote later that year. "The foundation as well as the building (the tower excepted) have held their own in a surprisingly creditable manner."

. . .

Horrifyingly, those three minutes of havoc were merely a prelude to the three days of destruction that followed—fires that in seventy-four hours consumed 508 city blocks and incinerated nearly thirty thousand buildings.

No single inferno arose. Rather, the small blazes sparked by the lengthy temblor merged into something much, much more. Large gas mains burst; small lanterns fell off structures and ignited once they hit the ground, sending combustible flares in all directions. Live electrical wires snapped. In the days that followed, flames stretched from south of Market Street past Rincon Hill, west toward Van Ness Avenue, then the dividing line between the central city and the neighborhoods of the Western Addition, and north to Telegraph Hill. Much of the Financial District was reduced to ashes and rubble, as were nearly all of Nob Hill's mansions. Finally, on April 21, shifting winds pushed the fire east instead of west, back over terrain that already had burned.

The full dimensions of the damage caused by the earthquake and fires during those three hellish days remain a mystery. This is especially true in terms of the cost in human lives—the Board of Supervisors in 1907 set the official death toll at 478 victims, but subsequent analyses put the number several times higher than that. The fires also left an estimated 225,000 people homeless, with more than 35,000 of them forced to shelter in rows of canvas tents or small wooden shacks. The short-term housing filled relief camps that were established in public parks, the Presidio military base, and undeveloped stretches of the city; the last one didn't close until June 1908.

In this pre-television, pre-internet age, the horrors of the earthquake and fire were publicized by means of such souvenir booklets as photographer James D. Givens's "San Francisco in Ruins," a "pictorial history" that billed itself as "EIGHT SCORE PHOTO-VIEWS of the Earthquake effects/ Flames' Havoc/ Ruins everywhere/ relief camps." Among the views of havoc we're shown: the pairing of "Wharf No. 7" and "Wharf No. 9," sagging wrecks of wooden sheds and unmoored piles just north of the Ferry Building. Another method of dissemination was the stereograph, a card with two nearly identical images that blended with lifelike depth when viewed through a stereoscope—a forerunner of 3D glasses that was invented in the 1850s. Urban devastation was particularly well suited for such a format, as shown by a card from 1906 where smoke billows behind a small "emergency hospital," with the dark silhouette of the Ferry Building "amid the encircling gloom."

Keeler turned out an entire book—*San Francisco through Earthquake and Fire,* a vivid exercise in first-person journalism that shows the writer's entrepreneurial bent. Rather than gaze transfixed across the bay from his home in the Berkeley hills, Keeler boarded the first westbound ferry he could, landing amid a disaster growing worse by the minute. "Just back of the Ferry tower and the stately rigging of the ships, the flames were running riot along the shore," he wrote. "The masthead of the ferry-tower was bent, stone had fallen from its walls and the great clock pointed silently the hour of fate— quarter past five." After he and the (few) other riders "hurried through the dark stone building," he stayed in the city for the next three days.

During that time, Keeler was privy to the tumult of Mayor Eugene Schmitz's command post, hurriedly installed in a dance hall where "tables were brought from a near-by candy store, one for each of the ten sub-committees." The next day found him joining a line of ad hoc firefighters on Telegraph Hill, or taking notes of such grim vignettes as "Looking down the narrow alleyways toward the wholesale district, I saw dead horses and demolished wagons amid piles of brick."

A few hours later, Keeler scrambled back toward the waterfront where tug boats were drawing water from the bay to try and contain flames being pushed east by the wind:

> But look, another path of fire has swept down from
> the hills to the docks! Nothing can save the Ferry
> Building and the wharves, we all agreed. But some-

thing did save them . . . the indomitable pluck and
courage of those men on the tugs, the deluge of
streams of sea water, the heavy blasts of dynamite.

Keeler wasn't shy about pouring on melodrama—"Never before was the ruin of a city consummated in a scene of such thrilling splendor," he writes at one point—and it was a spectacle made for hyperbole. The photos in Givens's album do not lie: Market Street's parade of office buildings, hotels, and popular theaters were reduced to charred shells. The Crocker family's Nob Hill mansion is shown in ruins; we see how East Street's wide cobblestone roadway buckled violently, leaving rail tracks twisted mid-air.

Don't look for a ravaged Ferry Building, though: As Keeler indicated, it weathered the horrors relatively well. The damage was real, so much so that engineers wrapped portions of the shaft in wire cables to keep it from shedding additional bricks or sandstone. But the base wasn't scarred by fire, nor did the tower crumple to the ground. Instead, the masonry that had encased the tower's steel bones was removed so the columns and girders could be repaired, with new rivets and bolts applied as needed. Once this was completed, a four-inch-thick shell of concrete was applied to the metal frame that weighed only half as much as the prior skin and provided additional bracing against seismic forces.

Restoring the tower took more than a year, leaving the structural steel exposed except for the cables that girdled it for added strength, yet ferry slips remained open and commuters streamed through the concourse as if nothing had happened. The structure served the region during those months in another way: the concourse that Brown had imagined as ideal for festive gatherings was pressed into service during the spring and summer of 1906 for meetings related to the recovery effort, be they organized by insurance underwriters, the chamber of commerce, or other interests.

The same urgent drive to move beyond the city's near-death experience translated into a building boom that began almost as soon as the last embers of the fires cooled. By July, makeshift commercial buildings lined Fillmore Street in the Western Addition. New housing was built deep in the Mission, and out west in the previously remote Richmond district above Golden Gate Park, and anywhere else with empty land and basic services. Downtown, after debris was hauled away, construction crews arrived to restore hotels and office buildings of recent vintage that had survived despite being gutted by fire—including Arthur Page Brown's Crocker Building, hollowed out yet still standing at Montgomery and Market Streets.

The mansion that Brown designed for Southern Pacific executive A. N. Towne near the summit of Nob Hill didn't fare so well. All that remained standing in the aftermath of the flames was the entrance with its six white marble columns. That ghostly image caught the local imagination so much that in 1909, the portico was given the name "Portals of the Past" and moved to the shore of Lloyd Lake in Golden Gate Park.

• • •

The speed of the recovery became a point of pride for boosters, no matter how ghoulish this might seem. "San Francisco deservedly ranks as one of the *Great Cities* of the world," one 1909 guidebook began, the reason being that "By the character and scope of her enterprises and progressive spirit of her people she turned what was thought to be an overwhelming disaster into a signal achievement for betterment in every line that makes for greatness of a city." An illustrated brochure from that same year bears a title that says it all: "San Francisco, California: Facts regarding the City of Courage and its transition into the City of Destiny will be found inside." This self-satisfied boosterism glossed over the reality that San Francisco also was a city that in the days after the earthquake talked of forcing an entire segment of its population, the Chinese, from the neighborhood where they had lived since the 1850s.

The first Chinese immigrants arrived during the Gold Rush and staked out a small district on the base of Nob Hill near the original Yerba Buena blocks, which prior arrivals were leaving for newer quarters. The Chinese population swelled in the 1860s and '70s, partly due to Charles Crocker: He and his associates recruited thousands of men from China to complete their half of the transcontinental railroad, pushing tracks over mountains and through arid terrains. Once that work was completed in 1869, many of the men returned to San Francisco and took on such jobs as shoemaking, cigar-making, and domestic work—blocked from more lucrative construction work by White men who often attacked them.

Such violence occurred again and again during the 1870s as the local and national economy sagged, and White agitators in San Francisco targeted Asians as scapegoats. The violence peaked during several nights of riots in July 1877, when mobs ransacked homes and businesses owned by Chinese, killing at least one Chinese man who was burned to death in a laundry. The riots ended but a new political force, the Workingmen's Party, trumpeted the slogan "The Chinese Must Go" and in October 1878 held a nighttime rally outside Crocker's Nob Hill mansion that vilified "Chinamen" and threatened Crocker with "the worst beating with the sticks that a man ever got."

The party's xenophobic drive to expel Chinese people from the city failed, but it succeeded in confining Chinese residents and businesses largely to ten compact blocks centered on Sacramento Street and what now is Grant Avenue. Nor were the prejudices against the community confined to working-class Whites. "The Chinese question was for many years one of the live issues in California politics," Keeler wrote in his chapter on Chinatown in *San Francisco and Thereabout*, "where much that is both curious and beautiful may be found." He left no doubt as to where he stood: "Chinese are in many ways useful and perhaps essential factors in the development of California," he wrote with patronizing condescension, but "to permit an unrestricted immigration of these people would be to court disaster."

The aftermath of the earthquake and fire seemed like an ideal opportunity by downtown powerbrokers to enlarge the office district by getting rid of Chinatown once and for all—relocating residents to the city's southern border, where one champion of a forced move owned one hundred acres of marshy land. But property owners and the influential Chinese Six Companies resisted, playing a powerful card in post-earthquake San Francisco: the economic one. One mid-May meeting featured neighborhood landlords reminding Mayor Schmitz and his cohorts "that Chinatown was one of the chief attractions for tourists and should be considered a valuable asset of the town," the *Chronicle* reported.

The efforts to keep Chinese people from returning to their former district fizzled out over the summer. Temporary wooden structures for returning businesses began to appear within weeks, and forty-three building permits had been issued by October. As recovery gained momentum, many of Chinatown's new buildings played up the most exotic aspects of what then was known as Oriental architecture, such as the curved roofs and colorful eaves of pagodas. By 1910, the district was more of a tourist attraction than ever, and the close-knit community helped bring San Francisco back to life.

· · ·

Rebuilding of another sort played out along Port-owned land, where the earthquake had scorched many wharf structures, and piers needed to be rebuilt to accommodate larger ships. In 1909, voters approved a $9 million bond for waterfront improvements. The measure provided the Port with the resources to refurbish the piers and to build its own train line, the State Belt Railroad, which would shuttle along the Embarcadero and gather or discharge cargo at each pier down to Mission Bay, which had become a plateau covered by Southern Pacific rail yards.

If the Belt Railroad was strictly business, the new piers and their city-facing bulkheads were designed to elevate the look of the waterfront. The ones south of the Ferry Building were done in a stripped-down Mission Revival style, with red tile roofs and an outer layer of plaster for a decorous adobe-like veneer. The piers to the north were rebuilt with subdued neoclassical facades.

The harbor commissioners weren't the only port operators trying to raise their game. The City Beautiful movement that caught the public imagination with the 1893 World's Fair was still influential, and San Francisco took note when New York upgraded the architecture of structures along the Hudson River. San Francisco's Port engineer confessed this in 1914, explaining how "to add to the attractiveness of the (water) front," the piers north of Market Street were "being designed on the model of Chelsea Piers in New York."

Things weren't nearly so stylish on the inland side of the

Embarcadero, where a prosaic mess of utilitarian buildings with storefronts occupied by saloons and cigar shops, shoe repair stands and pawn shops catered to the longshoremen and ship crews that made their living on the waterfront. A panoramic 1913 photograph, taken from the observation level of the Ferry Building's clocktower, conveys this well: the one- and two-story wooden structures flanking Market Street are easily lost behind the clamor of billboards and wall signs touting various whiskeys and lagers. Two stores offer "union made overalls." Hotel rooms on the few upper floors go for as little as 15 cents a night.

This is not a seedy stretch that somehow escaped the flames of the 1906 earthquake. The riot of structures indeed had been destroyed—and then put back into place pretty much the same as it was before, with no evident desire on the part of building owners to do anything other than reopen as quickly as possible. The name changed from East Street to the Embarcadero in 1909, but that was about the only difference.

"It is true our Ferry Building is striking and unique," wrote one observer in 1910, "but whatever good impression is made from the water side is lost the moment the visitor passes through the building . . . the semi-circle of temporary wooden buildings, topped with hideous signs, gives the city an air of crude provincialism . . ."

• • •

The Ferry Building rose above all this, in more ways than one.

The structure was never the tallest structure in San Francisco—that honor during the early twentieth century went to the 315-foot home of the *Call* newspaper at Third and Market Streets, which included a public cafe at the summit—but it had that gateway location and there was nothing remotely as tall within half a dozen blocks. Size didn't matter. The water-front icon is what lodged in the memory, the unquestioned confirmation that you had arrived. To send a postcard featuring the Ferry Building to a distant family member or a neighbor offered proof of your visit to the "the City That Knows How," as President William Howard Taft declared during his own trip in 1911.

Such physical evidence counted at a time when postcards were the most direct sources of imagery for bringing distant places into someone's home. Invented in Europe and first sold in the United States at Chicago's World's Fair, postcards only became widely accessible after 1898, when Congress dropped the mailing cost to a penny, half the rate for letters. Sales increased as printers increased their output to meet the demand from newsstands, drugstores, and any other retailer eager to devote a small bit of counter space to impulse buys; in 1913, when America's population was ninety-seven million, the US Post Office delivered 968 million postcards to peoples' homes.

Every city had them, with imagery shaped by a variety of motivations. Businesses used them as a form of advertising, free for the taking, which is why a twenty-first-century shopper at a flea market flipping through shoe boxes of old postcards will encounter long-gone hotels and restaurants and nightclubs. Postcard makers also wanted merchandise that would sell over time, so drawings or colored photographs of popular scenes were reproduced as long as visitors or boosters were interested in this or that popular sight.

As for what those attractions might be in San Francisco, there are clues in the ledgers of Carl Teich, a Chicago firm that in the first half of the twentieth century was the nation's largest postcard printer. Chinatown was popular, and the Cliff House restaurant perched above the ocean not far from the watery edge of Golden Gate Park. Portals of the Past made occasional appearances. So did Alcatraz, that odd exotic "rock" across the bay from Fisherman's Wharf that in the early twentieth century held a military prison.

But the Ferry Building, that was a perennial.

Many of the early twentieth-century postcards offer a perspective from inland looking north, the classical-yet-modern building juxtaposed with the bay and distant hills to underscore the natural setting. Others zoom in at ground level, letting us glimpse carriages and cable cars on hardscrabble streets, nods to the depot's workaday side. Some treat us to the water view, with the bay in the foreground and ferry slips the star of the show. Or the tower takes center stage in an otherwise typical 1920s urban skyline, the city's fabled hills adding a uniquely local touch.

These postcards are fascinating as artifacts; more than that, their popularity during this time suggests how the metropolis was perceived from afar. San Francisco's image isn't tied to skyscrapers and skylines nearly to the extent of cities in the early twentieth century as New York or Chicago; aerial views are more likely to emphasize the blue wrap of the bay rather than highlight downtown's tower-studded silhouette. There can be a sameness to the high-rise in Detroit and the high-rise in Houston, or the bulky blocks of Philadelphia and similar corners of Boston. But the Ferry Building's setting, plus its elongated dimensions and the blend of activities around it, was unmistakable.

In the same way that San Francisco boosters saw an ersatz depot as the ideal structure with which to represent their city at the 1904 World's Fair in St. Louis, postcard manufacturers saw a commodity that identified California's largest city at a glance. That larger context is made clear by one early postcard

Ferry Depot, San Francisco.   Royal Arches, Yosemite Valley, California.

Two California icons on one 1909 postcard. *Glenn Koch collection.*

that pairs an image of the depot's interior, potted palms lined up below the grand nave, with a depiction of California's most celebrated scenic wonder, Yosemite Valley. Two undeniable icons, one urban and one natural, united on a 3.5" by 5" rectangle of stiff paper.

A whole new set of postcard types went up for sale in 1915, when the Panama-Pacific International Exposition marked the culmination of efforts to show that San Francisco had emerged from the 1906 earthquake and fires more impressive than ever.

• • •

The official reason for the exposition was to welcome the opening of the Panama Canal, a marvel of engineering and construction that took ten years to build and opened the first direct shipping route between the East and West Coasts. But for San Francisco leaders and their supporters who had beaten out New Orleans to gain the support of Congress for the fair, the real hook was to show how suited their metropolis was to be the commercial link between the United States and Asia, and how the city's recovery made it—again in the words of President Taft—"an inspiration to the whole world."

The architect overseeing design of the constructed wonderland on 635 acres of filled land near the Presidio was Willis Polk, that former employee of A. Page Brown. The lone exposition building that remained in place after the fair's conclusion, the structure that most captivated San Franciscans, was Bernard Maybeck's Palace of Fine Arts, with its columned rotunda along a small lagoon, conceived as a melancholy evocation of "old Roman ruins covered with bushes and trees." Most of the fair had a more joyous tone, colorful and expressive with an array of attractions that managed at once to be theatrically transportive—Moorish towers here, Grecian domes there—and happily modern, with large "palaces" devoted to such themes as manufacturing, horticulture, and "varied industries."

Not that the fair was a world unto itself. Visitors from outside the region needed someplace to stay, and the convenient choice was one of San Francisco's hundreds of large and small hotels: "There are no old hotels in the downtown section of the city, for the fire of 1906 burned out everything in that district," one guidebook pointed out. The good news? "All of them now existing there are new, sanitary, and freshly decorated and furnished."

Almost certainly, those travelers passed through the Ferry Building. The transit depot played a key supporting role in the festivities, despite being located three miles east of the main event; the ferry slips served as the point of entry for most of the 18.9 million people who attended, with an estimated 500,000 of them from east of the Rockies. Those visitors could take home exposition paraphernalia that included a faux-gold paperweight that placed the Ferry Building in the center and relegated the phrase "San Francisco 1915" to the side, or tourist pamphlets extolling "The Exposition City" but featuring the tower on the cover. The building itself offered a prelude to the illuminated festivities that were a nightly feature of the so-called Jewel City. The outline of the tower was traced by incandescent bulbs—a flourish first employed during 1908 to mark the arrival of the nation's Pacific Fleet to the bay—and two sides were adorned with lights announcing "1915" in eleven-foot, six-inch tall numerals, above lettering that ran along the roof of the base proclaiming "California invites the world" on one side of the tower, and "Panama-Pacific Exposition" on the other.

We get a hint of the spectacles in "Mabel and Fatty Viewing the World's Fair at San Francisco," a nineteen-minute Keystone Film that's a glorified travelogue leavened by a few slapstick gags from comedians Fatty Arbuckle and Mabel Normand. A full minute of the silent movie is devoted to the stars' vessel pulling into a slip, the titles inform us, at the "Ferry Building where the vast throngs are greeted with the welcome sign and the heavy traffic is accommodated in every respect." Unlike the 1906 filmed ride down Market Street, the camera looks skyward to show us the large "1915" and the clock tower's statuesque presence. The short film concludes in a similar vein, lingering over "the great Ferry Building at night, showing the 1915 tower illuminated." It's as if Brown had conceived his depot to play the role of marquee.

After the exposition closed in December 1915, the mudflats that so recently had been filled in with loose soil were topped off with new housing to form an entire new neighborhood, the Marina District. At the foot of Market Street, the Board of

State Harbor Commissioners revised the fair-inspired rooftop lettering so that it boasted a new greeting:

WELCOME TO THE PORT OF SAN FRANCISCO

By all evidence, the good times on the waterfront would continue. The much-improved industrial port would modernize and prosper in tandem with "the wheels of the Juggernaut Progress." The Ferry Building would forever mark the prominence of an internationally known city surrounded by water, the gateway to a growing metropolitan region.

But one portion of the exposition suggested otherwise. A large section of the Palace of Transportation was given over to an assembly line for the Ford Model T, the nation's first automobile aimed at the mass public. The miniature factory had twenty-eight mechanics stationed along the fifty-foot line for three hours every afternoon, turning a skeletal chassis into a fully operational car in ten minutes.

Crowds often blocked the aisles around the biggest exhibit in a palace that included displays from two dozen other car makers trying to catch the public's attention. The biggest fuss came the day in late October when the assembly line was visited by Henry Ford himself, with fabled inventor Thomas Alva Edison as his companion, in town as guest of honor at the exposition's Edison Day later that week.

As the two men watched the cars-to-be being pulled methodically forward, workers adding more and more elements, Ford boasted how "they are coming out faster than that at the factory, now, since we improved it." Edison, then sixty-eight, just kept watching.

"Yes, I suppose so," he commented. "I dare say they will begin to spawn before long."

CHAPTER

———

FIVE

MOST BIG SAN FRANCISCO PARADES START AT THE FERRY BUILD-
ing and proceed up Market Street to City Hall. The parade on
February 26, 1933, began two miles to the west and had a far
different destination.

The festive march "was set in motion by the crash of a
bomb at 12:45 p.m.," the *Examiner* reported, and participants started marching west on Lombard Street from Van
Ness Avenue. The municipal band was first in line, followed
by a passel of elected and appointed officials and detachments
from every conceivable branch of the armed services—sailors
most of all, since the United States Fleet was wrapping up a
ten-day visit to the bay. Followed by the Boy Scouts, the Elks,
members of the American Legion and, wrote the *Chronicle*,
"scores of other patriotic and civic organizations and civilians
by the hundreds."

Quite a splash, and by all accounts the crowd of at least
one hundred thousand people turning out on a sunny Sunday
in February 1933 was the biggest that the city had seen since

the end of World War I. But this was quite an occasion: the formal groundbreaking for the Golden Gate Bridge. Or, as Mayor Angelo Rossi put it, "the greatest bridge ever designed by man, a triumph of engineering science, and a monument to constructive enterprise." His speech came during the ceremony that followed the two-mile parade that entered the Presidio through the Lombard Street gate of the US Army post and then descended to Crissy Field, with its shoreline view of the craggy strait soon to be bridged. The scale of the setting made the planned bridge all the more impressive, the idea that workers would eventually drape the opening with the longest single span of suspended roadway in the world—4,200 feet, with a 746-foot-tall tower at each end to hold it in place.

Rossi took the platform after a 250-voice choir sang "Hallelujah," the *Chronicle* reported, as the raucous crowd pressed close. He introduced Governor James Rolph, who extolled "the greatest engineering achievement of the age." There were more speeches, but people grew restless and overly jubilant audience members pushed forward in such numbers that the program was called to a halt. Guards formed a cordon so officials could do the ceremonial spading of soil; the 250 carrier pigeons that were to be sent aloft with fanfare were so frightened they cowered in their crate-like containers until "small boys . . . shooed them out with sticks," the *Chronicle* noted in a bemused tone.

The turnout was smaller but still exultant nineteen weeks later, when another groundbreaking of sorts occurred for an 8.25-mile span from San Francisco to Oakland—a bridge that would be the longest in the world. For starters, there was no parade: the main event was held on Yerba Buena Island, midway between the two cities and thus reachable only by boat. More than five thousand people showed up anyway, most of them arriving on the two ferries that went back and forth bringing invited guests and their families from Oakland and San Francisco to the forested US Navy base midway between the two. Similar crowds gathered where the bridge would lift off from Oakland and touch down in San Francisco at Rincon Hill, which a century earlier was the backdrop to sand dunes along Yerba Buena Cove's south edge.

A US Navy rear admiral personally greeted many of the visitors to the island where the main event was held. Governor Rolph stepped to the microphones again, this time to hail "the most highly significant monument of this era." Ex-president Herbert Hoover gave his first public remarks since leaving office in March before grasping a gold shovel to turn multiple scoops of dirt for photographers. Other dignitaries did the same and finally, at 12:58 p.m., Franklin Delano Roosevelt used a gold key at the White House to ignite a blast of dynamite that pulverized an island outcrop that needed to be cleared to make way for the eastern span of the bridge.

Amid all these flourishes that accompanied a nationally broadcast event, the most telling speaker bore no title: Charles White, a father of two who had been unemployed for fifteen months before he was hired to join the construction crew. "This bridge means plenty to me," he told the state director of public works, Earl Lee Kelly, who introduced him. "My house will be a happy one again."

Placing a recently destitute Everyman on the same program as the recently inaugurated leader of 125 million Americans helps to explain the enthusiasm on both days. The groundbreakings came during the fourth year of a national depression that had closed Bay Area businesses and factories while spiking California's unemployment rates from barely 3 percent in 1929 to 25 percent in 1933. There's a reason that FDR made time so early in his presidency to take part via the airwaves; not only would this be "the greatest bridge ever built," he told the radio audience, but the beginning of work on the Bay Bridge also "symbolizes the upturn that has come to our industrial life."

Wishful thinking and a politician's hype? Perhaps. What could *not* be denied was the emerging dominance of a new form of transportation. Personal automobiles were being incorporated into the daily lives of more and more Americans each year, people intoxicated by the idea that a four-wheel vehicle could give them the power to go where they wanted, when they wanted, ferry schedules and streetcar routes be damned.

The full extent to which the automobile would remake the nation's urban and regional landscapes was constrained at first by the burdens of a decade when prosperity proved elusive, and when labor strife in San Francisco and other cities threw that future into doubt. But as workers like Charles White toiled day after day, the coming impact of the bridges was obvious.

Another thing was obvious. The Ferry Building, once a symbol of San Francisco's national aspirations and modernity, would soon be consigned to the past.

· · ·

The Ferry Building entered the new decade in commanding fashion, still visual shorthand for one of the nation's most recognizable cities. The first movie version of Dashiell Hammett's *The Maltese Falcon* premiered in 1931 starring Bebe Daniels and Ricardo Cortez—and to show us where private eye Sam Spade does business, the movie opens with an extended water view of the towered depot and its slips. A painted image from the same perspective for years filled the cover of the

The Embarcadero in 1927, with the approach to Southern Pacific's automobile ferry at the lower right. *Glenn Koch collection.*

thick monthly guide published by the Hotel Greeters of San Francisco. And when Merrill Packing Co. of Salinas wanted a logo for its Frisco line of produce, the grower near Monterey selected a colorful, woodcut-like image of the clocktower at the foot of Market Street: "That was the symbol of San Francisco back then, my grandfather said," recalls Ross Merrill, the third generation of the family to run the company. "That's why he picked it."

But this singularity was nearing an end. The reason, of course, was the automobile.

Cars already were transforming the city's streets, despite the lack of easy access from the East Bay and Marin. In 1914, just over 14,000 cars and trucks were registered to San Francisco's 420,000 residents; a decade later the number of auto registrations crossed the 100,000 mark, and in 1930 there were 155,000 in a city of 634,000 people. The surrounding counties saw more dramatic jumps—going from 12,893 in 1914 to

235,184 in 1930, a year in which 4.5 million automobile ferry crossings were recorded in the region. Nor was the Bay Area a leader in the race to adopt the horseless carriage—one 1925 article decried how the region had "but one car to 5.1 persons," compared to the proportion of one car to two people in fast-growing Los Angeles to the south.

The streets of prosperous cities had never been idyllic: an 1878 article in an architectural journal described a chaotic norm in Boston where sidewalks were "jammed to suffocation" by pedestrians, and street traffic was at the mercy of any horse-drawn carriage or cart that stopped while "the horses attached to which munch their oats peacefully." But engine-powered vehicles changed every aspect of the situation. For starters, the newcomers were lethal: automobile fatalities nationwide climbed from roughly 1,000 in 1909 to nearly 10,000 a decade later, according to a study at the time. New York alone suffered 858 such deaths in 1922, when a medical examiner there stated the obvious by telling one newspaper "An automobile is a dangerous weapon." Cities such as Pittsburgh and Baltimore held "safety weeks," erecting large temporary memorials remembering the children lost during the prior year because adults driving cars killed them.

At the same time fatalities were increasing, so was the acceptance of automobiles as an inalienable right. Instead of governments requiring technology that automatically would turn off the engine if a driver tried to go above twenty-five miles per hour, as a Cincinnati ballot initiative would have required in 1923 (it was defeated, handily), pedestrians were classified as lawbreaking "jaywalkers" if they didn't cross the street in marked crosswalks and at decreed times. And while cities adopted regulations spelling out the rules of the road for drivers and pedestrians alike, individual planners and designers

floated ideas to make room for the growing number of cars—
whether it was a consulting engineer telling a Chicago business luncheon how the Chicago River could be topped by a
two-hundred-foot-wide boulevard, or prominent New York
architect Ernest Flagg's proposal that the city should sell off
large chunks of Central Park and use the proceeds to purchase
all private lots between Sixth and Seventh Avenues and build
a parkway from Lower Manhattan to Harlem.

Clear the way, cars will follow.

. . .

"Automotive traffic has everywhere shown a startling vitality wherever obstructions to its free use have been removed,"
was the observation of one not-disinterested national observer,
transportation consultant Miller McClintock. His career trajectory was an odd one: after graduating from Stanford University and spending two years as a courts reporter in San
Francisco at the *Bulletin*, he decided to return to Stanford to
study classical literature. Once his thesis was accepted and he
was teaching Chaucer, the married man of twenty-six shifted
gears again—heading off to Harvard University to earn a PhD
in municipal government. His dissertation was on "Street Traffic Control," and it attracted such notice that within a few
years the former classics lecturer was running the newly created Bureau for Street Traffic Research.

The bureau was affiliated with Harvard but funded by
Studebaker, a leading car manufacturer, and McClintock
didn't hide where his sympathies lay. "We are not interested
in planning city streets for less than an average speed of sixty
miles an hour," he told *Scribner's* magazine when it profiled
"the man whose job it is to stop the savage massacre and
mutilation by automobiles" on public roadways—basically

by getting people out of the way so cars would encounter as few obstacles as possible. Give McClintock credit, he lived the life he preached. He and his family settled in Scarsdale, New York, a twenty-four-mile commute to midtown, where from his office window he could look down on the viaduct surrounding Grand Central Station.

In the Bay Area, obviously, the biggest obstruction to McClintock's ideal of "startling vitality" was the 550-square-mile body of water that defined the region. San Francisco wasn't isolated—decades of growth were proof enough of that—but the peninsular setting that made it so memorable was also a hurdle that grew more aggravating as people were bewitched by the promised convenience of the internal combustion engine. As early as 1912, two ferries expressly built to hold cars on the lower level and passengers on top were sailing from Alameda to San Francisco: during one three-month period that first year the two carried 10,785 automobiles, 7,316 motorcycles, and 2,472 horse-drawn wagons. By 1920 there were slips for automobile ferries flanking the Ferry Building, and frequent weekend traffic jams as cars in pursuit of pleasure drives backed up along the Embarcadero. The following year, the Motor Car Dealers Association of San Francisco launched a Bridge-the-Bay movement that included full-page newspaper advertisements and lobbying throughout the year. Other boosters were more detached, but no less single-minded. When civic leaders invited St. Louis-based city planner Harland Bartholemew to produce a regional plan for the Bay Area—such efforts were in vogue at the time, and Bartholmew's firm specialized in them—the preliminary report in 1925 minced no words: the existing roadways were "totally incapable of properly serving probable future population . . . Bay crossings by bridge or tunnel are an immediate necessity."

Car dealers might agree. Local politicians and merchants might agree. But the final decision was up to the US War Department, which on several occasions between 1916 and 1925 rejected the concept of a bridge from San Francisco to Alameda County on the grounds that such a structure would impede naval movements through the deep channel that separated the city from Yerba Buena Island.

Undaunted, San Francisco in 1926 issued a national call for proposals to build a span to Alameda. The response: eighteen conceptual designs in thick brochures and blueprints, submitted by aspirants ranging from development consortiums and engineering firms to lone architects. One team proposed leveling the top of Telegraph Hill to create a site where the new bridge would meet "a great transcontinental passenger railway, rapid transit and automobile terminal with a magnificent hotel towering high above the hurrying passengers below." Another proposed a span that entered the city above the northern Embarcadero, automobiles touching ground to the west and commuter trains looping south on elevated tracks that ended at the Ferry Building. The rendering for this one is quietly startling. A bridge that's a ringer for what later was built hovers behind A. Page Brown's icon, looking as if it had been there all along.

Out of its depth, the Board of Supervisors hired three engineers to select a general route rather than a specific design. The trio returned in May 1927 with a report that explained why the best place for a cross-bay span to begin was Rincon Hill, a scenario that US Navy Secretary Curtis Wilbur curtly dismissed as "most objectionable from a naval point of view."

Case closed. But not for long.

In 1929 a new president was sworn in, Herbert Hoover—a former US secretary of commerce whose humanitarian work after World War I saved lives in Europe, but also a graduate of Stanford University who had never cut his ties with the Bay Area. Within months, he and California governor C. C. Young announced they were putting together their own commission. Its assignment? To determine *how* to make the bridge happen, not *whether* one should be built.

"There can be no question as to the necessity for such a bridge for the economic development of these communities," Hoover told reporters at his news conference announcing the commission's creation. When the group recommended the same route as San Francisco's consultants, Hoover later wrote wryly in his memoirs, "the Navy admitted it was high enough to do no harm to defense."

. . .

Compared to all this, the genesis of the Golden Gate Bridge was as straightforward as the structure that opened in 1937, a fusion of architecture and geography that shows both off to their best advantage. The idea had been discussed since 1916, when a *San Francisco Bulletin* journalist who studied engineering argued that "nowhere in the world has nature presented such an admirable site" for a grand suspension bridge. The state legislature in 1923 approved the creation of the Golden Gate Bridge and Highway District, and the War Department gave *this* concept its blessing. When voters in the district's five counties were asked in 1930 to approve $35 million in bonds, the case presented was vivid and blunt.

"Our people need the work," Rolph, then San Francisco's mayor, told one civic group. "Let us get this bridge across the Golden Gate and the East Bay Bridge under way."

A pro-bonds advertisement in the *Chronicle* sounded another theme, one both reminiscent of the 1890s and indicative of how times had changed. "Great bridges are milestones of progress," it proclaimed. "Today the point has been reached when the ferries, groaning under their burdens, are no longer sufficient to take care of San Francisco's transportation needs."

Opponents sounded what alarms they could. "Have we any assurance that $35 million is the final figure?" one statistician warned during a public debate. Engineers called the idea reckless since "a single span of 4200 feet is a great advance over such bridges as have proven their safety." Bay Area artists and writers signed an ad that declared, "The Golden Gate is one of nature's perfect pictures—let's not disfigure it."

Aesthetics, economics, intimations of apocalyptic danger: arguments of this nature would be sounded again and again in future decades by opponents of landscape-altering projects small and large. In 1930, thankfully, they had little effect.

· · ·

Through the debate and politics, the Ferry Building stayed busy. Nearly 50 million customers used the ferries as the decade began, the largest such system in the world. Newer ferries held more than two thousand passengers. The skyline now had sixteen buildings that were taller, but the Ferry Building still dominated the all-defining view from the east.

The Depression was real, no question, and the bleak times hit waterfront workers particularly hard: unemployed people have little demand for many of the items made from goods moving in and out of the Port, and this meant fewer ships with less cargo visiting the Embarcadero's finger piers. The tonnage reported by the Board of State Harbor Commissioners in its annual reports fell from 24 million in the 1928–30 period to 17.7 million in 1932–34. The commission laid off some of its workers; others had their time on duty trimmed from five to three days "with a corresponding reduction in income."

Though the Ferry Building had little to do with the workaday piers to the north and south, the two worlds overlapped directly outside. That's where longshoremen headed every morning at dawn in search of jobs, with as many as 4,000 laborers forming horseshoes around hiring agents from the various shipping companies who together might need 1,500 workers at best. Known as a shape-up, the ritual was used in other ports as well—but that didn't make it any less demeaning to the men forced to take part.

"More or less like a slave market," is how Harry Bridges, San Francisco's leading labor activist for decades, described shape-ups in 1934. The location intensified the emotions, especially when "at the moment of 8 o'clock, we were herded along the street by the police to allow the commuters to go across the street from the Ferry Building."

Another indignity? To take part you had to be a member of the shipowners' in-house union, holding up the small blue book to show you belonged. The agents controlled the selection. Who found work and who was left (literally) in the cold depended on those agents' favor, opening avenues for abuse and exploitation.

Efforts by the International Longshoremen's Association to topple this system were rebuffed throughout the 1920s, but FDR's National Industrial Recovery Act strengthened the hand of waterfront workers by giving them the right to belong to a union of their own choosing. Soon, all major West Coast ports had ILA chapters; when negotiations over wages and hiring practices stalled, union leaders on May 9, 1934, declared a strike from Mexico north to the Canadian border.

They were joined by teamsters and seamen, and within a week no freighters were pulling in or out of port.

. . .

The danger of violence was palpable from the strike's first day, when police on horses and motorcycles charged into a group of strikers protesting outside a pier where nonunion crews brought in by the shipping companies were being housed. Three weeks later, police fired gunshots into the air and shot tear gas canisters at strikers marching south from the Ferry Building in what the *Examiner* described as "the fiercest fighting yet . . . left scores of wounded and injured in its path." Piers were closed, rolling doors locked tight, and strikers kept the Port's freight line from moving up and down the Embarcadero. There were factions on both sides, some more militant than others, but the core of the longshoremen's demands were simple. They wanted jobs with a certain amount of dependability, where hiring conditions and hourly wages were spelled out in advance. They didn't want to stand outside in the dark cold outside the Ferry Building, hoping they'd get picked.

As July began, the city's power structure moved to break the strike. Mayor Angelo Rossi said the Port would reopen in early July, by force if necessary. Governor Frank Merriam announced he was prepared to deploy the National Guard. On July 3, fierce battles broke out, with one strikebreaker dying of a fractured skull. More than two dozen picketers and police were treated for injuries.

On July 5, memorialized by labor stalwarts ever since as "Bloody Thursday," matters came to a head. Police were out in force, allied with shipping companies determined to move cargo from pier sheds onto Belt Railroad trains and out to waiting markets. Strikers responded with barricades and hurled rocks and bricks from Rincon Hill, the emerging western anchorage of the Bay Bridge at their back. Two formations of police converged on the union headquarters near Steuart and Mission Street. Officers in uniforms fired at strikers. Three fell to the ground. Only one survived.

This was not some remote battle in an industrial corner of a sprawling metropolis—it was at the nexus of the Port and the city, in full view of office workers and shoppers and other people who never would have seen the horseshoes form at dawn and be cleared away by 8 a.m. On Bloody Thursday, when the fighting was at its worst, so many onlookers lined the Ferry Building to watch the fray that at one point, recounted the *Chronicle*, "mounted police rode through the arcade" to clear out gawkers. Then there was Josephine Fuentes, forty-two, whose streetcar was pulling up toward the Ferry Building when a stray police bullet pierced her in the temple, not fatally.

Violence paused on Friday while a stunned city took stock, strikers and bystanders alike. It was one thing to read of clashes elsewhere in a summer of economic strife—the month the waterfront strike began, strikers were killed by national guardsmen in Toledo, Ohio—but another to experience it at home. Governor Merriam used the lull to dispatch two thousand national guardsmen to the Embarcadero to impose order and, in the process, bolster business leaders' effort to portray the strike organizers as communists who wanted to seize control of the city. The Guard set up its headquarters in the Ferry Building above the grand nave, space usually occupied by state offices, only to move out eleven days later—citing overcrowded conditions but also "difficulties involved in barring the curious."

As the Guard relocated to a riverboat docked off Pier 3, the drama's final scenes were playing out. After a massive funeral and memorial march up Market Street for the two dead men, a general strike was called that closed the city on July 16 and lasted four days. The ferries were still running, which means people disembarking "saw an unusual sight," the *Chronicle* reported. "Army tanks crawled slowly along the waterfront."

Such a powerful action by labor was unprecedented in twentieth-century America, and the shipping companies and their business allies tried to get President Roosevelt to cut short a vacation in the Pacific and force a deal. "A lot of people completely lost their heads," he said later, referring to panicked politicians and business leaders. "They went completely off the handle."

The general strike ended on July 19, and longshoremen returned to work on the West Coast, though not until shipping companies had agreed to arbitration. The settlement ten weeks later included a six-hour day for workers, a decent pay raise and, perhaps most important of all, the establishment of hiring halls managed jointly by labor and the shipping companies. The shape-up with its horseshoes outside the Ferry Building was gone for good.

• • •

Work on the Bay Bridge stopped on July 5 because of the fighting between police and strikers on Rincon Hill, and didn't fully resume until after the general strike. Otherwise, construction of the new bridges proceeded with little disruption. And in the months that followed, open bodies of water were transformed, first by towers and then the main cables and then the roadways suspended from those cables several hundred feet up in the air.

As FDR's participation had shown in July 1933, the Bay Bridge was of more than local interest: it was to be the world's longest bridge, and at $77 million the most expensive ever built (the Golden Gate Bridge was $35 million). A pamphlet published in 1936 by United States Steel overflows with statistics—"the 70,815 miles of cable wire alone are sufficient to encircle the Earth nearly three times"—and a hyperbolic prediction that the structure would "stand as the largest bridge in the world for probably 1000 years." A company newsreel brought the process to life for national viewers with images of towers being assembled, cable being spun, heavy parts being fused to form a gravity-defying whole. After one clip in which workers sprinted across a wire-mesh catwalk, the camera panned down to a ferry on its westbound journey. The narrator summed things up:

> *Far below, the old ferry boats plowed stolidly along, soon to be replaced by trains of electric cars, automobiles and trucks, rolling along in an endless stream across the bridge that soars above.*

The big day came on November 12, 1936, when many of the dignitaries who had gathered for the sort-of-groundbreaking reunited to give laudatory speeches and then watch Governor Merriam use a blow torch to sever an iron chain at the Oakland toll booths. The motorcade headed west to San Francisco, where Mayor Rossi was on hand to replicate the ceremony and wield another blow torch—but with shorter talks this time, because at 12:30 the president was waiting at the White House to press a green "Go" button and allow public traffic to begin. Warships fired a twenty-one-gun salute while 250 naval aircraft performed swirling acrobatics above.

Deed done, traffic commenced. As did a three-day pageant to celebrate what one *Chronicle* headline proclaimed "A DREAM FULFILLED/ San Francisco's Isolation Ended

Forever." A Market Street parade the next day featured more than sixty floats, concluding on a somber tone with a flower covered float honoring workers who died during construction, including fifteen who plunged to their death. The final night's parade had the theme "bridges of the world," with one float holding an illuminated rainbow and another portraying a large fallen tree across a stream. The Golden Gate Bridge opened six months later—with FDR again pushing a button at the White House to open the lanes to the public—and ferry service between Marin and San Francisco ended after sixty-nine years. The exquisite span, with its sumptuous orange cables holding a 4,200-foot-long roadway between two 746-foot towers, transcended infrastructure to testify that progress can be infused with beauty. No other large bridge in America felt so intertwined with nature, so inherently at one with the forested ridges on either side.

The Bay Bridge supplanted the Ferry Building functionally, tying San Francisco to the East Bay and (figuratively) to the continent beyond. Then the Golden Gate Bridge replaced it symbolically. The newcomer became the structure linked to San Francisco in the popular imagination, a hold that has only grown stronger with time.

• • •

On the Bay Bridge's first anniversary, a *Chronicle* editorial gushed that 9,250,000 cars had used the span since its opening—"two and a half times the number of motor vehicles transported between San Francisco and the East Bay in the year before the span was opened." The editorial went on to state—favorably—that the bridge was proof of how "every sound facility creates new demands."

That demand also translated to congestion jamming streets

that already had been crowded with automobiles, so San Francisco hired none other than pro-car traffic consultant Miller J. McClintock to come up with a solution. He responded with a plan that looks ruinously destructive today, but then was welcomed as a blueprint for seamless times to come. With almost clinical detachment, McClintock studied local transportation trends and street patterns to find the best way to achieve, in his words, "the safe and seamless movement of vehicles and pedestrians." The dispassionate tone didn't hide his view that tweaks were no remedy for San Francisco's ills: the patient needed surgery.

"The only basic cure for the traffic problem lies in the construction of a system of automobile routes accurately adjusted to the free and safe movement of motor vehicles," he advised. This would be done by imposing "64.6 miles of limited way routes" on the city's existing street grid, offering "a complete and continuous physical separation of opposed streams of traffic." Some on the ground and some in the air, above existing conventional roads.

It's not as if there were no competing options: the city that same year asked voters to approve a $50 million bond to build a subway below Market Street and provide an alternative to clogged roadways. Voters said no. Auto-friendly roadways were the future. Streetcars had lost their allure.

Even the Board of State Harbor Commissioners was dazzled by the steel spans straddling the bay. In its 1938 report the Board made a point of welcoming "these mighty monuments," but conceding, "One of the problems which will require consideration in the near future is that of the utilization of the Ferry Building section of the waterfront following the inauguration of interurban railway service across the Bay Bridge and the discontinuance of the passenger ferries."

This was stating the obvious, especially after rail service began on the lower deck of the Bay Bridge in February 1939. The streetcars that so many East Bay commuters had used to reach westbound ferries could now travel all the way to a new terminal at First and Mission streets. The new terminus had no charm, with its hulking concrete columns and barebones façade, but that didn't matter. The passenger ferries would be docked permanently once intercity rail service began—a transition marked with defiant festivities on the Friday before Christmas 1938, when the 8 a.m. ferries from Oakland and Alameda were crowded with commuters singing carols and hurling streamers around decorated Yule trees. The tradition stretched back decades, and "the sense of loss became larger than the pulse of celebration," the *Chronicle* wrote. Many of these people had spent twenty minutes together each weekday morning, year after year after year. In a very real way, their festivities were also a farewell.

. . .

Commuters weren't the only ones feeling nostalgia as the shift occurred.

Herb Caen joined the *Chronicle* in 1936 as a twenty-year-old radio columnist, hired from the *Sacramento Union* by a publisher eager to bring youthful energy to the old daily. Born in California's capital city, Caen liked to claim that his parents had conceived him while visiting the Panama-Pacific Exposition.

Whatever his origin story, the wide-eyed newcomer embraced all aspects of San Francisco. On July 5, 1938, he began a daily city column in the style of Walter Winchell, the era's hugely popular New York columnist known for packing each installment with newsy gossip and wisecracking asides, three dots inserted between each item to give the patter syncopation. If Caen once joked, "I think I ran for a year before anyone knew I was there," there's no denying that he got around—and by the beginning of the column's second week, mixed into a batch of "Sightscene" items like "The Empire's Sky Room, where the sightseers buy one drink and get drunk on the view . . ." Caen ruefully if melodramatically pointed out, "The Ferry building, martyred by progress . . ."

For outsiders, though, the new mode of movement was the only way to go. One 1938 guidebook presented the choice for travelers this way: "You drove over one of the great bridges or you left the overland at Oakland Mole and . . . eventually found yourself in a narrow hallway in the Ferry Building, hunting for your baggage and none too favorably impressed."

The building *did* get a boost for twenty months when the Golden Gate International Exposition was held on Treasure Island—a flat four-hundred-acre oval of landfill linked to Yerba Buena Island and created especially for the occasion. The Expo featured floridly landscaped buildings clustered around the four-hundred-foot-tall Tower of the Sun, and nearly a quarter of the island was devoted to a twelve-thousand-car parking lot. But there was a ferry dock! Tickets were 10 cents each way; ferries departed their namesake building on the twelve-minute journey every fifteen minutes between 10 a.m. and midnight, with less-frequent runs until 3 a.m.

The exposition had more of a local focus than its 1915 predecessor, the rationale being to celebrate the completion of "the world's greatest SPANS OF STEEL,'" to quote one official guidebook. It also offered people a distraction from the still-tenacious Depression, a chance to wander the grounds and sample such attractions as the foreign pavilions, the fountain-studded courtyard, the exhibition-filled "palaces."

The San Francisco of 1999, as portrayed by US Steel on Treasure Island.
San Francisco History Center, San Francisco Public Library.

One of these was the Palace of Mines, Metals and Machinery, where visitors could gape at a forty-five-foot-long diorama
showing the supposed San Francisco of 1999.

This installation was the highlight of the exhibit assembled
by US Steel. Fresh off its triumphant construction of the Bay
Bridge, the huge company promoted the "breath-taking spectacle" in newspaper ads that asked, "Can you imagine what
San Francisco could be like in 1999? Our artists, designers
and engineers have." The "thrilling and prophetic glimpse"
of tomorrow's city on display at Treasure Island included
widely spaced residential towers south of Market Street, an
elevated roadway offering a straight shot from Telegraph Hill
to Russian Hill above North Beach, and a single Brobding-
nagian pier reaching into the bay from the south end of the

Embarcadero—a "modernistic transportation center" so large
it had a twelve-mile shoreline all its own.

"In the design all existing docks have been removed from
the waterfront," one US Steel release on the "waterfront of the
future" proudly explains, pointing out the obvious. "In their
place is a magnificent parkway and drive connecting the city's
two bridges."

The Ferry Building? It was nowhere to be seen.

PART II

RELIC

CHAPTER

———

SIX

LOOK DEEP INTO THE SHADOWS OF ANY LARGE CITY, PAST THE built terrain of structures and streets, into the plans and proposals that once loomed, and alternate landscapes can be glimpsed—an imagined realm that's beguiling and baffling and fearsome all at once.

Towers jab to startling heights, often where towers never touched down. Roadways meet in grand configurations, carving routes with no regard for their surroundings. Parks and plazas beckon in unexpected locations. When you *do* spot familiar buildings or settings, they might be taller and flashier than what you know to exist.

The most startling aspect of all? This realm is idyllic. The public spaces feature an attractive mix of people, never too many and never too few. Light traffic plies the streets. Architectural details are confident and crisp, rendered with seductive allure.

We know these imagined vistas aren't real. Our rational minds wince at the averted disasters, the misguided hubris, the developer schemes that went awry and the well-intentioned but naive manifestations of short-lived trends in city planning. Yet even the most preposterous visions can pull you in. Their purity offers an unfiltered glimpse of the ways that different generations and urban forces imagined *their* ideal city.

Not surprisingly, the virtual landscape grows most complex in contested locations. Instead of a single dodged bullet, stacks of what-ifs pile high. These are the places that people cared about, generation after generation, where movers and shakers—and ordinary people with the power of imagination—sought to make a statement about their city and its values.

These ghost landscapes, the dreams of unbuilt worlds, help to decode the fitful saga of the Ferry Building during the fifty years it spent in limbo after two brash new bridges took over its job. Nobody knew how to adapt the nineteenth-century depot to a modern region, or what to do with the matchless waterfront setting. Plan after plan came and went. Yet even as the landmark languished, it took on a new and urgent civic role. The Ferry Building represented what was at stake in a San Francisco torn by conflicting visions of what the city should become.

· · ·

When San Francisco's city planners in 1943 embarked on the ambitious task of rethinking their city for the second half of the twentieth century, they began with a 132-page document that reimagined the shoreline from the ocean to the bay.

The lure of a safe harbor is what brought the hamlet of Yerba Buena to life and allowed San Francisco to enter the twentieth century as the West Coast's leading metropolis. Now, with World War II raging in Europe and Asia, the region's importance to the nation was evident wherever you looked. At least a dozen army and naval installations ringed San Francisco Bay, from hospitals and arsenals to naval bases devoted to maintaining and supplying the Pacific Fleet. More than 1.6 million military personnel sailed below the Golden Gate Bridge en route to battlefields in the Pacific Ocean, many of them embarking from Fort Mason, one mile west of Fisherman's Wharf. Civic Center Plaza hosted army barracks and victory gardens; Treasure Island, not even five years old, was seized by the navy and made into a training facility.

Entire populations suffered, though battle lines were thousands of miles away: within months of Japan's deadly attack on Pearl Harbor in December 1941, the 4,500 San Franciscans of Japanese descent had been rounded up from twenty blocks of the Western Addition known as Japanesetown, local victims of a toxic nationwide brew of security fears and racism that led President Roosevelt in February 1942 to issue his executive order allowing the forced removal of Japanese-Americans from "military zones"—which included the entire West Coast. Some families had as little as six days to prepare. They were then bussed under armed guard to an "assembly center" at a former racetrack south of San Francisco, and from there to the hastily constructed, barbed-wire internment camps hundreds of miles from the Bay Area.

Their vacant apartments became homes to Black Americans who fled the harsh segregation of the American South seeking industrial jobs at facilities such as the Bethlehem Steel plant at Potrero Point. There, nearly twenty thousand workers repaired and maintained ships while building seventy-two military vessels between 1942 and 1945, including four cruisers and twenty-seven destroyers. The Western Addition always had had Black residents, but by 1943, the population there topped nine thousand.

This was total war the likes of which the United States had never experienced, and the summer of 1943 brought signs of victory ahead—from successful battles in the Pacific to progress in Europe. "LAST SICILY LINE BROKEN" ran the *Chronicle*'s banner headline on July 30, 1943, above a smaller article on the release of the first part of what the City Planning Department billed as "a comprehensive, coordinated plan and program."

We know now that the postwar boom would reverberate for decades, but San Francisco's municipal planners had no such assurance. Instead, they remembered the Depression's grinding turmoil, with its tensions that flared into the waterfront strike and Bloody Thursday. The shoreline plan was conceived in part to prevent those hard times' return, on the theory that job-rich infrastructure projects could help offer "protection of the city against those disorders and destructive forces which spring easily from mass unemployment."

A parallel threat, in the eyes of planners and decision makers, was that a traditional urban center like San Francisco was no match for the convenient enticements of the suburbs. The shoreline plan was blunt: "Some believe that the big city as we know it today is so inefficient, wasteful, and inhuman that it cannot survive in an age of technology and material progress. They hold that new forms of transportation and communication, new means of production, new standards of living and other social forces are destroying its reasons for existence." This didn't mean cities like San Francisco were doomed, necessarily—but as far as planners were concerned, the best defense was a good offense. "If we are prompt and aggressive, we can demonstrate the economies of forethought and coordination," they wrote. "The whole urban organism will be subjected to clinical examination and suitable prescriptions written."

What's illuminating though ominous in retrospect is the larger mindset of the plan, the glimpse into the era's psyche. The fears of an uncertain future due to local competition and larger economic forces were palpable, as was the confidence that wartime strategies could be applied to domestic revival. That, and faith in the value of top-down planning as practiced by the likes of Miller McClintock. Any notion that government should work *with* residents to improve on what already exists—a process that many cities in recent decades have come to embrace without question—doesn't figure into the equation. Better to define the problems as you perceive them, and then launch your counteroffensive.

This creed that big cities were at a crisis point, one where strong responses were needed, extended nationwide. The year before San Francisco released its shoreline plan, New York City published a set of public works programs "to provide employment immediately after the war"—because without it, planners warned of "a picture just too terrible to contemplate." As the war neared its end, the business-oriented Citizens Council on City Planning in Philadelphia issued a call to arms: "We must all overcome the inertia of complaisance and short vision. . . . We must blast our way into a clean new future."

Along San Francisco's shoreline, this mentality translated to a conceptual vision including a freeway running along the bay "to carry the highly important flow of heavy truck traffic along the margins of the city." New land for industrial development, and the housing that would be needed by blue-collar workers, would be created by filling at least 1,100 acres of tidal flats south of Potrero Point: "Until they are either dredged and made into deep water channels or filled and brought above the water, [tidelands] . . . contribute nothing to the advancement of the City."

Planners let the Ferry Building off lightly, though the structure and its surroundings are classified as "another blighted area in the making." The ferry slips would be cleared out to make room for anything from luxury liners to motorboats, perhaps with an area reserved for seaplanes touching down. The nave once filled with daily commuters could become a visitor's center with small museums related to maritime themes. A park in front with grass and flowering shrubs would be nice.

If all this seems vague—and it is—one reason might be that the report was published at a time when the militarization of the Bay Area had given the Ferry Building, at least temporarily, a reason for being. Southern Pacific's main waiting room held rows of triple-decker bunks for servicemen on leave, plus a Red Cross canteen and lounge. Seven daily ferries transported workers from San Francisco to shipyards in Richmond and Sausalito. "The war . . . has brought new uses for the Ferry Building and restored a measure of vitality to its surroundings," planners conceded. "The lower end of Market Street is once more important in the life of the City." But they add a caveat: "the present activities . . . are obviously temporary, and are due to disappear with the return of peace."

And once that happened?

"The Ferry Building can be kept as an antique, be put to better use or be removed," the planners write with an implicit shrug. What's more important, they emphasize, is that "the terminus of Market Street will always deserve special recognition."

...

After the war ended in September 1945, the Depression-like malaise feared by Bay Area leaders did not materialize. Quite the opposite. Servicemen from across the country who had passed through the Golden Gate on their way to the Pacific Theater chose Northern California as the place to begin their peacetime lives, beguiled by mild weather and a sense of possibility. Japanese families returned to San Francisco and found homes where they could, drawn to a familiar setting despite the injustice of having been uprooted by internment. Black residents who labored in factories on the home front, meanwhile, had little desire to head back south. There was both structural and personal racism in the Bay Area, including de facto segregation by many unions and employers, but this was nothing like southern states where Blacks were prevented from voting by poll taxes and literacy tests, and where segregation was enforced everywhere from schools to railroad cars. Lethal violence remained a threat there, too, as when a mob of White men in 1946 lynched two Black couples in a rural Georgia county. Despite a federal investigation, no one was ever charged in connection with the killings.

While individuals and families restarted their lives, civic leaders had larger goals. The triumphant end of conflict fueled the impulse for propulsive change, scrubbing the map and starting anew. A nation humiliated on the world stage by the Japanese attack on Pearl Harbor had responded with a vigor that would have been inconceivable a few years before, winning a world war on two fronts by mobilizing at a scale previously unimaginable—clearing routes in the ocean and paths through Europe, conjuring nuclear weapons and building

The Ferry Building in the early 1950s. *San Francisco History Center, San Francisco Public Library.*

Architect William Merchant's initial concept for the proposed World Trade Center, 1948. *William G. Merchant / Hans U. Gerson Collection, 1897–1998, Environmental Design Archives, UC Berkeley.*

ships and airplanes by the tens of thousands. All in less than four years.

The Ferry Building? By 1947, it had slid back into the torpor that planners had predicted. Southern Pacific still operated the transcontinental railway, but just two ferries traversed the waters between the Oakland terminus and the aging slips that served as the long route's final stop. A handful of cable cars still rolled down Nob Hill each day, thanks to a 1947 ballot initiative that thwarted City Hall's plan to replace them all with buses, but few transit lines bothered to stop at the foot of Market Street.

In a very real sense, the portal was a void. And in the new urban America, voids existed to be filled.

• • •

The lead headline on the front page of the January 22, 1948, *Chronicle* got straight to the point: "40-Story World Trade Center Urged for Ferry Building Site."

The headline wasn't intended as a warning—*beloved civic treasure at risk!*—so much as a sign of progress. The foot of Market Street would receive the "special recognition" desired in the shoreline plan. The Board of State Harbor Commissioners, which still managed the Port, had proposed the location. After all, said one commissioner, "If we fix up the poor old Ferry Building we still have a 50-year-old building."

The general idea of world trade centers dated back at least to the 1939 World's Fair in New York, where, even as the deadliest war in history neared, a building was devoted to the theme of "World Peace through World Trade." The end of World War II seemed to signal that such centers' moment had come, and civic leaders saw one as a way to reaffirm San Francisco as the trading gateway between the United States and the

Pacific Rim. New Orleans already had opened such a center in 1943. Why let another West Coast city cut in line ahead of San Francisco?

Not every local embraced the idea: "It's an outrage," one member of the city's Board of Supervisors told the *Chronicle*. "They might as well tear down the Eiffel Tower in Paris or the Statue of Liberty in New York." But other reactions echoed the letter writer to the *Examiner* who urged naysayers, "Wake up. Throw out those 1905 calendars . . . We're living in 1948. The past is past."

Equally sanguine was Leland Cutler, the president of the trade center authority. No fly-by-night huckster, the dapper Stanford graduate had built a formidable reputation as a business executive with a zest for civic projects, whether working to line up construction financing for the Bay Bridge or presiding over the Golden Gate International Exposition that spawned Treasure Island. This track record made Cutler an obvious choice to lead the trade center push: demolishing the Ferry Building "might meet with disfavor" among historians, he said the day of the announcement, but "a new and modern structure might, in effect, be a replica of the present building."

The quest was also embraced by the *Chronicle*, which followed the news story with a rhapsodic editorial praising the "logic" of clearing out the clutter of the past to move forward and seize the initiative. Rather than offering sentimental objections to the World Trade Center Authority's "bold proposal," the paper urged readers to view the swap of old for new in a different light—as "a monument to San Francisco's future."

That this future would be bigger, and emphatically different, was accepted across the board. As the planners were considering a new plan for the waterfront, there were studies underway to identify locations for a second Bay Bridge and a second Golden Gate Bridge to handle the traffic jams that the ever-growing number of commuters faced twice a day. Or consider the writings of Herb Caen, the young *Chronicle* columnist who was more popular than ever after returning from military service in Europe. He still dished out snappy observations and topical jokes, but readers particularly relished the smitten paeans to the city that was "glamorized a little by a wisp of fog." If such rhapsodies were sentimental, well, "the San Franciscan is hopelessly sentimental, and I am hopelessly San Franciscan."

Yet Caen agreed that the postwar strains were real. His chosen city's residents "can no longer sit quietly and ruminate on past glories," he wrote in 1948's *The San Francisco Book*. "The scenery? Beautiful, but no scenery can be quite as beautiful as a home to see it from." In a city with a population that grew from 634,536 to 775,357 in just one decade, he also challenged the idea of trying to protect "'landmarks' that serve no purpose today and have a doubtful importance as relics."

His next book was *Baghdad-by-the-Bay*, a celebration of his chosen city that became a national bestseller and downplayed current affairs. Yet when the Ferry Building makes an appearance, Caen sees nothing more than "this sad old pile of gray—dead and useless except for the clock that goes ticking on when all else is gone." In another chapter, he contemplates "the last rusty old streetcar rattling around the loop of the Ferry Building—old friends that have a lot to talk about, nothing to live for, and nobody to care anymore."

· · ·

The full reveal of the World Trade Center came in 1951 with the publication of a fifty-five-page prospectus on what the authors boasted would be "the most worthwhile major project in the annals of development in the west." The proposal had grown to nine blocks in size, three spanning a submerged Embarcadero and the other six perched on a mammoth pier that made A. Page Brown's vaulted concrete platform seem petite. In the center was the slab-like tower—"a landmark of massive simplicity"—surrounded by a vast plaza linked to Market Street by automobile ramps and to the bay by steps at a scale reminiscent of the ones in Soviet filmmaker Sergei Eisenstein's legendary 1925 silent classic *Battleship Potemkin.*

Schemes of this nature, eye candy unfurled with assurances that anything was possible, were nothing new to this stretch of the city. Think back to the Bay Bridge proposals of the mid-1920s, or John C. Pelton's eleventh-hour bid to recast the Ferry Building as a domed extravaganza. Now, though, government forces were the ones treating the urban terrain as a blank slate to be rearranged at will in service of a mega-development that supposedly would "foster international trade as a source of mutual understanding, which is prerequisite to lasting world peace."

The prospectus included letters of supposed support from officials that ascended in pecking order from the mayor of San Francisco to the US secretary of commerce, William Sawyer. Read closely, though, and much of the praise has a hollow ring. When Sawyer writes, "I am happy to encourage the citizens of California in their efforts to establish a World Trade Center in San Francisco," he's hardly signing on as an anchor tenant. And while Cutler no doubt was thrilled to secure a letter from Nelson Rockefeller, the New York multimillionaire with a web of international connections, his statement "congratulating the State of California on its forward-looking plans" doesn't amount to much more than a transcontinental pat on the back.

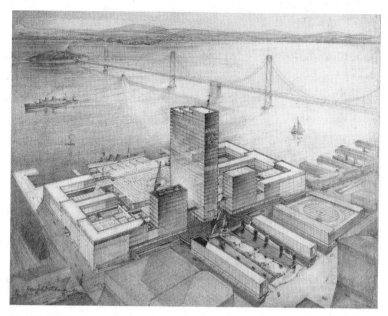

The World Trade Center as envisioned in 1951, with the Ferry Building replaced by a "landmark of massive simplicity." *William G. Merchant / Hans U. Gerson Collection, 1897–1998, Environmental Design Archives, UC Berkeley.*

The problem is that nobody could say what a world trade center would actually *do* on a day-to-day basis, or why it needed to be so large. The prospectus coincided with Cutler departing on a promotional trip to Asia after telling reporters that already "he has in hand tentative commitments to fill three buildings." A European expedition followed, but by then even the *Chronicle* was losing interest: Cutler's meeting with an Italian trade group in Rome was given a squib on an inside page beneath an article titled "Air Line Hostesses are Models for Aviation Day Travel Show."

The years of hyperbole ultimately resulted in nothing except a crude makeover of the northern wing of the Ferry Building so that it could house the trade center that opened in May 1956. Inside were displays from sixty nations, offices for

such trade-related outfits as importers and steamship companies, and services including interpreters and a small research
library. One of Brown's two ceremonial staircases was torn
out to make room for a new lobby clad in black marble. The
skylit nave was filled with two floors of office space. Modern
strip windows were added on the north and east facades. Yet
the opening-day festivities played up the pomp as if the original expansive vision had been realized, complete with a speech
where Cutler solemnly intoned, "if trade does not cross barriers, armies will."

If the saga of San Francisco's World Trade Center has its
hubris—"A Preview of Wonderland" is the title of the prospectus chapter on the proposed first phase—it shows the desire
of the Port and the city to present an updated image to the
world. The other thing it shows is the futility of large-scale,
long-range plans. Architects and urban designers might think
they can control the course of the future, but they're no match
for cultural and technological reality.

At the same time Cutler was touting how the proposed
World Trade Center would lure new business to the city, for
instance, the Port of Oakland was making itself the region's
dominant port of call. By 1950, the amount of cargo coming into and out of Oakland rivaled San Francisco, and the
harbor commissioners were scrambling to compete. Piers 15
and 17 were combined to attract larger vessels. Several piers
were designated as a foreign trade zone, a bid to tap into the
hoped-for business that the World Trade Center would bring.

None of this made much difference—and as the decade
neared its end, the harbor commission hired Ebasco Services,
a New York consulting firm, to analyze how the Port could
prepare for an age that was likely to move cargo in much different ways. Freight ships were growing in size, with shipping

companies demanding ample land around piers to load and unload. Produce and other goods that once arrived from the Central Valley on small vessels via the Sacramento River delta now entered the city on the back of trucks.

Ebasco proposed a strategy to focus maritime investment on the southern waterfront. The Embarcadero would be a transition zone, where piers deemed obsolete would make way for revenue-producing uses to subsidize the expansion to the south. As for the clock-towered landmark at the Embarcadero's heart, the one waterfront building that every San Franciscan knew, there was no recommendation at all.

"We leave the future of the Ferry Building in the lap of the gods," an Ebasco spokesman told the press.

• • •

The gods, one hoped, would be more charitable than the makers of *It Came from beneath the Sea*, a 1955 slice of B-movie sci-fi remembered mainly for the participation of special-effects wizard Ray Harryhausen. The story itself was standard 1950s matinee fare; scientists discover a horrible truth that higher-ups dismiss. A bit player scoffs and suffers the consequences. In the final reel—spoiler alert—all hell breaks loose.

In this case, "It" is an octopus of eye-popping enormity dislodged by an H-bomb test from the deepest recesses of the Pacific Ocean. Fast-forward through seventy minutes of story exposition, an unconvincing romantic subplot and the occasional glimpse of *really* big cephalopod appendages, and the protagonist nears San Francisco Bay. The Golden Gate Bridge doesn't fare well. Depth charges don't faze the hungry predator. One black tentacle slithers over the Embarcadero's stubby piers, another pokes through a bulkhead arch. Four sucker-studded arms ooze up to caress the Ferry Building's tower as the obligatory crowd of extras runs screaming—and then, then, then. . . .

Snap!

The top of the clocktower buckles. The concrete shaft crumples. According to the one side that briefly remains upright, it is 5:40 p.m. when what's done is done.

Harryhausen cultists are right: the special effects pack a retro punch. It's fun to see shots of 1950s San Francisco, slithering tentacles and all. We also get a hint of the Ferry Building's diminished iconic stature—while one snippet in the movie trailer is splashed by the lurid pronouncement "Golden Gate Bridge UPROOTED!," the phrase implanted on a glimpse of the clocktower's demise is a more general "Buildings Topple!"

However rudely *It Came from beneath the Sea* might have treated the Ferry Building, it's hard to view the destruction as anything personal. Simply put, you don't want to be a tall building along the water in a movie about a nuclear-powered octopus.

The real threat to the Ferry Building back then was from a much different source—not along the water, but above the Embarcadero.

THE PORT OF SAN FRANCISCO JUNE 1ST 1849.

A lithograph depicting Yerba Buena Cove as seen from Rincon Hill in 1849, after the Gold Rush began but before the young city's shoreline was transformed beyond recognition. *California State Library.*

One of the first detailed maps of San Francisco shows a city already intent on pushing eastward, into the bay. *David Rumsey Map Collection, David Rumsey Map Center, Stanford Libraries.*

FIG. 1.—VIEW OF NEW FERRY HOUSE AT SAN FRANCISCO, CAL.
Page Brown, Architect.   Howard C. Holmes, Chief Engineer.

A construction-era rendering that hints at civic ambitions—even though the dimensions of the tower are off, the magisterial bays at either end were never built, and the plaza was never so orderly. Engineering News, *July 29, 1897.*

A stereograph—one of many printed for mass distribution—showing San Francisco during the conflagration that followed the 1906 earthquake. *Courtesy of the Library of Congress, LOT 11523-5.*

Market Street and its surroundings a few months later, with the Ferry Building's clock tower shrouded for repairs. *San Francisco History Center, San Francisco Public Library.*

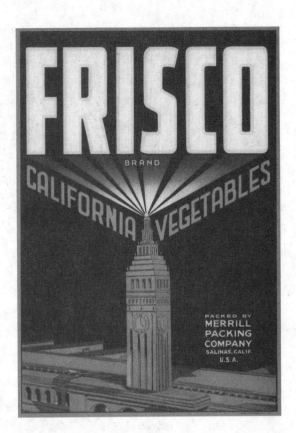

The Ferry Building's role
as cultural icon in the
1930s included a place of
honor on labels for Merrill
Packing Co.'s Frisco brand
of produce. "That was the
symbol of San Francisco
back then," says the current
owner. *Merrill Farms.*

The historic icon didn't
fare nearly so well—
destruction by a mutant
octopus—in the 1955
film *It Came from
Beneath the Sea. IT
CAME FROM BENEATH
THE SEA © 1955, renewed
1983 Columbia Pictures
Industries, Inc. All Rights
Reserved. Courtesy of
Columbia Pictures.*

The Bay Bridge during construction, a triumph of infrastructure that also hastened the decline of ferry service. *San Francisco History Center, San Francisco Public Library.*

Another sign of "progress": the Embarcadero Freeway on the rise. The viaduct opened in 1959, severing downtown from its shoreline until 1991. San Francisco Chronicle.

San Francisco's landscape of unbuilt visions includes this proposed bay span from 1926 that was to enter the city above Broadway, with a southern connection bringing commuter trains directly to the Ferry Building. *San Francisco Department of Public Works Proposed San Francisco-Oakland Bay Bridges Records (SFH 87), SF History Center, SF Public Library.*

"A terminal for aesthetic, culinary, recreational, and cultural experiences": I. M. Pei & Partners' ambitious makeover of the Ferry Building in the 1980s would have attached terraced wings along the bay. *Paul Stevenson Oles / Pei Cobb Freed & Partners.*

A reborn icon: The landmark's interior market, 2018. *San Francisco Chronicle / Jessica Christian.*

The Ferry Plaza Farmers Market in full swing—where organic growers meet serious foodies and sightseeing tourists. San Francisco Chronicle / *Michael Macor.*

The city changes but A. Page Brown's creation remains. During the Occupy protests that swept America in 2011, a tent city took root on the Embarcadero near Market Street. San Francisco Chronicle / *Michael Macor.*

Like so many parades in the past, the 2022 celebration of the Golden State Warriors' NBA championship proceeded up Market Street. This parade included Stephen Curry and his wife, Ayesha, atop a double-decker bus. San Francisco Chronicle / *Santiago Mejia.*

Bob Bastian's 1957 cartoon: "Hey, folks, HERE I am!" San Francisco Chronicle.

ON DECEMBER 13, 1957, AN EDITORIAL CARTOON IN THE *CHRONICLE* presented a take on the Ferry Building that bore no resemblance to the atmospheric postcards of prior decades. The clocktower had arms and a comically forlorn human face, its big round eyes peering over a prison-like double-deck roadway. From between blunt horizontal bars the clocktower's round mouth called out, "Hey Folks, *here* I am!"

The structure in the foreground, though caricatured, wasn't much different than highways going up in cities across the nation—a grimly functional artery intended to ease the path of automotive traffic and override those "obstructions to its free use" that car-loving transportation guru Miller McClintock had complained about in his studies before the war. What counted was minimum fuss for private automobiles and commercial trucks with somewhere to go. If the tradeoff included destroying family homes, or cleaving whole neighborhoods, or cloaking streets and sidewalks in shadows and fumes from above—that was a small price to pay for improving a driver's experience behind the wheel.

The difference between the Embarcadero Freeway and other highways then being built in cities across the country was the centrality and renown of the location. San Francisco's first elevated freeway was being imposed on the most cherished local vista imaginable: men and women accustomed to seeing the Ferry Building's reassuring poise punctuate the view down Market Street were now confronted by a sixty-foot-tall concrete freeway blocking the classical facade and closing off any sense of connection to the water beyond. Other freeways came earlier, in the Bay Area and elsewhere; San Franciscans were being shown, before residents of other large cities, what can happen when progress is pursued with no accounting for place.

• • •

Given the vitriol with which the Embarcadero Freeway is regarded today—certainly by those of us who remember the structure's bleak presence, and how the waterfront came back to life when liberated from its hulking girth—you might assume that the plans for a shoreline-severing "skyway" were met with outrage from day one.

Wrong.

Wade through newspaper clips and official studies detailing San Francisco's transportation metamorphosis after World War II, and what emerges instead is a militaristic strategy to impose a network of modern roadways onto the city's quirky collage of street grids and steep hills—a strategy built on the assumption that clearing the way from point A to point B was a matter of life or death for big cities. Cars were the future of urban movement, so a metropolis like San Francisco must accept car supremacy if it had any hope of long-term prosperity. The diagnosis by McClintock and other transportation planners was considered irrefutable. The question was how forcefully to apply the cure.

"The very survival of San Francisco as a healthful and efficiently functioning city is dependent upon resolving the not-so-slow strangulation which a deficient transportation system is inflicting," was the warning sounded in 1948 by the president of the city's Planning Commission, Ernest Torregano, in his introduction to a 428-page *Transportation Plan for San Francisco* that Torregano called "the only attack that can break the stranglehold . . . (and) check the forces of disintegration fostered by an outdated and inadequate system of transportation facilities."

Unlike the McClintock study, released at the tail end of the Depression, this one arrived the year after voters approved a $55 million bond for roads and transit. This timing might explain the assured tone of the report that followed the Planning Commission president's bombastic call to arms, a roadmap for remaking San Francisco that framed the task ahead by stating simply that "the city has two basic functions—it is a machine for production, distribution and services, and it is a place for living."

To keep the machine humming, the plan by the consulting

firm of De Leuw Cather and Co. mapped out an elaborate set of roadways to connect drivers with the world beyond their homes. People in the Sunset District below Golden Gate Park, for example, would be able to pilot their cars onto a new freeway that would slice through a corner of the beloved open space before heading east through the park's block-wide panhandle. The new highway would rise to meet the Central Freeway, another proposed addition, near Van Ness Avenue. From there our hypothetical Sunset District resident could drive above the fray toward the Bay Bridge, or descend into a partially submerged "parkway" that offered a clear shot north to the Marina District before curving back west toward the Golden Gate Bridge.

The consultants did suggest running express buses on new freeways, since "convenient and fast transit service may be expected to attract a considerable number of persons who would otherwise travel by automobile." But the plan's primary concern was the need for car-friendly infrastructure: "a thoroughly coordinated and balanced system of thoroughfares adequate to meet San Francisco's needs."

. . .

Politicians were happy to fall in line behind Torregano and his consultants, updating the city's master plan in 1951 to emphasize the need for additional expressways. The state already was building the Bayshore Freeway north from the peninsula along the edge of the Mission District, enlarging a preexisting surface highway through mostly industrial areas. San Francisco wanted the state's next investment to be a skyway extending from the Bay Bridge all the way up the Embarcadero, offering the exhilaration of gliding to the Financial District and neighborhoods like North Beach and Chinatown without having to slog through the blue-collar blocks south of Market Street. The first phase would reach as far north as Broadway; after that it would complete the bend around Telegraph Hill and run past Fisherman's Wharf, perhaps as far as the Golden Gate Bridge. Nobody seemed to mind, at least not at first. When the state agreed to fund the extension, the *Chronicle* hailed "a more rational solution of our ever-increasing traffic problem" and awaited "the spectacular scenic possibilities that can be realized by skillful engineering designs." The State Division of Highways went so far as to declare in one piece of bureaucratic propaganda that this and other planned skyways "will become synonymous with the city of San Francisco, restoring to its people and their visitors the opportunities of viewing the city which were lost with the departure of the ferries."

Put that way, you might think car owners were being issued flying carpets from which to savor "the beauty which has long been San Francisco's fame," according to state engineers. But in the fall of 1955, as groundbreaking approached, something remarkable happened: the city's business leadership had second thoughts. Bankers, developers, and the chamber of commerce began lobbying mayor-elect George Christopher to intervene with the state to curve the skyway several hundred feet to the west where it passed the Ferry Building—giving the onetime transit temple room to breathe, so to speak.

The belated crusade had the support of the State Park Commission, which went so far as to suggest that the Ferry Building could house a state historical museum—if, and only if, it had a proper physical setting. The grandly titled Citizens Committee for a Ferry Building Park took the cue, bringing in an architect and landscape architect to craft a speculative design for what was conceived as a twelve-acre plaza buffering the landmark.

"We accept the freeway's need and presence," the designers assured Christopher in a letter that December, one month before he was to be sworn in as mayor. Then they played the nostalgia card, hoping it might connect with a Greek immigrant who ran a small dairy as he climbed the political ladder to become president of the Board of Supervisors. The Ferry Building was "so much a symbol of another age," they wrote. "It only needs a use and setting. Both are now possible."

Chamber of commerce president Thomas Mellon led business opposition to the state-approved route that, he told the State Park Commission at one hearing, "will mar the face of the Ferry Building and lessen its value as a historic monument." Highway engineers were saying the altered route could cause a two-year delay and drive up costs, but Mellon and others argued that a world-class park would justify the expense in the long term. So did the *Chronicle*'s editorial writers: no longer exulting in the thrill of soaring above the city, they weighed in against "isolating and confining the Ferry Building in a two-story strait jacket, behind 10 additional lanes of surface traffic."

Alas, pragmatism won the day at City Hall as Christopher, along with the rest of the Board, voted to stick with the approved route rather than put everything on hold for sentimental reasons. The vote came after a hearing where, reported the *Examiner*, "proponents of the curved freeway, armed with an elaborate collection of sketches, diagrams and projection slides, failed to impress the board." Elected officials also shrugged off the city's planning director's argument that the approved route would "destroy the Ferry Building functionally and aesthetically."

City planners made one last push to soften the visual impact, hiring an outside architect to design a park that might convince the state to give the Ferry Building special status, even with the concrete wall close by.

Their choice was Mario Ciampi, an ebullient San Francisco native who had attended the classical Beaux Arts Institute in Paris in the 1930s before embracing the cause of fearless modern architecture. Too fearless, perhaps. Ciampi proposing lopping off the Ferry Building's wings and keeping only the campanile-like clock tower—his idea being that people on Market Street would be intrigued by the glimpse of grass and water beyond the viaduct, and then stroll underneath the concrete decks to explore such supposed enticements as a 620-foot circular pier with a lagoon and old ships inside it, a heliport to the north, and a cruise terminal to the south.

The city's main library displayed a model of Ciampi's unfettered shapeshifting for several weeks. Christopher, who was willing to see a park move forward as long as it didn't slow down the freeway's construction, lobbied the State Park Commission on behalf of the "dynamic plan" for the Ferry Building's immediate surroundings. The commission didn't budge; "I trust you're ready to throw this in the bay," its chairman told the mayor after being shown the model.

• • •

Quixotic efforts to do *something* about the freeway persisted as construction began. Business leaders suggested an underground tunnel where it crossed Market Street, but state engineers said this would cost $15 million. One paper called for shade-tolerant rhododendrons and azaleas to be planted below the skyway while adorning the clock tower with painted strips of blue ("like that of our fishing fleet, but lighter in tone"). City planners offered that gold paint might perk up the viaduct's concrete.

The Embarcadero Freeway during construction, 1958.
San Francisco Chronicle.

Mayor Christopher listened to all ideas, never budging from the position he took at his final supervisors' hearing: "We can't afford to sit idly by and twiddle our thumbs and take no action." It was a remark very much in the tenor of the push-forward age, coming from a moderate Republican who was elected mayor by a comfortable margin and took pride in cutting through red tape to make things happen.

As workers made their way up the Embarcadero, driving piles and pouring cement, it became impossible to pretend that change was for the better. The bay waterfront, San Francisco's original reason for being, was now a darkened backroad. The culprit? A boorish intruder that could not be ignored—not by office workers looking out their windows, not by Telegraph Hill residents looking down on a crude concrete gash, and not by anyone flummoxed by the rerouted traffic along the old piers. When the freeway opened in February 1959, there was no fanfare. Instead, the month before, the Board of Supervisors stunned state officials by voting to reject six of the ten approved freeways that the same Board had added to the city's master plan in 1951.

Though the De Leuw Cather plan had seemed inevitable when it was first unveiled, the first phase of Embarcadero Freeway became the *only* phase, its two decks halting abruptly at Broadway, five blocks north of the Ferry Building. The Central Freeway, which was starting to go up at the same time, was halted as well. Gone was the "Panhandle Freeway" that would trim the edges of Golden Gate Park—along with the "Crosstown Freeway" that would have cut past Twin Peaks through the middle-class residential areas of Glen Park and the Inner Sunset.

San Franciscans are nothing if not self-important, and local lore has dubbed this "Freeway Revolt" the first in the nation. The claim is an overstatement, as local legends often are. The Central Artery that ruptured several of Boston's oldest neighborhoods was delayed by lawsuits for several years before it opened in 1959. And even as New York infrastructure czar Robert Moses was pushing forward such destructive projects as the Cross Bronx Expressway that forced more than 1,500 families out of their homes, Greenwich Village activists successfully blocked his plan to cut Washington Square Park in half with a four-lane extension of 5th Avenue—not a freeway, but a powerful reminder that the power of planners like Moses wasn't absolute. The leaders of the Washington Square Park defense included Jane Jacobs, whose 1961 book *The Death and Life of American Cities* crystallized the idea that cities are not emotionless machines, but living organisms.

Still, the wider repercussions of San Francisco's "revolt" are undeniable. In 1989, surveying how freeways ran into citizen roadblocks in metropolises as disparate as Philadelphia, Miami, Milwaukee, and Seattle, urban historians Bernard

Frieden and Lynne Sagalyn wrote that "the San Francisco action . . . was a source of encouragement for highway opponents in dozens of other cities." Locally, the scale of the rejection was profound. Pulling the plug on what would have been state routes largely financed by the federal highway program scuttled $60 million that already had been committed to the city, as well as throwing $377 million of a $500 million program into limbo.

One state highway engineer "watched the proceedings . . . with some amazement," the *Examiner* observed. The *Chronicle* called the Board's vote "unanimous, seemingly compulsive and taken in full view of 162 freeway foes who crowded into the Board's chambers, sensing the kill." If nothing else, conventional wisdom had shattered. Politicians who at the beginning of the decade embraced the need for urban freeways, and residents who had craved automotive freedom above all else, could see that "progress" had a dark side.

• • •

The Embarcadero Freeway in and of itself didn't spark the wider opposition by neighborhood residents across the city who fought the engineers' plans for an interconnected set of supposedly efficient throughways. But that first early freeway validated their fears—they'd seen what happened on the waterfront, and they didn't want it happening to them.

The Ferry Building acted as a bellwether, a role it would come to play increasingly in the decades that followed. The way defenders rallied around it, though too late, rebuked the notion that character and heritage mattered nothing when weighed against "the economies of forethought and coordination," to quote the 1943 shoreline plan. As for the violence with which the Ferry Building had been severed from the city, that made the larger dangers plain to see. If a beloved land-mark could be treated so callously, was *anything* safe?

Or as one resident of Glen Park told the city's director of public works at a raucous 1958 hearing over plans for a free-way through that quiet hilly neighborhood: "The Ferry Build-ing situation gives clear evidence as to just what can happen when careless planning and thoughtless groups are given too much power."

The connection made by this resident wasn't random, as the Freeway Revolt was to prove. Despite the resounding vote of the supervisors in January 1959, several highway proposals kept coming back to life. One was the route that would have extended east through Golden Gate Park's panhandle to meet the Central Freeway. By this time, opponents weren't content to write dismayed letters or fill public hearings—the pushback included a festive 1964 gathering in the park that was orga-nized by twenty-six neighborhood organizations and attended by thousands of opponents.

Among the highlights: a short set of songs by folk singer Malvina Reynolds, whose 1962 song "Little Boxes" with its lampooning of "ticky tacky" suburbia became a hit after Pete Seeger recorded it.

At the 1964 protest, Reynolds debuted a new song, "Cement Octopus." You'd think she had just been watching *It Came from beneath the Sea*:

That octopus rose like a science fiction blight/
The bay and the Ferry Building are out of sight.

Once again, the Ferry Building served as a potent symbol. Functional or not, the structure excelled as a measuring rod and a rallying point. Widely loved and one of a kind, it was an ever-present reminder that many aspects of the landscapes around us are irreplaceable.

. . .

Without much fanfare, Southern Pacific won permission in May 1958 to end ferry service between Oakland and San Francisco. Its two remaining vessels—one a backup for the other— would be dispensed with, and passengers would travel the last segment by bus. The Ferry Building's original function was now fully obsolete.

"We at Southern Pacific regret the passing of the ferries," claimed newspaper ads that ran as closing day neared. "However, we must face the fact that the last remaining ferry boats are more an ornament than an efficient, up-to-date means of transporting train passengers across the bay." Service continued until July 30, with ridership so heavy the final week that extra runs were added. Which raises the question of where those patrons had been for the past decade. You can guess the likely answer: in their cars. "I haven't ridden this thing for 28 years," one man told a *Chronicle* reporter—"with a laugh"—on one of the final runs. "But it's a nice sunny day for a ride on the bay."

EIGHT

WHETHER YOU LOVED OR HATED IT—OR HATED IT BUT LOVED THE concrete behemoth's enticing ease—the Embarcadero Freeway offered a stunning ride on its upper deck.

Coming from North Beach, the journey began with a propulsive curve from Broadway that swung to the right as it gained elevation and showcased the Bay Bridge in its metallic stride across open water. The view into the city was both dramatic and daunting, a bulky clot of towers that thickened year after year, all of them lacking the chiseled romance that emanated from the terracotta-clad skyline the slabs had engulfed. They also blocked Twin Peaks and other hills that gave San Francisco a look like no other American metropolis. Construction cranes came and went, adding to the layered wall of rectangular forms that from some angles evoked bundled stacks of computer cards.

The view on the left, toward the bay? Same as it ever was.

The 1960s and '70s passed with no obvious change at all. You could barely see the graying piers below, where fewer and fewer ships pulled in or sailed out. The Ferry Building clocktower, at least, still had gravitas—but if traffic stopped moving and there was time for a close look, the driver would realize that the landmark had seen better days. The dignified old friend looked faded, in need of new paint, and the driver might wonder if big new buildings like the ones to the right would soon begin to line the bay as well.

Fair question. Because the freeway's upper deck placed you in the middle of San Francisco's ongoing struggle over the kind of city that it wanted to be.

· · ·

In many ways, the story of San Francisco during these decades mirrored that of big cities across America. Municipal governments were eager for developers to build high-rises, hoping that corporate shafts might reverse suburban sprawl. Urban renewal leveled neighborhoods with Black or low-income residents, from young families to retired longshoremen in single-room-occupancy hotels, who deserved much better than cruel displacement and flattened memories; in San Francisco's case, the buildings covering dozens of blocks of the Western Addition were razed after planners classified the heart of the district as a "blighted area" that could be redeveloped to become a new frontier with "all the beauty and restfulness of the suburbs combined with all the advantages of 'the City.'" In reality, thousands of residents were displaced. Newly built public housing deteriorated rapidly. Large barren lots stayed empty for decades. To the extent there had been blight, what followed was worse.

Nor was the upheaval confined to the built terrain. The number of homicides in San Francisco climbed from 36 in 1960 to 109 a decade later and 138 in 1975, similar to increases in older cities across the United States. The lurid local strain culminated in 1978 with the assassination at City Hall of Mayor George Moscone and Harvey Milk, the city's first openly gay supervisor, by an ex-supervisor who had once been a police officer.

If crime and destructive urban renewal projects marred San Francisco in this period, the city was reinvigorated by fresh variations of the social and cultural forces that throughout the city's history have taken root in "an ideal place for a poet and artist to live, especially one who considered himself a kind of expatriate," in the words of Lawrence Ferlinghetti, who arrived in 1951 after a train journey from New York that culminated in the short ferry ride from Oakland.

Had he been on a bus, it's unlikely that Ferlinghetti's first impression would have conjured up such imagery as this recollection fifty years later:

> Approaching the Ferry Building, he stood on deck and saw a small shining white city, looking rather like Tunis seen from seaward, a Mediterranean city, with small white houses on hillsides, brilliant in January sunshine.

The son of an Italian immigrant, Ferlinghetti had commanded submarine chasers in World War II and studied at the Sorbonne before moving to San Francisco, where he was in the vanguard of what became known as the Beat movement— opening City Lights Bookstore in 1953, publishing poets like Allen Ginsberg and Gregory Corso and writing his own poetry collections such as *A Coney Island of the Mind*. He remained on the scene as beatniks were followed by the young people branded as hippies by the media, and the gay men and lesbians who moved into neighborhoods that working-class residents were leaving behind for the suburbs.

The draws included the proximity to nature, the reputation for tolerance and diversity, the notion that San Francisco was the rare American city that welcomed nonconformists. "In the Eastern states, you feel two-dimensional," Alan Watts, whose writings on Zen Buddhism rippled through the nation's counterculture, said in 1961. "San Francisco reminds you that you have a third dimension as well." All this enriched an experimental stew where individuals felt free to challenge the powers-that-be. Sometimes on national issues, such as the opposition to the war in Vietnam or the discrimination and economic inequality that persisted in America despite the passage of the Civil Rights Act in 1964. Other fights were local, like stopping freeways or trying to prevent new buildings from climbing so high.

Amid this upheaval was the enduring presence of the Ferry Building—a steadying force in some ways, a statuesque rebuke in others. The generational shifts that had made it superfluous, such as the triumph of automobiles embodied by the Embarcadero Freeway, helped in an odd way to amplify its cultural importance. Elsewhere, newer towers gradually obscured landmarks like Los Angeles City Hall or Boston's Custom House Tower to the point where it was easy to forget they were there. But with a powerful waterfront setting, and tall corporate intruders kept at (figurative) bay by the ungainly viaduct, the Ferry Building stood apart. Isolation could be read as something like defiance.

. . .

The same month that City Hall halted the Embarcadero Freeway, Cyril Magnin unveiled Embarcadero City—an audacious

Cyril Magnin (left) and Governor Edmund Brown at the unveiling of Embarcadero City. *San Francisco History Center, San Francisco Public Library.*

plan that left the Ferry Building standing but acted as if it did not exist.

There were gauzy renderings from an impossible perch high in the air, discreet clouds adding a hint of romance. The governor was on hand, along with the mayor and a state senator. To stoke anticipation, the plan was teased beforehand in a sneak preview that the chosen recipient, the *Chronicle*, splashed across page one. "Investors will be fighting to come in," Magnin, the chairman of the San Francisco Port Commission, assured the reporter. This new waterfront, he predicted, could make San Francisco "the greatest city in the world."

Orchestrated product launches were old hat to the fifty-nine-year-old Magnin, who had turned one of his family's department stores, Joseph Magnin, into a thirty-two-store West Coast success known for its chic anticipation of fashion trends. No mere bureaucrat, Magnin served on charitable boards and was a patron of the arts. He made the rounds at night though he did not drink, lived for decades in a penthouse atop a Nob Hill hotel and was the city's (unpaid) chief of protocol for much of that time. He also befriended politicians of all stripes, including Goodwin Knight, a Republican who was elected governor in 1953 with financial support from Magnin, a Democrat.

When Knight asked Magnin to chair the Board of State Harbor Commissioners in 1954, the retailer signed on even though "I didn't know a thing about shipping," he recounts in his autobiography. He skimmed a pile of maritime books and then got down to work, rebranding the agency as the San Francisco Port Authority and selling voters on a $50 million bond measure to upgrade the Port "using the merchandising techniques I'd learned my whole life in the business." The victory felt good but he took it in stride: "I was born with the ability to make people see things my way."

He seemed to have hit the mark once again, judging by the positive initial reaction to Embarcadero City, which proposed to line the seawall between the Ferry Building and Fisherman's Wharf with an abundance of attractions designed for the Port by architects Ernest Born and John Bolles. The old finger piers would make way for platforms holding a colorful modernist buffet of structures, including a performing arts center and a skating rink. A retail street and an eighteen-thousand-seat convention hall. A cruise ship terminal and a whole lot more.

"Bold and imaginative" was the verdict of Governor Edmund Brown. The architects likened their approach to "a continuous world's fair." Everything would be privately financed, Magnin assured the press at the unveiling, and predicted, "It won't be a matter of finding investors—but of selecting the ones we want." He also offered a sop to the nostalgics: "most of the antiquated piers" would be replaced, the *Examiner* reported, but Magnin assured listeners that a few would remain intact "to retain a maritime atmosphere along the entire waterfront."

Magnin's aim wasn't simply to jazz up the Embarcadero. He, like the consultants at Ebasco, saw the need to reinvent the Port that now was his responsibility.

Throughout the 1950s, the cross-bay rival Port of Oakland had continued to expand, helped by its proximity to railroad freight lines and the new freeways connecting the Bay Area to California's Central Valley. These traditional advantages of location and convenience were amplified by the rise of container shipping—the now-universal system in which cargo is placed beforehand into metal containers that can be transported on a freight train or the back of a flatbed truck to dock, where they're lifted onto ships by gantry cranes. This sped up the shipping process enormously. It also required fewer longshoremen than traditional "break bulk" cargo, in which a single vessel might hold everything from bags of coffee beans to barrels of olives, coils of steel, and bundles of copra, the dried coconut meat that for decades was San Francisco's top import from the Pacific islands. The cargo often was stored in the sheds atop finger piers for days at a time, tying up space and slowing things down even more.

The container age began in 1956, when a converted World War II tanker sailed to Houston from Newark, New Jersey, with fifty-eight metal truck trailers bolted to its deck. Within two years one of San Francisco's largest Port tenants, Matson Navigation Co., was using containers to ship goods to and from Hawaii. By 1960, Matson had its first container-only vessel, as the maritime giant founded in the city in 1901 began investing in larger container ships. Larger ships create a need for larger port facilities, and Oakland had room to grow—unlike the Embarcadero, where the finger piers were cramped and the new overhead roadway offered little room for big trucks and cranes.

Factors like this explain why Ebasco's 1959 report called for concentrating new shipping investments on spacious Port-owned land to the south. That same year Magnin began his pitch for Embarcadero City, treating the Embarcadero as real estate that, with the right packaging, could generate profits to help fund the Port's maritime improvements.

But treating a historic waterfront as a development zone was more fraught than other forms of marketing, as Magnin and fellow proponents of Embarcadero City and subsequent proposals were to learn. Everyone had an opinion—especially with the Ferry Building standing tall amid the commotion, a figurative question mark about the wisdom of casting aside what endured, for what power brokers said was needed.

Skepticism about the Port's chosen path received a national airing when *Holiday* magazine, a popular travel journal of the era, devoted its April 1961, issue to San Francisco. The reason for such extensive coverage, the editors explained to readers, was to give writers and photographers leeway to explore a city that "embodies culture, sophistication, taste, and a self-assurance that can take even the rise and proliferation of the beatnik in stride." One article was by novelist Calvin Kentfield, a former seaman who recounted a lazy waterfront stroll with just one jarring moment: an encounter with Magnin, who gushed to him how Embarcadero City "will be the most beautiful thing, the most beautiful thing. Can you imagine?" Kentfield could do so too well. "I wouldn't like anyone to think I'm not for progress," he wrote, "but I'm sure Mr. Magnin will forgive me if, for now, I withhold my unbridled enthusiasm." Kendall was realistic enough to acknowledge in his piece that working waterfronts like the Embarcadero evolve "day to day, minute to minute," except in a single spot.

> One thing that does not change is the Ferry Building . . . The Ferry Building was once the focus of the Bay. Now its slips are vacant and its concourse quiet, but it remains, nonetheless, the heart and brains of the harbor.

· · ·

In 1962, Mario Ciampi again was hired by City Hall to envision a park beneath the Embarcadero Freeway. The determined visionary promptly resurrected his idea of removing the wings of the Ferry Building. He also upped the stakes by proposing office towers on new landfill in the bay on either side of Brown's campanile. A gesture of this sort, he enthused, would create "a dramatic beginning for Market Street." (Drama takes strange forms.)

"We'll study anything," Magnin said after agreeing to let the city's official tire-kicking include the state-owned Port land. "I'd just hate to be the one who suggests tearing down the Ferry Building when the people hear about it."

When Magnin made his quip, he might have been thinking about one of the few people in San Francisco who was as influential as he was: Herb Caen.

Mario Ciampi's 1962 waterfront vision, including two modern towers on new piers to the Ferry Building's east. *Prelinger Library & Archives.*

Writing six columns a week, described by *Time* magazine as "probably the most loyally read columnist in the U.S.," Caen was no longer a proponent of the need for assertive change. More and more, he shared fears about what his adopted home might become.

"Damn and doom me for a reactionary if you will, but I still find a cable car more cunning than a freeway built across the graves of houses that once knew laughter and tears," Caen wrote in June 1959—a reference to the Central Freeway, which consumed several blocks of Hayes Valley in the Western Addition before being halted by the Freeway Revolt. His frustration grew more pointed a few paragraphs later: "Does it matter, now, that the Ferry Building was once the most important building in town; it will disappear too, one of these days, and then a fresh batch of newcomers will wonder why YOU'RE so upset, Newcomer turned Old-Timer."

Days after Ciampi's renewed pitch for Ferry Park, Caen fired off a full-column diatribe against "a bad joke in the worst possible taste," no doubt hastening the rapid descent of that trial balloon. "The line, and I don't mean a mythical one, must surely be drawn at the Ferry Building. I can't think of a landmark I'd fight harder to save."

Ciampi's plan was so extravagantly impractical it soon sank out of sight despite having been commissioned by the planning department. No revolt was needed. But as the 1960s drew to an end, two development proposals surfaced that, for Caen, marked the crossing of the line. This time, he and Magnin were on opposite sides.

. . .

Ferry Port Plaza, announced in 1969 and formally submitted in June 1970, would have replaced Piers 1 through 7 with a seventeen-acre platform stretching 1,300 feet into the bay. The mega-pier would hold a single building stretching west from the Embarcadero with eight stories of shops and offices at one end, a ten-story hotel at the other and, in between, a linear glass atrium to connect the two wings. One of architect Chuck Bassett's sketches showed a sailboat bobbing in the water and—shades of that 1957 editorial cartoon—the Ferry Building peeking through the multistory glass passage.

Immense though the proposed plaza might be, the developer stressed that "high rise buildings are not a part of Ferry Port Plaza plans"— a tacit reference to the *other* proposal flanking the Ferry Building, a forty-story office tower that United States Steel sought to erect on a new triangular pier beginning directly to the south. The high-rise would be accompanied by a cruise terminal that US Steel would build free of charge; this benefit, boosters argued, justified the tower even though it was four times the height of waterfront zoning that the Port had agreed to the prior year as part of a larger plan for the Embarcadero.

Architect Charles Bassett's sketch of Ferry Port Plaza, with the Ferry Building
visible through its glass atrium. *SOM.*

"We are in the process of building a beautiful frame for the
beautiful picture of San Francisco," Magnin said with pride.

Caen assessed the pair of projects much differently—as "the
Whale," in the case of the horizontal Ferry Port Plaza, and for
the sky-bumping US Steel monolith, "the Giraffe."

Those nicknames appear in a 1970 column memorably
titled "Shove It Up Your Skyline," which was built around an
interview with architect Bassett of Skidmore Owings & Merrill, the firm designing both projects.

*When I first saw a model of Ferry Port Plaza, I ven-
tured to Mr. Bassett, "It sort of overshadows the
Ferry Building, don't you think?" He was offended.
"Who cares about the goddamn Ferry Building?" he
snapped. "If I had my way, I'd tear it down . . . it's*

*nothing but a bus depot with a tower. In fact, I'd tear
down every old building in town except City Hall."*

Whether or not this vignette is gospel truth, it makes for
lively reading. So does Caen's aside that "Mr. Bassett gets
quite emotional in defending his pets." The column ends with
Caen inviting readers to join the crusade: "At noon today,
there will be a walk along the waterfront by those who say
'This far and no farther.'"

Several thousand people turned out for the march, which
culminated with everyone releasing balloons at the Ferry
Building. The pre-march rally included two bona fide celeb-
rities, film idol Paul Newman and actress Joanne Woodward.
The couple had flown from Los Angeles that weekend for a
film festival tribute to Newman, then forty-five, and before
returning home they stopped by to lend what the actor called
"moral support." "San Francisco is probably one of the last
great cities," Newman told a reporter covering the march,
"and projects like this will ruin it."

Ultimately, neither the Whale nor the Giraffe found homes
on the Embarcadero. Ferry Port Plaza was blocked by the Bay
Conservation and Development Commission, a regulatory
agency founded in 1965 because of public concerns over development threats to what remained of the natural shoreline. The
commission had final say on projects along the bay, even if
cities or counties gave them the green light; as far as the young
agency was concerned, clearing out five piers to create a single
mega-pier would not do. Then US Steel called it quits when the
Board of Supervisors voted that waterfront heights could not
exceed 175 feet, period.

Nobody was more dismayed by all this than Magnin, who
left the Port Commission in 1974—a self-described "futurist,"

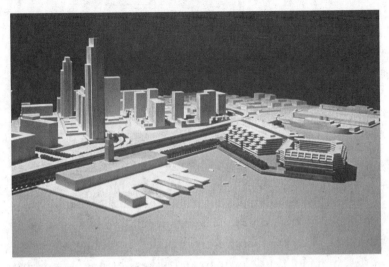

Model of waterfront with Ferry Port Plaza, 1970 (right). *Courtesy Jeffrey Heller.*

but also a person who genuinely loved his life-long home. In his 1981 autobiography, he reiterated his belief that "the waterfront should have been redeveloped with sensibility." You can imagine the author shaking his head: "The times were very much against us . . . I thought I could accomplish something. But there were too many blockades in my way."

In hindsight, it's easy to dismiss these initiatives that went astray as trivia for planning buffs. Not so. Look at the battles along the Embarcadero as a process of elimination—determining what people *didn't* want on their waterfront, be it excessive height or massive piers or development that treated the shoreline as a blank slate. From this, perhaps, better options could emerge.

Unbuilt realms can frame the future, too.

NINE

WHILE THE FERRY BUILDING LANGUISHED, AND LITTLE HAPPENED along the Embarcadero, the transformation of an old chocolate plant into Ghirardelli Square showed that fresh takes on urban life could flourish in historic shells.

The block nestled against Russian Hill just west of Fisherman's Wharf had been evolving since 1893, when chocolatier Domingo Ghirardelli purchased 2.5 acres that contained two small manufacturing buildings and plenty of room to grow. As the family business prospered, the block filled with handsome brick structures including a clocktower modeled on a French chateau—a neighborhood landmark enhanced by the aroma of freshly made chocolate floating past the nineteen-foot-high letters that spelled out the family name. But time moves on, and in 1962 the company, now owned by a conglomerate, moved across the bay to a modern plant and put its old home up for sale.

Enter William Matson Roth, a well-connected local businessman in his forties whose family had founded the shipping line that was betting its future on container ships. Roth decided that all but one of the aged structures on the site would remain, and he'd fill them with small shops. Below the clocktower, Ghirardelli would operate a cafe selling ice cream and chocolate to sweets-seeking visitors. There was a cable car stop outside and a parking garage tucked underground.

Only five shops and restaurants were ready on opening day, when Mayor Jack Shelley praised the conversion's "imagination, ingenuity and love of beauty" before throwing a switch to illuminate the Ghirardelli sign that had been dark since World War II. People were entranced nonetheless, and within five years the square was attracting an estimated fifteen thousand visitors daily to its fifty-five shops, fourteen restaurants, and two theaters.

The project was a popular success as well as an economic one, and a big reason was that Roth and his design team grasped the changing nature of what drew people to San Francisco: they wanted to feel like they were part of a continuum, where new sensations and experiences didn't clash with what came before. This was true of Ferlinghetti with his "Mediterranean city," just as it was true a half century before when Keeler celebrated the coexistence of "juggernaut progress" and billowy nature. Ghirardelli Square, consciously, set out to cloak modern consumer convenience in a familiar ambiance: "We wanted from the beginning to create a place that San Franciscans would enjoy and not just tourists," Roth commented at the time.

Compare this to the alteration that the Ferry Building underwent at roughly the same time, on Magnin's watch, when the landmark's south wing was overhauled to create new Port offices and leasable real estate. The nave was chopped into small offices with low ceilings that banished the historic skylight from view, while a concrete slab was inserted to create an additional floor of office space.

"Although outwardly unchanged, the entire south half of the second-floor nave would be unrecognizable to those who last visited over a year ago," boasted the Port's in-house newsletter (as if this was a good thing). "Even Port employees . . . could get lost in the new complex of corridors and offices."

The Embarcadero scene outside was disorienting, as well. There was the viaduct, a glum presence with hundreds of metered parking spaces underneath. Directly to the north, where Ferry Port Plaza would be proposed a few years later, the neoclassical bulkhead fronts to each pier retained a certain workaday romance despite fading paint and a shabby air. The Belt Railroad still rumbled by a few times each day, though less and less often as years passed. But the storage shed on Pier 7 went up in flames in 1973, to be replaced by a parking lot atop the remaining piles. The sheds and piles behind Pier 5's bulkhead were dismantled. Pier 1's 706-foot-long shed only held parked cars. The piers to the south were sadder still, several lost to fire and others rotting at their own chosen pace.

If the details were specific to San Francisco, the bleak larger reality was shared by ports across the country and around the world that had come of age in the nineteenth and early twentieth centuries: global shipping was leaving them behind. In New York, the industrial waterfronts of Manhattan and Brooklyn were largely quiet by the 1970s. Boston's port was in decline. So was Philadelphia's, since container ships by the late 1960s were too large to navigate the Delaware River.

For all the grief he took at the time—and his tin ear in terms of what people wanted, experientially, from their waterfront and their city—Magnin grasped the profundity of what loomed more than his critics who insisted the Embarcadero could return as a working port. Oakland's ascendency became obvious after 1967, when that city opened its first container terminal. Matson Lines soon moved east, followed by its competitors, and during the next four years the amount of cargo going in and out of San Francisco fell by more than half, while that of Oakland nearly doubled. But even as the Port redoubled its efforts to modernize its southern piers—which Magnin sought to fund through revenues from the Whale and Giraffe—unions resisted the idea of large-scale changes between Mission Creek and Fisherman's Wharf. "Some people seem to think the waterfront should be phased out and devoted to rose gardens," fumed Morris Weisberger, head of the unions' Maritime Trades Council. "This, to me, is silly. The waterfront built San Francisco."

. . .

Not that there wasn't plenty of conventional development going on in San Francisco, as any commuter on the skyway's upper deck could attest.

Call it the shock of the new: twenty-five office and hotel towers in or near the Financial District were completed between 1963 and 1972, with a dozen of them taller than the Russ Building, a masonry cliff of radiant terra cotta that had topped the skyline since the Great Depression. One of the temples of commerce from the early twentieth century that fell victim to change was Arthur Page Brown's Crocker Building at Montgomery and Market, demolished with little fuss in 1966 to make room for a thirty-nine-story, 528-foot high-rise clad in dark granite and accompanied by a small public plaza.

The towers that went up were of varying merit, as towers always are, but most stuck to the midcentury corporate ideal—rectangular floors stacked one on top of the next, no sculpted silhouette, a flat top. More often than not the windows were flush with the skin, not for design reasons, but to

The Transamerica Pyramid as seen from Columbus Avenue, 1970.
San Francisco Chronicle.

placate developers who wanted to pack every possible square foot of rental space into the project that they could. The buildings did their job. As far as their creators were concerned, that was enough.

The one exception to this norm, and San Francisco's most controversial tower of the era, was what we know today as the Transamerica Pyramid—a steep, 853-foot concrete triangle that opened in 1972 and was nearly twice the height of the Russ Building. The oddly shaped skyscraper was for a small insurance holding company that wanted to make a splash; architect William Pereira of Los Angeles responded by presenting the chairman with nine options based on forms including an oval, a needle, and an angled spike. The triangle won.

As if this wasn't provocative enough, Transamerica intended to build its new headquarters at the corner of Washington and Montgomery Streets, smack between the traditional Financial District and historic Jackson Square, where the two- and three-story brick buildings date back as far as 1852. That corner also marks the starting point of Columbus Avenue, a diagonal boulevard that leads into North Beach; Ferlinghetti's City Lights was three blocks away.

Horrified critics from around the country rushed into battle. The *Washington Post*'s architecture critic recoiled from Pereira's "height of hideous nonsense." The *Los Angeles Times* fulminated against "antisocial architecture at its worst." *Newsweek* bemoaned a tower that would be "wrong in any city" but "particularly wrong in . . . easily wounded San Francisco."

Closer to home, protestors on one occasion gathered outside Transamerica's office while wearing dunce caps that proclaimed, "Stow The Shaft." The city's own planning director fought the design, describing it to *Time* as "a 'look-at-me' building that does not complement the buildings near it." But the Planning Commission brushed all objections aside—and the day that the Board of Supervisors gave the final green light, Transamerica quietly pulled permits so construction could begin the next morning, before opponents had time to file lawsuits.

Even now, it is hard to imagine a more stark contrast between two architectural icons than the Ferry Building and the Transamerica Pyramid. The former conjured up a "monumental gateway" by using traditional design styles to signal the maturity of then-young San Francisco. The latter defied urban norms to generate a head-turning symbol for an upstart company. Yet the very shape that repelled so many people is what made Pereira's pyramid iconic once the shock wore off. Five years after the tower's completion, *New York Times* architecture critic Paul Goldberger flew west for an up-close look. His verdict? A column praising "the one brightening element" in a skyline that "otherwise has become a deadened mass of boxes."

The pyramid today is unforgettable, and unforgettably linked to San Francisco. The same holds for the Golden Gate Bridge and, yes, the Ferry Building. They resonate.

. . .

When Hollywood stars lent their influence to cheer on the protestors battling the Whale and the Giraffe, or East Coast architecture critics expounded on the rare virtues of San Francisco, they sent a message that this city had a character unto itself. It had *authenticity,* to use a word that in the twenty-first century has become a real estate cliché.

There was nothing new to this belief, which generations of parochial Bay Area residents held as a matter of faith. It's also what had attracted visitors to the city as far back as the 1915 Panama-Pacific International Exposition. The difference in the 1960s and '70s is that many people who regarded the city as a model feared they saw that model at risk. Caen was an obvious example. Another was *Holiday* magazine, which returned in 1970 to the city that it had celebrated in 1961 as a place where "the legend, the myth, the spell persist in clinging."

No longer.

"The loveliest of American cities is in mortal danger of total disappearance," the editors warned in a letter at the front of the magazine. "There is the remorseless brutalization of a uniquely delicate skyline, and the obliteration of everyone's view."

That take was mild compared to a lengthy dispatch from Nicholas von Hoffman, who at the time was one of the *Washington Post*'s most combative and celebrated columnists—"an irreverent intellectual who wrote like a dream," in the words of legendary *Post* editor Ben Bradlee. Von Hoffman kicked off by declaring that "growth and progress are ruining a city its inhabitants love with a zeal unmatched anywhere else." He reminded the affluent *Holiday* readers how "San Francisco is probably the only city in the world to stop a freeway in mid-course" after "an appalled citizenry interposed itself." But Transamerica's pyramid was on the rise ("an 853-foot sharpened spike . . . of unsurpassed mediocrity"), and new battles kept breaking out.

"San Franciscans have fought and are fighting to hold onto their city, which is still a delight," von Hoffman reported. "They're losing."

• • •

As towers rose to the west, and developments were battled to a standstill on the north and south, the area around the Ferry Building once again became a part of how people entered and left the city.

The most futuristic, or so it seemed at the time, was the 1961 debut of helicopter service from alongside the Ferry Building to San Francisco International Airport. The ten-passenger amphibious helicopters provided an eight-minute flight for $6.50, about the same as cab fares at the time, but service ended in 1970—the same year that ferry service to and from Marin returned. The instigator, ironically, was the Golden Gate Bridge and Highway District, the descendent of the government agency that built the bridge that took the ferries' place to begin with. Now it was seeking ways to reduce traffic congestion on the span; the two ferries it purchased to launch the route often ran late, service was infrequent, and passengers were dropped outside the Ferry Building and then had to walk underneath the Embarcadero Freeway—"but even a fake ferry is better than none," wrote Herb Caen, who couldn't resist taking a ride on opening day.

A Sikorsky helicopter, part of the short-lived SFO Helicopter Airlines, touches down alongside the remodeled Ferry Building. *Collection of SFO Museum.*

The real innovation at this time was the construction of BART, the Bay Area Rapid Transit system. It was conceived in 1956 to whisk commuters from all nine regional counties into San Francisco's Financial District—an attempt to contain what the consultants described in their first analysis as the danger of "what now is referred to as 'urban sprawl'—that is, almost unlimited spread in any direction." The only counties that chose to sign on were Alameda, Contra Costa, and San Francisco, but construction began in 1964, and the East Bay portion of the taxpayer-funded system debuted in 1972. The San Francisco line began running a year later, and in

September 1973 the 3.8-mile transbay tube opened to connect the two sides of what then was a 71.5-mile system.

There was no Ferry Building stop, even though the double-bore tunnel that links Oakland to San Francisco goes directly underneath the building. Not only that, it *cuts through* some of the wooden piles that support the concrete foundation. To do this, steel columns were driven down to bedrock along the outline of where the tubes needed to be. Girders were inserted amid vaulted arches and connected to the columns, creating a scaffold-like frame to support the weight above it. Once everything was connected—a new foundation beneath the foundation, in a way—the tunnel was bored through several hundred of those eighty-foot-long trunks of Oregon pine. The only visual evidence of this endeavor is at the back of the Ferry Building, a tall chimney-like structure that was needed to provide ventilation for the subterranean tube.

Which means that the Ferry Building, literally, got the shaft. The benefit, theoretically, was the addition of a waterfront plaza that BART needed to allow easy access to the site. But the bayside space turned out to be a nondescript sequel to Ciampi's overheated dreams, with a squat restaurant space wrapped around the ventilation shaft in a clumsy effort to put lipstick on a structural pig.

• • •

A few years after BART began transbay service, City Hall and the Port began work on yet another waterfront plan. This one suggested the city might have learned lessons from the misfires of recent years. An extensive citizen advisory group was appointed beforehand, the theory being to get potential foes involved from day one, and the document approved in 1980 was built on the realization that regular people wanted to experience the area as they chose, at their own pace. A pedestrian promenade would run the length of the Embarcadero, including stretches that hadn't had sidewalks up until then. Derelict railyards on the inland side of the Embarcadero, between the Bay Bridge and China Basin, would be replaced by mixed-income residential blocks.

The Belt Railroad—still running once a day or so, largely to placate diehard longshoremen who insisted that break bulk cargo had a future—would remain. The two decks of concrete above? The report minced no words: "Remove the existing elevated Embarcadero Freeway."

As for the Ferry Building, the plan emphasized that changes along the Embarcadero must defer to "a landmark structure symbolic of the City's ties with the Bay Area and the World"— and nearby development must "maintain the physical prominence" of the icon.

All this sounded promising. So did the Port's announcement in the summer of 1978 that it would invite developers to restore the landmark. Rather than leap at whatever they might bring to the table, as with the Whale and the Giraffe, development parameters were laid out in advance. The goal of the competition, like the plan's explicit recommendation to remove the Embarcadero Freeway, was to get serious about restoring the luster to one of San Francisco's foundation elements, and exploring what its potential might be.

The Ferry Building during the prior twenty years had played a civic role far different than anything that its creators could have imagined. It had inspired people who loved the city to fight for an urban landscape that they valued, and to articulate why those values mattered. The question now was whether protecting the past could include giving an icon new life, not just warding off change.

CHAPTER

———

TEN

The Howard Street stub of the Embarcadero Freeway, 1972.
San Francisco Chronicle / *Joe Rosenthal.*

LOGICALLY, THE BALLOT MEASURES IN JUNE 1986 TO TEAR DOWN the Embarcadero Freeway should have passed by landslide margins.

San Franciscans famously had loathed the double-decked concrete intruder since before it opened in 1959. Mayor Dianne Feinstein and the Board of Supervisors were united in their desire to replace the mile-long viaduct with a landscaped boulevard that would "once again let us see our waterfront," as Feinstein concluded her argument in the election's voter information handbook. Her pitch was flanked by endorsements from all parts of the city's political, economic, and cultural spectrum. One person calling for the viaduct to vanish was the developer of Pier 39, a wildly popular tourist and family mecca that had the look of an ersatz fishing village and had opened in 1978; another was Jack Morrison, who fought Pier 39's creation and had been the only member of the Board of Supervisors to vote against the Transamerica Pyramid back in 1969. Also weighing in: Lawrence Ferlinghetti, the revered poet who still presided over City Lights Bookstore, was among the authors of a plea that the waterfront should be "graced by a grand promenade."

The freeway defenders in that handbook? Few and far between. One argument was signed by several leaders of the local Republican Party, hardly a ringing endorsement in an increasingly liberal city. Another was from the San Francisco Taxpayers Association, which routinely challenged any measure involving public expenditures. The only elected official against the idea, Supervisor Richard Hongisto, warned vaguely that tearing down the freeway "will aggravate an already bad traffic problem" and "be very expensive." More studies were needed, critics agreed; they didn't say what those studies should be.

Then came election day, and logic was turned on its head. The people who wanted to get rid of the supposed scourge were no match for an opposition that preferred to see nothing happen at all rather than take a chance on the unknown. Both measures went down to lopsided defeat.

A similar dynamic was playing out around this time with the Ferry Building: a proposal that had been touted in 1981 as the best chance yet to revive the faded landmark's former glory had foundered. Instead of being rejected by voters, it was in limbo and headed to court.

The story lines were different, and in the case of the Ferry Building, we're better off as a result. But each saga fit with a larger trend during the 1980s. The culture of opposition that had emerged during the 1960s, the tenacious and often inventive resistance to top-down initiatives that threatened the city's quality of life, had hardened into force of habit.

Feinstein called the defeat of efforts to remove the Embarcadero Freeway "a vote for the automobile." One of her campaign leaders fingered a different culprit. "We did everything we could short of collaring people on street corners," he said the day after the election. "But the general reaction to everything is 'no.'"

. . .

When the Port held its competition at the end of 1978 to revive the Ferry Building as a civic destination, the contender that emerged victorious was Continental Development Co. The Southern California firm vowed to honor the heritage while creating "a grand public gathering place," but the details sounded cheesy from the start. The second floor would showcase "an international bazaar with an array of ethnic restaurants opposite shops of the finest quality imports of each country." The interior's maze of atriums and escalators bore no resemblance to Brown's clean linear design. A glass-enclosed annex to the north would hold a large fern bar.

Ah, the 1970s. If a fern-draped singles bar wasn't your style, a "turn-of-the-century Vienna-style coffee house" at the building's south end would feature live classical music and "is intended to become a San Francisco tradition."

Watchdogs promptly sounded the alarm. Most vocal of all was the *Chronicle's* architecture critic at the time, Allan Temko, who published a lengthy column savaging what he called a "cheap-o concoction"—or, to remove any doubt as to where he stood, "a minimal business strategy to make a bundle on one of the greatest waterfront sites in the world without doing justice to its real potential."

Continental took the hint, ditched its design team, and brought in a lead architect of undeniable stature—I. M. Pei, who had received acclaim for the recently completed East Building at the National Gallery of Art in Washington, D.C., and was beginning what would become his firm's most famous project, the remake of the Louvre in Paris. On a visit to San Francisco in September 1980, he affably struck the right notes by reminiscing about his first glimpse of the Ferry Building in 1935 when, as a seventeen-year-old on his way from Shanghai to start college on the East Coast, his ocean liner pulled up to Pier 28. Pei assured reporters that "I have to get a feel for the City" before starting design work. As for the sealed-in warren of offices filling what had been conceived as a depot bathed in natural light, he was politely aghast: "I can't imagine locating in this place and not having that (Bay) view."

The conceptual design made public a few months later went to the other extreme: hollowing out the inside, enlarging the skylight so that it would be as wide as the nave and creating a wide passage from Market Street to the water with a full-height glass wall on either side. Temko applauded the "brilliant promise" of what he described as "a contemporary glass palace." Equally enthusiastic about the proposal's "tremendous potential" was the new mayor, Dianne Feinstein.

Feinstein had assumed the executive desk in November 1978 after her predecessor, George Moscone, was assassinated in his

City Hall office by one of Feinstein's former colleagues. That gruesome act of violence—Dan White also shot and killed Harvey Milk, the gay supervisor representing the Castro—brought a somber promotion for someone who had run for mayor twice during her ten years on the Board of Supervisors. Despite being a pro-business moderate, Feinstein was no fan of what had been happening along the Embarcadero; while serving as the president of the Board of Supervisors during the battle over the US Steel tower, she had released a letter to the mayor, Joseph Alioto, telling him, "The Port must recognize that . . . San Franciscans do not want high-rises on the waterfront."

In a way, Pei's design was an update of Ghirardelli Square. But the obvious template was an East Coast success story: the revival of Boston's Quincy Market in 1976, which took a powerful but long-neglected enclave of granite and brick warehouses from the 1820s and revived them with contemporary gusto as Faneuil Hall Marketplace.

The developer of that project, James Rouse, made the cover of *Time* and was praised by the magazine for his "unique and uncanny ability to blend commerce and showmanship into a magnetizing force in the inner city." Nor was his Boston success a fluke; Rouse updated the formula at Baltimore's Harborplace, a cluster of new retail pavilions that helped spark the revival of a derelict waterfront far tattier than the Embarcadero. He went on to restore St. Louis's palatial Union Station, and turned a cluster of brick survivors in Lower Manhattan into South Street Seaport.

As is often the case in America, innovation spawned knock-offs and replication. By the early 1980s, it seemed that every large- and mid-sized city with an outdated but decent-sized historic building was opening what became known as festival

A rendering of the retail galleria with the proposed renovation of the Ferry
Building in the early 1980s. *Paul Stevenson Oles / Pei Cobb Freed & Partners.*

marketplaces. Some were former transportation depots, such
as the former Union Station in downtown Indianapolis, or a
cluster of railroad structures on the Monongahela River in
Pittsburgh that were repackaged as Station Square. In Washington, D.C., the landmark Old Post Office from 1899 received
a 1983 makeover with boutiques and eateries around an eight-
story skylit pavilion. The aim was to offer a sense of history
and place that suburbia could not match, but with a concentrated selection and energy akin to a successful shopping mall.
Or as Pei's firm claimed in a brochure describing its project,

"the readaptation and recycling of once-important facilities, rich in historic legacy, has a way of reviving urban morale."

What Pei and his lead designer James Ingo Freed conceived was a mannered contemporary structure that happened to hide behind a nineteenth-century facade. The floor of the nave would be removed, including the tile mosaic of the state seal that somehow had survived all past renovations, to carve out a floor-to-ceiling "galleria" lined by mall-like bulbed store-fronts. Four terraced levels of new office and retail space would step down toward the bay on either side of the central wall of glass.

"This is a masterplan animated by the deepest sorts of humanistic instincts," the brochure insisted. "Once func-tioning as a terminal of transportation, the readapted Ferry Building will function as a terminal for aesthetic, culinary, recreational and cultural experiences."

. . .

While the plans for the Ferry Building inched forward, efforts to demolish the Embarcadero Freeway hit high gear.

As early as 1973, Feinstein had vowed, "I'm determined that that freeway come down, if I have to become totally gray-haired in the process." Once she became mayor, her admin-istration started making the case to regional transportation and planning agencies that the viaduct was no longer wanted, even though it carried fifty thousand cars a year. The surface boulevard sketched out in the recently approved plan for the southern Embarcadero would suffice to handle the displaced traffic, they argued, and much of the cost could be covered by state and federal funds already promised to the city.

In November 1985, the Board of Supervisors voted over-whelmingly to bring sunlight back to the Embarcadero.

Feinstein signed the legislation in a ceremony held in a parking lot beneath what she called a "concrete monolith that divides our neighborhoods." Other cities were starting to make similar moves: on the East Coast, engineers with the Massachusetts Department of Transportation were planning to replace Boston's much-loathed Central Artery with an underground highway. New York's West Side Elevated Highway, a lumbering single-deck viaduct mostly built in the 1930s when Manhattan's working waterfront still flourished, was on the verge of being dismantled to make way for a surface roadway and extensive parks. The Freeway Revolt had evolved from battling proposed intruders to, also, trying to take down the old ones that blocked a new generation of residents from creating the city they desired.

But if environmentalists and neighborhood activists saw their quest in the context of what could be *gained*—"the waterfront will be opened up to sunlight and fresh air," in the words of the Sierra Club—skeptics focused on what could be *lost*, beginning with direct access from the Bay Bridge to the districts north of Market Street. This wasn't just the complaint of Bay Area residents who liked their straight aerial shot to North Beach or Chinatown, such as the Alameda County supervisor on one regional agency who said he'd support tearing down the Embarcadero Freeway when his San Francisco counterparts "stop using freeways in the East Bay on their way to Sacramento and Tahoe." One of the only two supervisors who voted against the measure, Richard Hongisto rounded up signatures to put the issue on the ballot. Such a tactic was nothing new in San Francisco: Feinstein herself was the target of a recall attempt in 1983 that was launched by the far-left White Panther Party—"We're on the Marxist, Leninist, Maoist, Castroist side of most questions," one member told the press—after she signed a measure banning handguns. That recall lost by an 80–20 margin, but over the years they've often been successful. Hongisto's move opened the debate to people who might never attend a City Hall hearing. It also tapped into visceral concerns about the state of affairs in San Francisco, a vague but powerful emotion.

The election coincided with a fresh bout of voter fears that downtown development was out of hand. Construction cranes were visible in all directions, spreading beyond the Financial District skyline into the blocks south of Market Street, with two dozen large office projects approved between 1980 and 1985. What if removing the freeway allowed them to spill east, imperiling the waterfront yet again?

"Development interests are urging this forward," Hongisto darkly confided to the *Los Angeles Times* before the supervisors' vote.

This ominous notion, and the reality that a generation of San Franciscans had grown to rely on the freeway, was a powerful counterpoint to the visions conjured up by people eager to reunite the Embarcadero and the inland city. Ask Herb Caen, who turned seventy in the spring of 1986 and seemed increasingly frustrated with the changes around him. His daily column was as nimble as ever in its mix of jokes and name-dropping and blind items ("Which famous private club is violating its union contract by paying workers under the table for private parties to avoid pension benefits? Right the first time . . ."), but his sentimental take on San Francisco had soured from the early years when he urged the city forward, or drew lines in the sand to defend aspects of his chosen home that were of unquestioned value.

"Save the Freeway is not a slogan I'm comfortable with," Caen admitted as Hongisto's initiative was heading to the ballot. So why vote "no"? "This city has lost its way and probably needs all the freeways it can get, if only to show us how to get from point A to point B. Point C seems to be beyond us."

Dismiss such views as short-sighted, a sour funk, but Caen was saying what a lot of people felt—a pessimism that was more than a match for detailed land-use plans and earnest rhapsodies about how taking down a freeway would bring the Embarcadero to life. Consider the two measures themselves. Freeway defenders presented voters with a simple yes-or-no vote on whether or not to tear down the freeway, the idea being that voters would rather stick with what they knew. The rival initiative, placed on the ballot by Feinstein and six supervisors, went into laborious detail stressing the potential good things to come, asking voters if they wanted to "replace part of the Embarcadero Freeway if it would increase public access to the waterfront and improve traffic . . . (with) a tree-lined six-lane boulevard."

· · ·

Each vote was advisory, lacking legislative force. Everyone agreed that if either one passed, political dynamics were such that all systems were go.

It wasn't even close. The ballot measure in support of a landscaped boulevard was rejected by a 58–42 margin in the election on June 3, 1986. Hongisto's yes-or-no vote lost by more, which was what the freeway-lovers wanted all along.

Hongisto was exultant: "She got in the ring with a gorilla in terms of these issues," he said of Feinstein afterward. "And you know you can't beat a gorilla."

Feinstein didn't bother trying to give the debacle a positive spin.

A model showing I. M. Pei & Partners' design for the Ferry Building and its surroundings. *Thorney Lieberman / Pei Cobb Freed & Partners.*

"It was a vote for the automobile," she told the *Examiner.* "The voters had the idea it's up there, so let's not take it down."

· · ·

By the time voters chose a double-deck freeway over a wide-open waterfront, Pei and Freed's vision of a Ferry Building that melded old and new had joined the unbuilt landscape of the Embarcadero, another what-if that never came to pass.

There was no grand denouement, no civic election or citizen march, just a drumbeat of dissension. Fisherman's Wharf merchants, already feeling the sting of Pier 39's success, complained that the ambitious project would rob them of customers. San Francisco Tomorrow, a development watchdog cofounded by Morrison in 1970, complained each time the proposal changed (which was often). The Planning Commission worried that the complex would become "the Rodeo Drive of San Francisco," in the words of one skeptical commissioner. Every objection had merit, whatever the motives. And with each regulatory delay or design tweak, costs continued to climb.

There also was the strange twist of the World Trade Club, an offshoot of the World Trade Center that had another twenty years remaining on its lease for a wood-paneled space with wide-open bay views. The 1,800 or so club members included sixty-seven foreign diplomats, and they were in no hurry to trade their posh nook for a spot elsewhere along the bay, the deal offered by Continental. Though there's no evidence that the club lobbied City Hall in private, the membership included its full share of attorneys who'd be happy to defend the lease in court if need be.

"The club is a matter of habit," one former president shrugged to the *Chronicle*. "You want to minimize the disruption of your membership."

If the World Trade Club was a bastion of thick tablecloths and white linen pomp, the scene below grew more frowzy with each passing year. Piers 15 and 17 still held a cotton warehouse, and rolls of newsprint arrived at Piers 27–29 on ships from Canada. But many piers along the Embarcadero had devolved into parking garages or storage space, or were subdivided into small offices where the rent was cheap.

"It basically was a moribund industrial area," says Diane Oshima, who joined the city's planning department as an intern in 1980 and retired from the Port in 2021. The Port operations back then were so anachronistic that Oshima remembers one staffer whose sole job it was to keep track of all the agency's keys to all the doors on all the buildings and piers that it owned. Maintenance trucks parked inside the Ferry Building on the ground floor—or as employees called it, the basement. That's also where old records and planning documents were kept, "stacks and boxes of all this crap."

Which doesn't mean the raffish atmosphere and bayside nooks weren't seductive. Oshima and her future husband loved wandering the nooks along the Embarcadero—"If you were out here, you were by yourself"—and when they decided to marry in 1988, they held their wedding in the restaurant that clung to BART's ventilation shaft, lights of the city glittering above them to the west.

• • •

Diane Oshima's wedding took place two years after the Embarcadero Freeway was given a new lease on life, and the same year that the Port Commission voted to end Continental's development option on the Ferry Building because of the lack of progress. As for all those downtown cranes, their days were numbered. San Francisco voters had narrowly approved a measure to cap the amount of new office space at less than one new Transamerica Pyramid each year.

Forty years of the postwar city had come to this point: the excesses of planning a city from the top down, be it scorched-earth urban "renewal" or disruptive freeways or waterfront mega-projects, had met their match in civic activism. Such activism was needed and worthwhile. It also could curdle into a blinkered resistance to anything that might *perhaps* be harmful.

As often is the case, other cities took their cues from San Francisco. The Bay Area suburban hubs of Walnut Creek in the East Bay and San Mateo to the south imposed height limits. Seattle passed downtown controls similar to San Francisco's in 1989.

That said, every city is unique. One thing that sets apart San Francisco is its proximity to the San Andreas fault that in 1906 destroyed much of the city. The fault that on October 17, 1989, came to life again.

PART III

REBIRTH

CHAPTER

——

ELEVEN

THE LOMA PRIETA EARTHQUAKE THAT STRUCK THE BAY AREA AND beyond on October 17, 1989, may have been America's first natural disaster to be broadcast live on nationwide television, without any advance notice.

The 6.9-magnitude temblor wasn't a hurricane that looms for days on weather charts before reaching land. Nor was it a volcanic eruption like the one that tore the top 1,300 feet off Mt. St. Helens on May 18, 1980, and killed fifty-seven people, a cataclysm preceded by weeks of small earthquakes. Even the octopus in *It Came from beneath the Sea* was being tracked as it neared the Golden Gate Bridge.

No, when the San Andreas fault unleashed its force after eighty-three quiet years, it did so in almost absurdly theatrical circumstances—twenty-one minutes before the first World Series game to be played in San Francisco since 1962, with the San Francisco Giants hosting the Oakland Athletics at Candlestick Park. Sportscasters Al Michaels and Tim McCarver were dissecting highlights of the first two games, the fan-packed upper deck visible behind them, when static fuzzed the image that froze as Michaels' voice broke in, "I'll tell you what, we're having an earth—"

And the screen went silent and black.

A green placeholder "World Series" image appeared a few seconds later as the audio feed continued, airing the nervous excitement of the Candlestick crowd that had just felt terrifying waves of motion ripple through the ballpark, including that upper deck balanced on suddenly precarious-looking columns. "Well, I don't know if we're on the air," Michaels could be heard saying in an adrenaline-fueled voice: "Well, folks, that's the greatest open in the history of television, bar none!"

"We opened with a bang!" McCarver blurted.

"I guess you can hear us," Michaels jabbered. "We'll be back, we hope, from San Francisco in just a moment!"

• • •

Michaels and McCarver wouldn't resume their broadcast for another two weeks. Instead, devastating images riveted the television audience, nightmarish views commanding national attention. A fifty-foot-long section of the upper deck of the Bay Bridge had snapped loose and slammed into the lanes below, leaving one car hanging mid-air but somehow killing only one person. The death toll was exponentially higher in Oakland, where forty-two people were crushed or burned to death when a mile of the Cypress Freeway near the city's port buckled and then collapsed; cameras captured a dystopian scene of professional fire fighters joined by neighbors with forklifts and ladders, attempting to pull out survivors. In San Francisco's Marina District, which sat atop the site of the 1915 Panama-Pacific International Exposition, the soil that had been poured into marshes seventy-five years earlier liquefied and turned to mush. Buildings lurched off their foundations and burst into flames, a fiery disaster made all the more haunting that night by the serene backdrop of the Golden Gate Bridge.

The lens broadened the next day to take in scenes such as downtown Santa Cruz, ten miles from the epicenter of the earthquake, where historic brick buildings that hadn't been structurally reinforced crumpled to the ground along the open-air Pacific Garden Mall. In San Francisco, there were the stark remains of a post-1906 building at Sixth and Bluxome Streets where an unreinforced brick wall buckled abruptly and crushed seven cars, killing five people. One man inside the structure described how the wall "just blew out like an explosion . . . there was nothing but blue sky."

Absent from these scenes was the Ferry Building where, as in 1906, the heavy arched foundation resting on those trunks of Oregon pine held firm. The lone sign of visible damage was the tower's tilted flagpole; a military helicopter hovered low the following Sunday to lift it off, only to lose grip and send the flagpole into the landmark's roof like a dagger. Workers cut the unexpected spear into foot-long pieces and carted them away, leaving the cupola bare until a replacement was lowered into place by another helicopter at dawn, eleven months later.

The Embarcadero Freeway was another story.

The structure hadn't collapsed like the Cypress Freeway across the bay. But the two viaducts were of the same era, and the highway that had opened thirty years prior was closed to traffic almost as soon as the last cars could find off-ramps following the quake. A few hours later, the sky dark, the scene was visited by L. Thomas Tobin, executive director of the California Seismic Safety Commission. What he encountered was ominous, Tobin told state legislators that week, with deep diagonal cracks traveling up five of the ten concrete columns

he examined. Before he could inspect other ones, or take photographs of the fissures, police guarding the scene said his time
was up—they were concerned the structure might topple onto
the bureaucrat.

"If the quake had continued for another five seconds," one
engineer told the legislators at a special hearing three days
later, "we think the Embarcadero Freeway would have failed."

· · ·

Years later, a report by the United States Geological Society on
Loma Prieta's impact on roadways confirmed that the structure "had the same inadequate reinforcement details as many
of the other damaged double-deck viaducts . . . in fact, it was
similar to the collapsed portion of the Cypress." What saved
the Embarcadero Freeway, the scientists determined, was the
compact route: the column-supported curves necessary to pivot
onto the waterfront, plus the lateral support of on- and off-
ramps every few blocks, gave the Embarcadero viaduct a stability its East Bay cousin lacked.

By the time that analysis was released, however, the ungainly
structure was long gone.

The weekend after Loma Prieta, construction workers
erected wooden supports around the columns and below the
lower deck so that people could reach the waterfront if they
needed. BART ridership between San Francisco and the East
Bay more than doubled during the month the Bay Bridge was
out of commission, from a weekday average of 105,000 to
nearly 229,000. The Bay Bridge reopened in mid-November,
and Caltrans, the state's department of transportation, said
full repairs could be done within eight months.

But all those people who had spent years fighting the freeway on the traditional issues—it was ugly, it marooned the

Ferry Building—had a potent new weapon that they flourished with melodramatic glee: "It's not a question of whether it's coming down; it's a question of whether it's coming down on people or whether we're going to take it down," warned one supervisor who introduced a resolution calling for the viaduct to go. Freeway foes who had been active in the 1986 election began meeting in homes on Telegraph Hill to plot strategies. The urban design committee of the city's chapter of the American Institute of Architects released a thirty-page report on how a viaduct-free Embarcadero would be a long-term plus for the waterfront.

As the calls for demolition continued, an unexpected voice joined in.

. . .

Like so many people on the left end of the city's political spectrum, Art Agnos hit town in the full flowering of the sixties: he grew up as the son of Greek immigrants in Springfield, Massachusetts, working after school with his father in the family's hat cleaning and shoe shine shop. As the two polished customers' shoes, the father would lecture the son in Greek about the importance of getting a college education. That way, some day, Art would be the one getting *his* shoes shined.

The son took the hint and went to Bates College in Maine, where he developed an interest in social issues. There was a two-year stint in the US Army—"exactly what I needed at that point in my life"—and he earned a master's degree in social work from Florida State University. Degree in hand, Agnos hopped on a Greyhound bus and headed west. "Three days later I was in San Francisco," he likes to say, "and I've been here ever since."

The gregarious newcomer got hired by a housing nonprofit

and found an apartment on then-working-class Potrero Hill. Soon he was volunteering on election campaigns, and in 1968 he joined the staff of one of the city's state assembly representatives, Leo McCarthy—a post he still held in 1973 when, after a community meeting on the night of December 13, he was talking with two women when a man walked up and shot him twice at close range, above the left hip and below the heart.

As the seemingly random and often lethal shootings continued, they became known throughout a terrified city as the Zebra killings. By the time that the suspected assailants were arrested on May 1, 1974, fifteen people had been killed and at least eight others wounded. At one point San Francisco police began stopping any Black men who even vaguely matched a composite drawing of one of the suspects, which inflamed tensions all the more. A federal judge ruled the profiling unconstitutional within a week, but more than five hundred Black men had already been pulled over. Four men went on trial the next year; three were convicted of murder. Agnos took the witness stand to testify and pointed out on his shirt where the two bullets had entered his body.

Despite the trauma of the shooting, with injuries to his lungs and colon that required a year of convalescence and rehabilitation, Agnos returned to McCarthy's staff—and when Potrero Hill's assembly district had an open seat in 1976, Agnos successfully ran at McCarthy's urging. He was reelected five times, forging alliances with community groups, and as Dianne Feinstein prepared to leave the mayor's office in 1987 because of term limits, Agnos joined the scrum. He won the race easily, billing himself as a neighborhood candidate who wasn't in downtown's pocket and gaining endorsements across the political spectrum, from the Police Officers Association to the Sierra Club.

Art Agnos kicks off demolition of the Embarcadero Freeway, February
1991. San Francisco Chronicle.

The latter's support aside, Agnos was known as a champion
of social causes, not environmental ones. His political incli-
nation after Loma Prieta was to steer clear of a crusade that
voters had drubbed just three years before.

"I wasn't inclined to swing at first," he admits, using a baseball analogy. "I didn't have the vision, and I had all these other
things coming at me. People would say I should tear it down,
but I didn't want to add more turmoil at a difficult time over
an issue that had already been defeated at the polls."

This wasn't an issue that a mayor could duck, he found
out. Agnos was being lobbied by all sides. Chinatown leaders such as Rose Pak—a vocal supporter during the 1987
campaign who had pull with neighborhood voters—would
meet with him privately and insist the neighborhood's
visitor-driven economy would die without easy freeway
access. Freeway advocates would leave the office and in
would come his advisors to reiterate their view that removing the elevated artery would open a new landscape of

possibilities for San Francisco, its waterfront, and the relationship between the two.

"The more I learned, the more it appealed to me," Agnos says now. "They made such an amazing case, I decided I *wanted* this. It could be my legacy."

Even in the aftermath of an earthquake, doing away with the Embarcadero Freeway was no simple task. Commuters wanted their elevated route back in action, and so did shopkeepers in Chinatown and Fisherman's Wharf who insisted the closure was why shoppers hadn't returned after Loma Prieta. When the Board of Supervisors took up the issue, six months after the earthquake, the Board chambers couldn't hold all the Chinatown merchants and restaurateurs who closed their businesses for the afternoon to voice their dismay at City Hall. Four hours later, the Board voted by a bare 6–5 majority to allow demolition if the federal government would help pay for it. Another 6–5 vote followed that summer to reaffirm the plan; the loudest "no" vote came from Terence Hallinan, a feisty progressive born in San Francisco who called the proposal "totally crazy" and proclaimed to the overflow crowd, "we're not tearing the freeway down to have parks and waterfront, we're tearing this down to sell . . . more high-rises."

Supervisor Wendy Nelder also voted "no," aligning herself with the fears about the economic impact on Chinatown and its neighbors.

"I'm not willing to sacrifice . . . the families in this city who depend on their jobs in the area," Nelder said. "Do we take advantage of the fact that there was an earthquake . . . in order to get a better view of the Ferry Building?"

After all this, the start of demolition in February 1991 had the air of a civic festival. The mayor took the controls of a red hydraulic battering ram to punch the first hole in the upper

The scene outside the Ferry Building, 1991. *Darius Aidala, San Francisco History Center, San Francisco Public Library.*

deck as fireboats launched cascades of water into the air and the San Francisco Gay Men's Chorus sang "San Francisco, Open Your Golden Gate." Dianne Feinstein, who the next year would be elected to the US Senate, also was on hand. After more than a decade failing to pull down the structure using the tools of government, she exulted, "It just needed that push from Mother Nature."

The demolition proceeded with efficient speed, and by the time it got to the Ferry Building, where Diane Oshima was now working for the Port, contractors had the routine down pat. A crew would cart in rocks that were spread around the next doomed section, a bed of rubble to keep falling concrete from caroming in unprotected directions. A battering ram would move in and jab at the columns to weaken them, then shove the destabilized columns and beams so that they toppled onto the rock bed below. Cart off the debris and start all over again.

"It was amazing," Oshima said recently. "It also was *really* loud. Those (Ferry Building) windows were *not* insulated."

Seven months after the festive kickoff, Agnos was running hard against four opponents to win reelection. As the last concrete columns came down, he stepped before an enthusiastic crowd of several hundred people to boast: "Today we celebrate not just the end of demolition, but the beginning of renewal for a spectacular waterfront that for 32 years has been blighted by a concrete monster."

Politics factored into such events, Agnos is quick to admit: "I was trying to get a picture wherever I could. We wanted to show people that something was happening, that we were bringing the city back." But the photo-ops were to no avail. After being forced into a runoff election against former police chief Frank Jordan, a conservative by San Francisco standards, Agnos was defeated by 7,616 votes.

To this day, Agnos insists that he became a one-term mayor because of his role in bringing down the Embarcadero Freeway. "I'd been on the ballot seven times, and I had always won somewhere around 70 percent of the vote" in Chinatown and nearby neighborhoods, he mused over lunch. "In 1991, Chinatown, I got 30 percent . . . When you lose a tight election and get blown out in the northeast corner of the city, that's not a coincidence."

Indeed, after winning Chinatown and North Beach by a 64–46 margin in 1987, the mayor lost those northeast neighborhoods to Jordan in the 1991 runoff by 58.5 to 41.5 percent. The legacy had proved to be a political albatross.

"Frankly, I was depressed for six months after I lost." Agnos says today. "But I finally realized I'd gotten defeated for doing the right thing. I'd do it again in a minute."

. . .

The deconstruction of the Embarcadero Freeway, and the political price that Agnos paid, shows the extent to which a single convulsive event can knock a city's trajectory in a different direction, even as the underlying character of that place remains constant. Look at the experiences of New York and New Orleans. One was the target of a terrorist attack that killed 2,753 people, destroyed the city's two tallest towers, and left blocks of Lower Manhattan uninhabitable for months. The other was ravaged by flooding that took more than 1,800 lives and initially caused the city's population to fall by 50 percent. In each case, the future of the city was called into question, yet each violent disaster served to reaffirm the city's essential character, bringing new vitality and, if anything, a recharged sense of purpose. The challenge to San Francisco wasn't as stark as what those two American metropolises faced twelve and sixteen years later—but anyone who lived through it knows the earthquake was an inflection point. Too many people had died. The physical damage was too apparent. Some reactions were simple, such as the state tightening building codes to require new structural support for unreinforced masonry buildings. At a deeper level, the Loma Prieta earthquake forced the question of what should come next.

In the decade after the earthquake, San Francisco remade itself in lasting ways. City Hall simultaneously was modernized and restored to its original splendor, including a fresh coat of gold leaf applied to the regal dome. In Golden Gate Park, Loma Prieta prompted the trustees of the Fine Arts Museums of San Francisco to commission an engineering report on the seismic stability of the M. H. de Young Memorial Museum;

the consultants reported back on the "high potential for partial collapse" if another major earthquake hit. The trustees took the hint, and a striking contemporary museum opened in 2005 to replace the old collage of different wings from different eras. A much bigger change came to the Western Addition's Hayes Valley, which had been torn apart by the Central Freeway in the late 1950s. Residents saw the freeing of the Embarcadero and pressed for a similar act of liberation in *their* neighborhood, which led to its replacement by a tree-lined boulevard that concludes at a community green. This also opened up public land that became surplus property when the viaduct came down, and has since been filled with roughly one thousand residential units, half of them reserved for low-income residents.

Nothing was easy, and nothing was quick. City Hall's remake was ridiculed as "Taj MaWillie," a slap at then-mayor Willie Brown, who made the upgrade a personal priority. Voters twice rejected public funding to build a new de Young inside the park, which prodded wealthy supporters to raise the money themselves. The Hayes Valley story was most convoluted of all: there were four separate ballot measures between 1997 and 1999 on whether the elevated Central Freeway— still in service but structurally obsolete—should be rebuilt along the same path or as the ground-level boulevard desired by neighbors. The first election came out on the side of the freeway fans; the next three favored the boulevard, and it finally opened in 2005.

Yes, the city was as fractious as ever. But the earthquake had left visible wounds on the urban landscape. They couldn't just be left to fester.

"If there's a cataclysmic experience like an earthquake, it makes people anxious to *do* something," recalls Jay Turnbull,

a preservation architect whose firm Page & Turnbull saw business soar after 1989, providing historic guidance on projects
at century-old downtown landmarks where seismic upgrades
were paired with meticulous restorations. "The earthquake
created this avalanche of things that needed to be done, and
maybe you could make things better while you were at it."

· · ·

How did the Ferry Building fit into all this? At first, not particularly well.

By the time the Embarcadero Freeway's 120,000 tons of
concrete had been carted away in 1991, the icon's fate was as
murky as at any time in the past fifty years. A. Page Brown's
design never relied on frills or intricate flourishes, as did other
transit depots of the era. Its visual force stemmed from the
march of classical assurance at a civic scale, every detail adding to the overall effect. But as its one hundredth birthday
neared, air conditioners jutted randomly from some windows.
Other windows were blacked out. Fire escapes cluttered the
facades. A boiler room protruded from the bay-facing wall, a
sad substitute for broad ferry slips.

Inside, the ground floor of the space renovated by the Port in
1962 held parking spaces for agency vehicles, one level below a
law firm and two levels below the Port's dingy offices crowded
with bureaucratic detritus. The northern half of the building
still had those 1950s add-ons that looked more incongruous
each year, including a modernistic cocktail lounge facing the
Embarcadero that radiated all the glamor of a strip mall.

Continental Development and its I. M. Pei designs were now
history, with all lawsuits related to the project dismissed after
an out-of-court settlement, two weeks before freeway demolition began. Yet the fears of waterfront changes were as strong

as ever: San Francisco voters in 1990 had narrowly approved a ballot initiative to ban hotels along the water and impose a moratorium on development of Port-owned land until a land-use plan was approved for the entire 7.5 miles.

Two four-story hotel proposals underneath the Bay Bridge had lit the spark; they were modest by the standards of the Magnin era, but once the Port Commission approved them, that was enough to rally diehard Embarcadero stalwarts for another campaign. They included none other than Supervisor Richard Hongisto, then preparing to run against Agnos for mayor (he came in fourth), who argued in the voter information pamphlet that "hotels on the waterfront will wall off the bay."

Seven years passed before the Port Commission and the Bay Conservation and Development Commission were able to complete the land-use plan. But the slow procession of public meetings, environmental studies, and bureaucratic negotiations was time well spent. Unlike past decades when state regulators would intercede to halt overly aggressive Port projects, as with Ferry Port Plaza, the two sides agreed up front in terms of what was and wasn't allowed. The southern waterfront would still be reserved for industrial maritime activities. From China Basin to Fisherman's Wharf, parks and popular attractions would be encouraged, in new structures as well as old.

"We can give the Port the flexibility it wants, if it gives us the uncovered bay and the public access we want," Will Travis, the BCDC executive director, said at the time. Much later, in his oral history, Travis explained how the two agencies made peace and moved forward.

For years we at BCDC and the port staff were bat-
tling with each other. Then the port director and I

got together and said, "Look, I don't care which of
us is to blame. We're both responsible for the fact
that the San Francisco waterfront is a pit and we're
not going to put up with it anymore."

As plans go, the 219-page document doesn't get the blood
racing (unless you're enthralled by subdistrict spreadsheets of
accessory uses). But the ambitions were clear: "This Plan is
intended to alter the course of history at the Port."

And why not a hint of bravado? At the most fundamental
level, the difference between this initiative and prior ones is
that the potential was plain to see. The Embarcadero might
still have a raw feel—those parking lots that had lurked
beneath the freeway were still there—yet the acreage where
cable cars had pivoted laboriously at the conclusion to "A Trip
down Market Street" was taking on a festive air. The wide
sidewalks promised in 1980 were being installed, adorned
with historical plaques and public art. Tracks for a new streetcar line were being laid in place of the Belt Railroad, which
shut down in August 1991. For the first time in decades, the
waterfront felt like a place where good things could happen.

• • •

As the 1931 Lincoln slowly rolled up Market Street, roars of
pleasure erupted each time another stretch of people glimpsed
the eighty-year-old man inside.

It was an event without parallel in American history, a civic
parade honoring a daily journalist. He had arrived in town
to take a job in 1936 and never left. Now, on June 14, 1996,
he was the guest of honor for Herb Caen Day, cheered by an
estimated seventy-five thousand people who lined Market
to watch a motorcade that also included cars holding civic

Herb Caen shows off a 49ers helmet presented him by the football team's owner
on Herb Caen Day, 1996. San Francisco Chronicle / *Deanne Fitzmaurice.*

luminaries, elected officials present and past, and such local
legends as comedian Robin Williams and baseball immortal
Willie Mays.

The parade concluded, where else, in front of the Ferry
Building—dismissed by Caen in his youth as "this sad old
pile of gray," and then defended on multiple occasions by the
middle-aged columnist because "I can't think of any landmark
I'd fight harder to save." Now he was a man entering his ninth
decade who the previous month had confided to readers that
he had lung cancer, and inoperable cancer at that: "I have had
two chemotherapy sessions so far, with the promise of many
more to come." More poignant still, that diagnosis came a
month after Caen was awarded a special Pulitzer Prize "for
his extraordinary and continuing contribution as a voice and
conscience of his city."

The formal program was held beneath the Ferry Building's

clocktower, in front of the magisterial entrance, with a stage facing the Embarcadero where crowds were gathered to watch the celebration. The guest of honor sat with his wife on one side and venerated television news anchor Walter Cronkite on the other—the two became close friends in London during World War II—while the gathering was treated to maniacal ad-libs by Williams, wry reflections by Cronkite, and music by everyone from rocker Huey Lewis to a jazz band and "Cabaret" star Joel Grey. The master of ceremonies was Mayor Brown, who for years lunched with Caen each Friday.

Brown had the object of affection step to the microphone after the broad sidewalk from Fisherman's Wharf to China Basin was officially dedicated as "Herb Caen Way . . ." (complete with the three little dots that were his trademark).

"There are five living mayors here!" Caen observed with a laugh. "Obviously the grand jury hasn't been doing its job." Mostly, though, he basked in the affection and the setting, his periodic gloom about San Francisco's evolution nowhere to be found.

"God, I love this town," the honoree burst out at one point. He reminisced about his youth, arriving from Sacramento as a new *Chronicle* employee, "coming out through the Ferry Building into this incredible maelstrom of noise and streetcars and newsboys."

As Caen left the stage a few moments later, gingerly descending into the crowd with Brown at his side, the jazz band kicked in. Hundreds of balloons were let into the air, the same as after that march to protect the waterfront that Caen had promoted in his column twenty-five years earlier.

The clocktower, the classical arches, the contrast of weathered gray stone and vivid blue bay—there could be no better setting for this bittersweet bash. The Ferry Building's presence said San Francisco every bit as much as the beaming presence of Mr. San Francisco himself.

Caen died eight months later. The Waterfront Land Use Plan was approved four months after that. The next chapter in the life of the Ferry Building was about to begin. This one, unlike all the ill-fated initiatives of the prior sixty years, was the one that came to pass.

CHAPTER

———

TWELVE

CRAFTING VISIONS FOR URBAN LANDSCAPES ISN'T THE SAME AS making them reality, as the contentious arc of San Francisco and its waterfront since World War II makes abundantly clear. But by the late 1990s, San Francisco's waterfront was showing real signs of life.

The revival stretched beyond the crowded onetime events, like Herb Caen Day or the offshore fireworks on New Year's Eve. New housing was beginning to fill blocks on the inland side of the Embarcadero, south of the Bay Bridge. At China Basin, on land where a port maintenance facility had been, the San Francisco Giants in 1997 broke ground for a privately funded ballpark the year after voters gave the project their blessing.

Ferry service was on the increase, too. Before Loma Prieta there was the line from Marin and patchy service from Vallejo, near Napa, a forty-five-minute journey at best, but the month-long closure of the Bay Bridge forced East Bay government officials to assemble an impromptu armada that captured the imagination of commuters. Within a decade, regional trans-portation officials had launched a transit authority to offer alternatives to bridges and BART when crossing the bay. There was a push to buy ferries and build gates behind the Ferry Building and in several cities along the bay.

Plenty of other American cities were refurbishing their own industrial waterfronts, as well. In New York, derelict piers along the Hudson River were merged with portions of the land opened up by the removal of the West Side Highway to create a 550-acre linear park featuring such private attrac-tions as Chelsea Piers with its recreational array of offerings from tennis courts to a driving range for golf. In Boston, the 1998 opening of a federal courthouse on a curving waterfront site known as Fan Pier was the first step in the city's effort to remake a dormant waterfront district along Fort Point Chan-nel, which prospered in the late 1800s handling raw cargo such as coal and animal hides but by the 1980s consisted of a handful of old brick warehouses amid acres of parking lots. The transformations also reshaped inland cities where river-front manufacturing had declined, such as Minneapolis with the revival of obsolete mills along the Mississippi River inter-laced with distinctive newcomers like the towering home of the Guthrie Theater. In Louisville, the conversion beginning in 1998 of scrapyards along the Ohio River into Waterfront Park spurred the blossoming of a district filled with apart-ments and restaurants plus a basketball arena and Louisville Slugger Field, a minor league ballpark.

San Francisco, in other words, was part of a larger move-ment to tap into the visceral appeal that proximity to water has for people on land. If there's an icon nearby—think Syd-ney Opera House, or the aquariums along the shore of cities such as Boston and Baltimore—then all the better.

The Embarcadero of the late 1990s mostly had potential, such as the new streetcars and sidewalks that were being installed, and the ballpark set to open in 2000. But that potential explains why four strong development teams responded to the Port's call in May 1998 for proposals involving "the high quality rehabilitation of the Ferry Building as financially successful, premium space . . . providing both a focal point on the waterfront and an integrating link with Downtown."

One bidder was William Wilson & Associates, a large developer that specialized in Silicon Valley office parks and joined with Christopher Meany, who had impressed preservationists with his restoration of the Flood Building, a 1906 survivor next to the cable car turnaround at Powell and Market Streets. Wilson provided the resources and experience; Meany, then in his mid-thirties, liked the challenge of making a great old building relevant again. This team was the only one to propose the revival of Brown's original centerpiece—the grand nave that had run the full extent of the second floor from north to south. There'd again be the layered drama of marble tiles underfoot and skylit trusses up above, just as when commuters rushed from the ferries to descend the grand staircases into the city.

A move like this meant removing all the office space that had closed off the nave's volume during the building's nadir, and re-creating the arches and moldings and brickwork that originally framed it. Port planners were captivated: in the words of the staff report dissecting the four proposals, bringing back "the original and preeminent grand public space of the Ferry Building would be a remarkable achievement."

There was a catch, a big one. At the same time Meany and Wilson proposed the full spatial restoration of the nave, they wanted to cut two long holes into it so that people on the ground floor could look up and feel like part of history. The only portion that would be retained would be the central stretch with its mosaic of the California state seal.

Port planners acknowledged "problematical preservation issues" with the audacity of this approach. But the counterargument was compelling.

When A. Page Brown conceived the grand nave, it had a functional purpose—to serve as a concourse where large volumes of people could reach or depart their vessels without claustrophobic confusion. The ground floor mostly consisted of baggage storage, ticket counters and a few waiting rooms that attracted few patrons, because upstairs was more fun. The twenty-first-century Ferry Building would operate in a much different way, with private offices filling nearly all the space along the second-floor nave; the ground floor would be the public area, with retail space along passageways allowing people to walk directly through the building to a bayside promenade. A visual link to the skylight and nave added historical context to the public experience.

Bustling memories of the golden era might be cherished by preservation purists, but the days when individual ferries discharged as many as 2,300 people from the slips onto the concourse were long, long gone.

When the staff offered its final assessment to the Port Commission that November, the Wilson team came out on top. "We knew they were going to make this work," recalls Alec Bash, one of the Port's planners at the time. "They recognized the importance of the Ferry Building, and what it means to the waterfront and the city." The commission agreed by a 4–1 vote.

. . .

One factor in Wilson and Meany's favor is that they had hired architects with local DNA. The design team was led by the firm SMWM, which already was working on a renovation of Pier 1 that would fill the old shed with offices for the Port and other tenants.

The "S" in SMWM, Cathy Simon, grew up in New York and moved to San Francisco in 1969 with her husband-to-be, poet Michael Palmer. "The Bay Area was such a different place from the East Coast at that point, so open and free," Simon said recently. "The East Coast was buttoned up, and totally man-oriented. Here, you could go to interviews and not be the only woman in the room. You could think about starting your own firm," which she did in 1985.

The retail designer BCV Architects had offices in North Beach; Hans Baldauf, the partner in charge, came from a family so entwined in Bay Area food culture that his father installed the first pizza oven at Chez Panisse, the Berkeley restaurant created by California cuisine pioneer Alice Waters. The third firm was Page & Turnbull, which had done historic analyses of the Ferry Building and nearby piers dating back to the 1970s.

Once the Wilson-Meany team won the competition, Meany took Simon, Baldauf, and a few others across the Atlantic Ocean to experience food retailing in London, Paris, Milan, and Venice.

It sounds like a junket, and nobody denies the quality of the food and drink consumed along the way. But the focus was on the details of experience—why retail scenes in the heart of European cities often radiate a sense of immersive discovery that Americans rarely find at home in even the most ballyhooed shopping malls. The old Covent Garden in London impressed them with the rawness of structure, where the structural bones of cast iron underscored the integrity of the food and wares on sale. In Paris, long walks from arcade to arcade and public market to public market revealed a common denominator: in each of these classic spaces, the visitor navigated what felt like a blurred sequence of intoxicating sensations.

"No doors, no windows, just merchants pulling out everything into the streets," Simon reminisced. "We were struck by the messiness of it all. The energy was infectious."

The most direct impact of the trip, in terms of what eventually got built, involved the layout of the ground floor. The competition proposal called for a set of fairly conventional retail spaces. Once the travelers returned home, plans changed: they decided to push the retail spaces ten feet into the central passage, narrowing it, banishing glass walls wherever possible and instead securing the front of each storefront or stall with artful metal grills.

If they chose, retailers could extend another six feet into the passage during store hours to display their wares. An upside for the developer? The compressed layout created several additional retail stalls, snug and shallow but injecting more life.

"It's what makes it a civic experience, rather than a bunch of storefronts lined up in a row," Baldauf says. He likens the passage to Paris' Rue Mouffetard, a narrow two-block street market, "spilling out, the notion of immediacy, spilling out."

Simon had another motive on the trip—to sway the developers' team on the merits of a bolder, more European approach to preservation, "the idea we shouldn't be afraid of contemporary interventions in historic buildings." That's why, in Venice, she walked them through the Olivetti showroom designed in the 1950s by Carlo Scarpa, an architect revered by other architects for his adventurous fusion of old and new. This example, a jewel box-like shop within a sixteenth-century arcade along the Piazza San Marco, is punctuated by features like a blunt concrete staircase that seems to hover in the air.

"Chris *hated* Scarpa," Simon says, laughing at the memory. "I completely failed at my mission."

Whatever the merits of unapologetic modernism, Meany knew better than to try and push things too far.

Bay Area preservationists already were wary of what might happen to an old friend that had survived decades of disrespect; part of Bash's unofficial job description was to keep history buffs from raising too many objections, too loudly.

A conservative approach also was essential to the bottom line—more than $9 million of the project's funding was tied to the sale of the federal historic tax credits, which provide a financial boost to the rehabilitation of historic buildings. But such credits aren't allowed unless the National Park Service signs off.

The sticking point involved slicing open the tiled floor of the nave; "I'd rather see the Ferry Building sit vacant for 100 years than see the nave desecrated," one preservationist told Jay Turnbull. State regulators balked, even those who were willing to bend rules to help the project along.

To resolve the impasse, Meany flew east with a quite different entourage than the one that went to Europe, including the project's real estate attorney and political consultant. The lone architect on the trip was Turnbull, the head of the firm whose role in the project included the vetting of the historical credibility of the design.

"By the time we left for Washington, everyone was thinking 'what kind of deal can we propose' . . . we give a little, you give a little," Meany shrugs two decades later. "'How can we make this work?'"

It didn't hurt that when Meany's small group met with

the National Park Service team, a staff member stopped by from the office of Congresswoman Nancy Pelosi from San Francisco. She wasn't yet the top Democrat in the House of Representatives—that would come in 2001—but she clearly was on the rise. That aide's brief visit to welcome everyone wasn't by accident. As Turnbull saw it, "The idea was that this is politically important in California and, by God, get someone there."

Meany made his pitch to remove the equivalent of seven bays, or 210 feet, on either side of the great seal, leaving only the far ends and the central section intact, arguing that "if this was going to be a *public* building, the true nave was the 1st floor." Park Service staff didn't want to lose more than a three-bay stretch to the north and a three-bay stretch to the south. The final verdict? They met halfway: two sections containing five bays each could be removed, 30 feet by 150 feet, one on each side of the state seal and its tiled surroundings.

"It's a classic developer strategy: always ask for more than you want," Turnbull suggests with a smile. Asked what he contributed to the meeting, the architect just laughs. The sole reason for his presence was in case somebody wanted to explore the architectural ramifications of the impasse, the inherent tension between preservation and change in urban contexts.

Nobody did. They were there to get things settled, and head back home.

· · ·

As the new decade dawned, construction crews started on the real work at hand—to transport an oft-altered structure from 1898 into the twenty-first century.

Restoring the classical grandeur required gutting the interior

The reshaping of the Ferry Building's interior, 2000. The nave's tile mosaic floor is covered with plywood for protection. *Tom Paiva.*

and removing all the outer walls except for the west-facing facade, a task made more difficult by the decades of renovations by various tenants with various motives. "There was demolition going on for months," recalls Alan Kren, the project manager for the structural engineering firm Rutherford + Chekene. The sections where the building had been "modernized" for the World Trade Center were especially difficult, with thick concrete walls that served no obvious purpose: "We blew out tons and tons of stuff . . . So much of it was total crap."

The floor of the nave was treated with more care, covered for protection after the thick tile-topped flooring in the doomed bays was cut into two-foot by two-foot panels and then stored in a warehouse outside San Francisco. The team hoped to keep the original skylight, but the materials were so decayed that the decision was made to rebuild from scratch, meticulously replacing the 644 original panes with double-glazed updates for better insulation.

After deconstruction came the installation of new structural elements, both for seismic strength and to delineate the spaces that would be occupied by vendors, restaurants, and offices. Interior details evocative of 1898 were installed, such as the beige tiles along the ground-floor retail arcade. Only a short stretch of the second-floor wall had survived, clad in the last of the Tennessee marble that had lined the nave. Those panels were cleaned while the other walls were finished off with sheetrock and painted in a complementary hue. Arched wooden windows that had allowed light into the waiting rooms for the long-gone ferries were found stored away; they were cleaned and repaired and placed along the foyer of a custom-built conference room for the Port Commission that faces the bay, due east of the state seal.

Most fastidious of all was the rebirth of the tile mosaic floor, done by (in Simon's words) "two guys on their knees for nine months." It was a slow but subtly magical process. The first step involved blasting the surface with walnut shells, a specialized technique used to gently buff loose carpet adhesive when sand-blasting would be too abrasive. (As part of the postwar renovations, carpet and vinyl had been applied pretty much everywhere except on top of the seal.) Then the mosaic tiles were washed in place and re-grouted. When tiles were missing—such as spots where the floor had been cut through to insert an elevator and fire stairs for the World Trade Center—they were replaced using the stockpile that had been salvaged from the deconstruction.

Nothing about the reclamation was easy, not even something as seemingly basic as installing the utility pipes. The building sits directly on the foundation's concrete slab, so there's no basement or crawl space. The only way to add plumbing for shops and restaurants was for workers to climb into row boats with their tools and head beneath the building at the lowest possible tide, day or night. Using floodlights to guide them, and ropes to steady their boats amid the ricocheting tides, workers would drill into the peak of each groined vault, where the concrete was "only" three feet thick. Then, workers hustled to get as much done as they could before tides rose too high. The pipes had to be stainless steel so that salt water wouldn't corrode them—and tough enough to not be damaged *too* much by flotsam and jetsam swept in from the bay.

"It's like being in the catacombs down there," says Kren, the structural engineer. "When the tide is really low, you see a beach that has formed along the seawall. Crabs and stuff like that."

• • •

As construction crews worked from their rowboats and scaffolding, the developers worked to secure tenants for the ground-floor marketplace.

Meany always envisioned smaller shops and a culinary theme, but details beyond that were fuzzy until Europe brought things into focus. "The places that worked best were quirkily idiosyncratic, adaptations to their world," he recalled in 2022. "The thing that hit us was, we have to mine what's in San Francisco—what is our local thing?"

The path they chose seems obvious now, if not downright clichéd: put Northern California food culture front and center, emphasizing the fresh-grown virtues of organic food close to home. You could buy the ingredients and dazzle friends at home, or meet at the Ferry Building and savor the surroundings along with your food and wine.

Food as signifier of place was nothing new. Part of Ghirardelli Square's early luster was the range of you-are-here offerings, from Ghirardelli's branded sundae shop at one end of the consumer spectrum to Cecilia Chiang's upscale Mandarin restaurant at the other, said at the time to be a first in the United States. The Mandarin dazzled the likes of Herb Caen but also a young Alice Waters, who grew close to Chiang and later reminisced in a magazine interview about Chiang's banquets for friends, "Always creating a harmonious whole" so freshly sourced that, for instance, "you would only ever have bamboo shoots in the spring at just the right moment." That evolving Bay Area appreciation for experiences tied to the locale is one reason the Continental Development scheme for the Ferry Building never felt right, with its food court-like "international bazaar" and stage-set Viennese coffeehouse.

This time around, twenty years later, the aim was a destination that evoked the ethos of freshness and local sourcing. As surely as the original intent of the Ferry Building was to signal travelers from the east that they were entering a sophisticated metropolis, the reinvented space would nod to the aspiration for a kind of gustatory nirvana. Wines from Napa and Sonoma. Bread and cheese summoned forth with artisanal care. The fetish for seasonal produce epitomized by Chez Panisse and its farm-to-table peers—or more precisely by the weekly farmers market that since 1994 had operated on Saturdays outside the Ferry Building, along the Embarcadero where the freeway once passed overhead.

The market had begun as a one-off event to publicize the need for a market downtown, then blossomed into a destination for customers drawn to the bounty of small farmers and ranchers (and the like-minded social scene). If they chose, the shoppers could see themselves as part of something larger, a movement billed as the fusion of big-city consumers and regional farmers by the nonprofit running the market, CUESA—as in "Center for Urban Education about Sustainable Agriculture."

"Everyone who really was part of the food community shared a commitment" to such values, Meany says, looking back. He and his wife Michele, who handled the retail leasing, started reaching out to leading figures of that self-defined community with a pitch that Meany in retrospect boils down to, "We're creating a house. We'd like all of you, at this philosophical moment in the Bay Area, to be here."

One of the first to sign on was Cowgirl Creamery, an organic cheesemaker.

"When they talked about their vision, it really intrigued us," recalls Peggy Smith, who worked at Chez Panisse before she and her partner, Sue Conley, in 1997 bought a barn and opened a showcase of West Marin food makers in the tiny downtown of Point Reyes Station. They soon were making fresh cheeses of their own, and the accolades followed.

Conley, for her part, was thrilled at being asked to take part: "They didn't ask to look at our profit-and-loss sheet, they just wanted the best cheese."

Second-generation mushroom grower Ian Garrone was recruited from the Saturday market where his stall, Far West Fungi, had a cult following. At the age of six he had entered the trade, so to speak, breaking down boxes for his parents in an old military hangar where they grew exotic mushrooms in laboratory-like conditions. When Ian graduated from college, he convinced mom and dad to let him open a stall at the Embarcadero market. Michele Meany reached out to the family not long after that.

"I think it was 'these guys are scrappy, they're showing up, let's get them in here too,'" Garrone muses today. "It sounded like fun."

Garrone ended up in a small stall across from a pork rancher and a fishmonger. At the other extreme, the Meanys sought a few large restaurants to help make the building a nighttime destination. The last one to sign on had a much different pedigree than farmers markets or the Berkeley food scene: Slanted Door.

The restaurateur was Charles Phan, whose family fled Vietnam during the collapse of South Vietnam. They ended up in San Francisco, his father working as a janitor and his mother as a seamstress while Charles dropped out of UC Berkeley before getting intrigued by cooking. In 2005, his extended family pooled their credit cards to buy a small building in the Mission District on Valencia Street, what then was a funky strip where Mexican immigrants overlapped with lesbians, punks and 1960s holdovers.

Slanted Door's contemporary take on Vietnamese food quickly attracted a far wider clientele—including then-president Bill Clinton, who took his daughter Chelsea there for lunch in 2000. After a move to larger quarters near the Embarcadero in 2002, Michelle Meany approached Phan about opening a noodle stand in the Ferry Building. Phan made a counteroffer.

"It came to me in the shower—that's where I get all my best ideas," is how Phan tells it twenty years later. He knew one large corner space was empty, so he called the Meanys with his pitch: "I want to move the Slanted Door to your building, here's what I need and can afford, period, and you have 48 hours to decide."

It was a big ask, and Wilson and Meany no longer were calling the financial shots: William Wilson's company was

The restored nave and skylight, with a new third-floor pedestrian
bridge. *Courtesy of Noah Berger.*

now owned by Chicago-based Equity Office Properties Trust.
The Ferry Building was one item in the portfolio of a property owner with 380 buildings and 95.5 million square feet of
space, and higher-ups in Chicago wanted to review any sizable
leases. But before the deadline expired, Phan had his deal.

· · ·

Profit margins were tied to the two floors of office space along
the nave, where Meany and Wilson anticipated an average rent
of $65 per square foot, almost 20 percent above the going
rate at the time for Class A offices in the Financial District.
Ambitious—except that the late 1990s was a boom time in
the Bay Area where, after decades, the economic and cultural
divide between San Francisco and Silicon Valley to the south
began to blur.

This period is remembered now as the dotcom boom,
which briefly made sensations out of companies like Pets.

com, a short-lived start-up that built its ad campaigns around an abrasive sock puppet. But there was more to it than that. Established South Bay technology firms were looking for large blocks of space in San Francisco, where more and more of their younger workers wanted to live. Silicon Valley's boom times also meant big business for the bankers and attorneys in San Francisco who handled much of their business.

At the same time it pursued the Ferry Building, in fact, the Wilson company purchased four sites south of Market Street with an eye to the Silicon Valley connection—a project it dubbed Foundry Square, with a freeway onramp two blocks away that offered a straight shot down the peninsula. By contrast, the appeal of the Ferry Building was tied to the older city. A landmark structure on a resurgent waterfront in a prosperous metropolis had to be a safe bet.

Then the dotcom boom went bust and tech companies retrenched, including one Silicon Valley mainstay that had signed a lease for two of the Foundry Square buildings but canceled its expansion plans. This was followed by the attack on the World Trade Center by Al Qaeda terrorists on September 11, 2001. That murderous horror occurred 2,500 miles from San Francisco, but it deepened a recession that already was underway, because nobody knew what might come next. At the Ferry Building, all the retail tenants with signed letters of intent put their deals on hold in the days after 9/11. An investment firm that had been planning to move to the office space upstairs called off negotiations.

"Those were two of the worst years of my life," Meany says now. "The world's falling apart, the building's essentially empty, but we can't just stop construction." Finally, as opening day neared, the real estate law firm Coblentz, Patch, Duffy

& Bass leased half of the office space. The rumored rent was $38.50 per square foot, barely half the anticipated amount.

Through all this, work continued. Many of the original retail tenants were coaxed back. New ones like Slanted Door came aboard. The farmer's market signed on for three days weekly, with plans to host live cooking demonstrations in the open arcades once lined with ticket counters for the ferries.

As the spring of 2003 drew near, construction was nearly complete. The Ferry Building was ready to go. Simon liked what she saw, even if the design was more conservative than she originally had wished.

"I had all these ideas! I wanted to embrace change, and have people think of the building in a completely radical way," Simon says now. "But at some point I realized, 'get over yourself. Don't be so academic and intellectual. This is a building that people love.'"

CHAPTER

———

THIRTEEN

AFTER ALL THE FALSE STARTS, THE DASHED HOPES AND UNBUILT visions, the Ferry Building's return to public life was a low-key affair.

The small but growing band of ferry commuters could enter the building on their way to and from work beginning March 21, 2003. The first retail tenants opened in April, one selling coffee and one selling chocolate: two small lures pulling people in to linger, to admire the rebuilt skylight through the newly opened nave or enjoy such small surprises as the muted tile mosaics, fifteen inches square, offering cameos of crabs or olives or figs, details of nature's bounty. A more celebratory taste of what might lie ahead came when the Ferry Plaza Farmers Market debuted on the last Saturday of April, marking its return to the Ferry Building area with a ribbon-cutting at which CUESA founder Sibella Kraus raised a figurative toast "to the small farmers and vendors" and vowed, "Our dream is that San Francisco will be the first American city to link itself with its farmland."

Ceremony out of the way, thousands of people mingled in high spirits to purchase fresh produce and take in the scene—or as one customer explained to a reporter, "squeeze and smell and taste." Their tactile lust for organics sated, patrons ventured inside and, merely by their presence, conjured up an atmosphere of vibrant potential that left everyone wanting more.

More soon followed.

. . .

The shops opened one by one, each newcomer adding to the larger momentum. By the time the tower's clock was restarted in mid-June—an event that included a private champagne reception for dignitaries and an enormous cake shaped like you-know-what for everyone else—85 percent of the retail spaces were spoken for. Two-thirds of the office space upstairs was leased. Four months later, the National Trust for Historic Preservation awarded the icon one of its ten Preservation Honor Awards for the year.

Hometown accolades could go to parochial extremes, as when *Chronicle* restaurant critic Michael Bauer hailed "a magical convergence of past and present" in one article, and "a shrine to the Bay Area's obsession with food" in another. But the gushing didn't stop at Bay Area borders. *Gourmet* magazine devoted several pages to "San Francisco's brilliantly original idea of an urban market." *Bon Appetit* was almost as effusive as Bauer, dubbing the restored landmark "a kind of cathedral for the city's food-worshiping population . . . it's the reason why San Francisco still ranks as one of the country's top destinations for foodies."

More importantly, the Ferry Building reclaimed its place as the crossroads of an increasingly global city.

When England's Prince Charles visited the United States in

King Charles III, then Prince Charles, at the Ferry Building in 2005 with Queen Consort Camilla, then Duchess of Cornwall. San Francisco Chronicle / *Liz Hafalia*.

2005, the final leg of his goodwill tour included an afternoon at the Ferry Building, where Mayor Gavin Newsom walked him through the nave and security guards with high-powered rifles were posted high in the tower, above the four clocks, to keep discreet watch over the surroundings while the prince gave a speech on environmental issues inside. He and his wife Camilla, the Duchess of Cornwall, then browsed the stalls: "We talked about British pigs," one pork vendor told a reporter. Camilla happily accepted a brownie from a chocolatier.

Bill Clinton attracted 3,500 fans who stood in line to be scanned with magnetometers by Secret Service agents before entering the San Francisco outpost of Book Passage so the ex-president could sign their pre-purchased copy of his autobiography, *My Life*. In 2007, the secretary-general of the United Nations, Ban Ki-moon, was given a tour of the building. With less fanfare, Maureen Hardy of BCV, who had been the firm's project architect during the transformation, received so many

Fireworks during the week before Super Bowl 50, 2016. *Courtesy of Jim Stone Photography.*

requests for tours from fellow designers and civic groups that she drew up a six-page list of talking points.

Gay Pride parades began nearby every June, antiabortion marches every January. When the Fiftieth Super Bowl was hosted by San Francisco in 2016, the tower wore a black banner with the logo draped below the clock facing the city; an enormous illuminated "50" glowed above, just like the "1915" that announced the Panama-Pacific International Exposition.

The key here is that Wilson Meany's design team understood the art of illusion whereby a historic building is calibrated to be in sync with modern-day needs. The retail corridor's dimensions would be cramped if not for the sliced views of the skylight above, that hint of timeless urbanity above the daily buzz. The theatricality of the market stalls is leavened by the muscular steel columns and beams that have been there all along. The place names stenciled along the frieze above the public passages are a throwback to the 1875 Ferry House;

now, the likes of Lakeport and Gilroy and Marshall are included not because they are Southern Pacific destinations, but for their association with Northern California's bounty.

If there's an element of make-believe in all this . . . so what? Architecture has always had a theatrical aspect that takes its cues from the past. Look at the historical motifs employed by Arthur Page Brown and his firm the first time around: The deep arcades facing west were a nod to the formalities of classical design. The powerfully composed clocktower was inspired by the Giralda bell tower of Spain's Seville Cathedral. Such gestures served to enhance the stature of San Francisco's "monumental gateway," as the *Examiner* put it in 1893—since, to quote the Board of State Harbor Commissioners, "first impressions are the most lasting."

. . .

It takes more than atmospheric architecture to make a business a success, however.

Ian Garrone learned this at Far West Fungi—he opened in 2004 with eight varieties of fresh mushrooms and soon learned that commuters or tourists passing through the marketplace are different from locavores lingering over their favored stands at a farmers market.

"We had no idea what we were getting into," he confesses. "After the first week I realized, 'This isn't working. We need more variety.'"

The homegrown mushrooms were augmented by travel-friendly mushroom products, from a dried "organic cultivated mix" to powdered European porcini. With time there were medicinal mushroom oils ("tinctures," to be precise, $20 for a bottled ounce as of 2023). Surprisingly tasty mushroom jerky. And yes, consumer goods like tote bags and T-shirts and $45 hoodies with the Far West Fungi logo. The rationale for the latter? "Tourists always want to take something home, and in summer they always need an extra layer of clothing" due to San Francisco's omnipresent fog, Garrone explains.

"The core of business, we thought, was going to be the locals in the area. They are—on Saturdays. We've learned we need to try and make ourselves as relevant as possible."

All the tenants had to accommodate themselves to the particularities of the scene.

Upstairs, the Coblentz firm found that arranging two floors of office space in an elongated U around the nave meant windowless inner corridors so long that different carpet patterns were deployed along the way to make long walks less dreary. When attorneys asked about the private offices they'd be getting, the answer from the partner in charge of the move, Todd Brody, was a succinct "small and *very* small." The views were great, but the tightly spaced structural columns between the window bays clamped down on private space.

Down below, retail tenants needing to install new pipes or fix old ones had to dispatch repair crews underneath the concrete foundations in small vessels, once again scheduling the work in tandem with the lowest tides. "We've sent crews below, the boat would flip and we'd lose the tools," recalls Olle Lundberg, architect for Charles Phan of Slanted Door, which finally opened in June 2004. "We're lucky we didn't lose the workers."

But with the particularities came the payoff.

In the case of Slanted Door and its earthy yet elegant Vietnamese food, Phan's 150-seat restaurant filled up night after night, year after year. It helped that he received multiple awards from the influential James Beard Foundation, and was profiled in the *Washington Post* and the *New York Times*. But

The Ferry Building marketplace, 2010. San Francisco Chronicle / *Michael Macor.*

the location helped fuel the allure that pushed annual revenues in pre-pandemic years as high as $19 million, making it California's highest grossing independent restaurant.

For Garrone, selling mushrooms in a cultural icon pays benefits far from home.

"I can be doing sales calls to places in Miami or Los Angeles, and I don't hear back," he says. "Then I'll stop by their restaurants when I'm traveling, or meet them at a food conference, and they'll say 'You're from San Francisco? Do you know that great place at the Ferry Building?' It's happened so many times."

Cowgirl Creamery flourished from day one. The range of cheese offerings was exquisite, with each order carefully cut for the customers by hand. Then there was the one-night-only event each year when the Specialty Food Association came to San Francisco for its annual Fancy Food Fair: Conley and Smith would take over the grand nave and host a party for their cheesemaking peers from around the world. "The admission was one pound of their cheese that they were most proud of," Conley recalls fondly. "It was the hottest ticket in town."

. . .

For someone not part of the "food-worshiping population," to quote *Bon Appétit*, the aura of the Ferry Building as a culinary citadel could be a little much. An easy place to find obscure mushrooms and boutique goat cheese, but the necessities of daily life? Maybe not. As Todd Brody of the Coblentz law firm puts it, "People were very proud of having offices there. But if you wanted a cheap sandwich, you had to take a walk."

Then there were the complaints from the other end, that the temple was being debased by too much popularity. *Food + Wine* magazine might place the Ferry Building among the top twenty-five food markets in the world. Real estate analyst Cushman + Wakefield might single it out as "one of the best examples of the modern food hall in the United States." To the true believers, that itself was cause for concern.

"In the food world, success is a double-edged sword," Paolo Lucchesi wrote in a 2018 *San Francisco Chronicle* piece headlined "Does the Ferry Building Still Reflect the Bay Area's Food Culture?" The paper's food editor at the time, Lucchesi didn't focus on leasing rates or who "should" be there; rather, he explored the increasing number of tenants with ties to global commerce—how the cachet surrounding the building in food circles added a luster that, in turn, helped catch the attention of investors.

Lucchesi included the tale of Blue Bottle Coffee Co., which by then had outposts stretching from Boston to Japan, all nestled in a pristine white decor that couldn't be more different than the woodsy aura of old-school coffeehouses. It first attracted a following with long lines snaking through the Ferry Plaza Farmers Market, each customer waiting for their beans to be ground before the barista slowly poured loops of hot water over them, stirring gently all the while. After opening a small space on an alley in San Francisco's Hayes Valley, Blue Bottle graduated in 2009 into a corner stall within the Ferry Building. Before long, its investors included the celebrity likes of U2's Bono and skateboard legend Tony Hawk, and the founders sold a two-thirds interest to the Swiss conglomerate Nestlé in 2017.

"The Ferry Building was never perfect, nor will it ever be, but it had a clear, if impossible, vision," when it re-opened, Lucchesi wrote in 2018. "Now, 15 years later, its businesses are full of investment firm money and corporate interests."

Two years before the piece, Cowgirl Creamery had its own change of ownership.

Conley and Smith were in their sixties by 2016, with ninety-five employees and two small plants in the North Bay producing a dozen varieties of cheese. They still had Tomales Bay Foods in Point Reyes Station. They had added a sandwich counter next to their Ferry Building shop, and the monthly rent for the two stalls was $36,000, up from $10,000 for the cheese shop alone when they opened in 2003.

"We just realized we were getting up there. We had to figure out how we were going to leave this company," Conley said. The solution? They sold Cowgirl Creamery to Emmi, a Swiss dairy cooperative with $3.3 billion in net sales at the time.

· · ·

Global economics was not an issue with the Ferry Plaza Farmers Market. Instead, it periodically came under fire as a precious world unto itself.

Yes, Alice Waters was a Saturday morning regular, pulling into a parking spot reserved for the doyenne of California cuisine. Martha Stewart stopped by whenever she was in town. Britain's "Naked Chef," Jamie Oliver, did a cooking demo for NBC's popular *Today Show* from what he called "one of the best farmers markets in the world." But that sheen rubbed other visitors the wrong way. The skeptics included a revered figure in the pantheon of culinary sustainability: Carlo Petrini, who rose from protesting the arrival of a McDonald's in Rome's historic core to founding the "Slow Food" movement. In writing and lectures he expounds on the importance of "the strong connections between plate and planet," so foodies in 2007 took note when his book *Slow Food Nation* described a trip to the Saturday market (as a guest of Waters, no less) in tones of sniffish disdain:

> *Alice Waters introduced me to dozens of farmers: they were all well-to-do college graduates, former employees of Silicon Valley, many of them young. Meanwhile their customers, most of whom seemed to be actresses, went home clutching their peppers, marrows and apples, showing them off like jewels, status symbols.*

So much for a planned book signing at the Ferry Plaza Farmers Market. Nor did it help that Petrini's subsequent letter to CUESA would make a defensive politician proud: "I want to apologize for any offense caused by this passage . . . the translation of this passage was, unfortunately, not as accurate as it should have been."

On the populist end of the spectrum, roaming cult-food provocateur Anthony Bourdain visited San Francisco in 2009 for his Travel Channel show "No Reservations." Tearing up and down hills in a black Ford Mustang, with a running commentary that gleefully mocks the city's leftist affectations, it's no surprise Bourdain introduces his segment on the Saturday market by calling it "a magnet for the food-fetishizing elite." We see clips of a blue cheese vendor, and customers cooing over baby artichokes, while Bourdain's voice-over confides, "I wanted dearly to hate them."

What stopped him? All the samples were great. His simple pork tamale plate from the popular Primavera stand at the back of the market was terrific. "The people here are, like, really nice and more often than not the stuff they're selling is superbly tasty," he concludes. "It's hard for me to be against this."

That said, some people involved with the farmers market knew their Saturday ritual could seem over the top. "I think people really have to be careful about their price," a member of the market's board told the *New York Times* in 2005. "It becomes cause for ridicule if they're not."

Christine Farren, who has been with CUESA since the Saturday it first wrapped stalls around three sides of the Ferry Building, made the same point in 2022.

"Our reputation as being an elitist, bougie market with produce that's too expensive—that has always existed," admitted Farren, who became the executive director in 2020. "We're a lot more than that, but you can't deny the image if that's what people see."

• • •

When negative perceptions stick, the underlying appeal of a destination can erode. Tourists might still come by, or suburban residents who want their Big City outings to be predictable. But if a once-hot destination goes cold, the stigma becomes hard to reverse.

This happened with Ghirardelli Square, the forerunner to festival marketplaces that debuted in 1964 and initially was embraced by locals and tourists alike. The glow began to fade as it became *such* a mass sensation, and any clear sense of mission was lost. When "Bing Crosby's San Francisco Experience" debuted in 1970 with special effects in a customized cinema ("a volcano of sound and color . . . absolutely designed to turn you on!"), Herb Caen's reaction was a tepid "It's all a little vague to me, too." Add an ever-rotating roster of tenants that at one point included a shop specializing in Harley-Davidson accessories, and city dwellers found other places to go.

After a succession of repackaging efforts during the 1980s and '90s—and after the Ferry Building made Ghirardelli feel totally dated—new owners launched the most thorough makeover since William Roth had stepped in. The historic buildings' upper floors became a posh version of timeshare condominiums, where people could pay $275,000 to purchase a room of their own, thirty-six nights a year. Ghirardelli's ice cream and chocolate shop remained popular as ever, but the new batch of tenants was anchored by Cellar360, a multi-winery tasting room where "wine country casual will blend with San Francisco sophistication," and which emulated Bing's experience by closing a few years later with little notice.

As much as anything else, Ghirardelli Square was on the wrong end of a gradual but inexorable shift of San Francisco's center of cultural and social gravity. An early sign of this came in 1995 when the San Francisco Museum of Modern Art opened near Third and Mission Streets around the corner from Moscone Convention Center. The Giants' ballpark opened five years later at the south end of the Embarcadero, close enough to the water that right-field homeruns sometimes land in China Basin. The team's move sparked the conversion of the dormant railyards of Mission Bay into what now is a neighborhood of housing and health-related offices and labs, reinvigorating the working waterfront in ways that no long-shoreman would have expected.

That's part of what makes the reborn Embarcadero compelling—the utilitarian seawall has come to function as a corridor that allows glimpses of the city in its diverse strains. History abounds, but new attractions flare up along the way. Some areas are overly precious, others need repair. Infrastructure shapes the experience. Nature shapes it all the more.

The walk north still includes long stretches lined with the bulkheads of the finger piers erected in the years after 1912. Only a handful continue to fester as parking garages; instead you have Lazarus-like Pier 1, which escaped demolition for Ferry Port Plaza to be deftly restored in the early 2000s by private developers and SMWM. Behind the Pier 3 bulkhead, a discreet new building was added in 2007 and leased by Michael Bloomberg's media empire in a deal that worked out to $100 per square foot—well over twice the rental rate that Coblentz had secured at the Ferry Building a few years before.

The most audacious makeover of all is Pier 15, where cotton long was stored. It reopened in 2013 as the Exploratorium, an interactive science museum with a rumored cost of $300 million when the exhibits are figured in. The unusual institution began life as an experimental pop-up during the ferment of the 1960s; it financed its permanent home with help from donors including General Motors and United Airlines, though not without sacrificing such creative flair as a public art installation that sends fog swirling four times daily around a diagonal footbridge between Piers 15 and 17.

Head south instead of north and things are choppier—a procession of spaces and experiences that don't fit together particularly well, but show you why today's San Francisco can intoxicate some people and infuriate others.

There are quiet revelations like Pier 14, a 637-foot-long breakwater topped by a walkway that opened in 2006 and is barely wider than a college dorm's corridor; the compression of the elongated space makes the splendor of the bay seem more expansive the further out you go. But then you come to the theme-park nature of Rincon Park, a neighborhood green where two gaudy upscale restaurants opened in 2008; one, Waterbar, debuted with a decor that included two 1,500-gallon aquariums. The park's centerpiece is over the top, too: "Cupid's Span," a sixty-four-foot-tall sculpture of a bow and arrow by pop art masters Claes Oldenburg and Coosje van Bruggen that was commissioned by Gap Inc., the clothing empire with its headquarters across the street. Too much? Keep walking underneath the Bay Bridge—a muscular show unto itself—and order a hamburger and beer at Red's Java Hut. It's a wooden shack alongside Pier 30 that dates to the years after World War I and still feels like a joint where port workers would grab a bite at the end of their shift.

"An espresso is nowhere to be seen," Bourdain noted approvingly on "No Reservations." "Any time you begin to doubt the wonderfulness of San Francisco, really, all you gotta do is come here."

. . .

Purely in a business sense, the Ferry Building was an unqualified success.

If the initial office leases came in below what had been anticipated, the new tenants made up the difference. There was another, less obvious impact: being part of the team that summoned the Ferry Building back to life paid dividends as you pursued additional deals. In the decade that followed the project's completion, Meany recalls, "the only thing anyone said about our company was '*they* developed the Ferry Building.'"

This was true though the majority owner, Equity Office Properties, bought out Wilson Meany's remaining stake not long after the building opened. Equity was purchased by the even larger Blackstone Group in 2007. The new owners kept Michele Meany as their retail broker but took over management of the building.

The 2008 recession deflated the high hopes of a resurgent Ghirardelli Square, sending vacancies past 50 percent, yet the Ferry Building kept adding new tenants. When America's economic disparities fueled the Occupy movement of 2011, protestors commandeered a bocce court in a little-used plaza at the foot of Market Street and set up several dozen tents for two months. Ferry Building managers complained to City Hall of cellphones stolen from retail counters by the campers, but any loss of business was imperceptible.

In other words, the crowds kept coming—plenty of tourists and plenty of locals, too. Most of those early tenants who gloried in the ideals of the Bay Area's sustainable food community remained, yet the mix slowly broadened to take in shops like Heath Ceramics, a vaunted creator of understated pottery that dated back to 1948 and crafted its wares in San Francisco and Sausalito (Heath also made plates and mugs for Blue Bottle, a natural fit). Other stalls were leased to food operations that brought street cred from hipper neighborhoods: Humphrey Slocombe ice cream from the Mission, Daily Driver bagels from Dogpatch, not far from where the Bethlehem Steel shipyard that helped win World War II was being primed for redevelopment.

Whatever the details of who was in or out, the ongoing

evolution of the Ferry Building and the Embarcadero reflected a city still wrestling with how it wanted to be perceived by the world. The transformation by no means was unique— with traditional shipping and manufacturing consolidated far from city centers, cities across the country and around the world continued to recast their waterfronts. A shoreline with parks and cultural attractions is almost to be expected today in any city touting its quality of life. But the new reality has extra resonance in this region named for the body of water that it enfolds. In the twenty-first century, no setting compared in terms of offering Bay Area visitors and locals the chance to exult in the *urban* waterfront. The Embarcadero and Ferry Building marked the idealized fusion of nature and city—choreographed in some spots, excessive in others, but enthralling all the same.

. . .

After a decade of ownership, Blackstone took stock of San Francisco's ongoing real estate boom and gauged that there was money to be made. The lease with the Port for the Ferry Building was put on the market, and in October 2018, the remaining forty-nine years of control were purchased for $291 million—a deal that worked out to more than $1,000 per square foot. Allianz, a German insurance behemoth, paired with Hudson Pacific Properties, a real estate investment trust based in Los Angeles and "focused on epicenters of innovation for media and tech," according to the firm's website.

The pair said all the right things: "We take our stewardship of this world-renowned San Francisco landmark seriously," Hudson's CEO declared in the obligatory press release when the sale was announced. With less fanfare, the new owners brought in a branding consultant from New York City and held focus groups to gauge how a top-grade attraction could generate even more value. Google leased roughly forty thousand square feet of office space at a reported price above $110 per square foot. Hudson also embarked on physical upgrades to the building, patching cracks in the Colusa sandstone and painting it in a hue which, after historic preservation reviewers gave their approval, was named "Ferry Building Gray."

By May 2023, the clocktower was shrouded in net-draped scaffolds. The paint job was nearing its end. And in the intervening years, the world had changed.

. . .

The fourth season of "Somebody Feed Phil," a celebration of gustatory tourism that airs on Netflix and stars Phil Rosenthal, devoted its second episode to San Francisco. No sooner do the opening credits fade than we see what Phil says "may be my favorite place in town"—the Ferry Building, luminous in dusky half-light, romantic and archetypal at once.

There's none of Bourdain's pugnacious mockery from Rosenthal, creator of the popular 1990s sitcom "Everybody Loves Raymond." Phil visits the icon with "my old friend Alice" (Waters, of course), sampling the produce served with breakfast at Boulette's Larder—"it's like eating jewelry!" Phil exclaims—before lunging into an enormous porchetta sandwich from Roli Roti, a food truck that pulls up on Saturdays and routinely attracts lines of more than fifty patient carnivores.

As if the shtick weren't awkward enough, the season's episodes were released on October 30, 2020, seven months after COVID-19 upended American life. The only acknowledgment of the lethal pandemic that had the residents of cities like San Francisco wearing masks and fearing personal contact was Phil's clumsy recounting of the 1906 earthquake, casting it as an affirmation of good times ahead: "I love the evidence that no matter how dark it is, everything can have a rebirth. . . . What I'm saying is, there's hope, people."

Which meant that as viewers watched the outgoing Rosenthal hugging every chef he sees, Ferry Building merchants in real life placed stickers on the floors outside their stalls warning people to stay six feet apart. A dozen tenants closed shop. Slanted Door went on hiatus.

The farmers market stayed open, but the number of vendors diminished. Those that remained weren't allowed to serve prepared food due to concerns about spreading the virus—a blow to CUESA's finances, since hot-food spots like Roli Roti and Primavera pay the market a percentage of gross sales on top of weekly rent.

"For a while it was just us, just us who live in the city," Christine Farren said in terms of her customer base that first year. "Now we know more of our regulars by name."

Farren had joined CUESA as an intern the week before the market's homecoming in 2003. The internship turned into a paying job, and Farren eventually became director of development. Then COVID hit and she soon received what she calls "the most unceremonious promotion ever"—the post of executive director for a nonprofit wondering if it had enough money to stay afloat.

After Farren and other staffers got the finances in order, they focused on making CUESA's markets more welcoming to people of different races and classes. One form of outreach involved broadening the farmer mix—not by kicking out anyone, Farren emphasized, but "as there's natural attrition, you're very deliberate about who you bring in . . . we don't need another coastal strawberry grower." The nonprofit also used a state grant to set up a program where CUESA matches spending for needy families up to $15 each visit, which translates to a $45 weekly food subsidy if they shopped on Tuesdays, Thursdays, and Saturdays. To keep the program operating year-round, the nonprofit added $45,000 from its own coffers in 2021, raised through private donations.

"If we want this farmers market to be more inclusive, we have to put our money where our mouth is," Farren shrugged.

In 2022, CUESA became Foodwise, an admittedly vague term of uplift (the term "honors the wisdom in all of us," we're told on the website), that nonetheless helps send a message that sustainability isn't simply a matter of extolling the virtues of organic family farming; it requires making healthy, nutritious food available to all Bay Area residents.

"People are thinking more systematically now," Farren suggested a few months after the name change. When she returned to the topic a few moments later, she was more blunt: "The good food movement needs to grow, and the only way to do that is to make it less white."

. . .

Even if his Ferry Building episode made viewers cringe, Phil hadn't been wrong about there being hope. After a COVID vaccine became available in 2021, the Ferry Building stepped up efforts to bring people back inside. Each door was locked in an open position, the better to provide cross-ventilation. Hand sanitizers stood alongside signs proclaiming "Welcome back! Your safety is our priority." Outside Acme Bread, an original tenant that operates a full bakery behind its counter and sales area, a chalked sandwich board cheerfully suggested that patrons think of social distancing as the equivalent of two baguettes, end to end.

Visitors would also notice vacant storefronts, a rarity in pre-COVID days, though management had covered several

Making do: the marketplace in 2022. *John King.*

with festive floral displays—bundled silk flowers in pink and red and purple and white, the ones in the middle forming a single giant heart.

"It's a very popular, Instagrammable site," Drew Gordon, an executive vice president at Hudson Pacific, suggested during a tour, pointing out two young women who looked like tourists, laughing as each took turns posing for the other.

Other empty storefronts periodically held retail pop-ups, an effort to enliven things while reaching out to communities that in the before times had little presence on the scene. But here again, darker currents of topical life cast a cloud: when Derek Tam, a maker of Hong Kong-style Dragon Beard's candy, was spinning malt syrup into festive food before a small delighted crowd, a man grabbed Tam's cell phone. Tam told him to put it down, reached for the phone—and the man hit him in the face and told him to go back to China.

None of this was unique to the Ferry Building. Racist violence against Asian people spiked nationwide following COVID's descent. Vacancy rates inside the landmark were low compared to other parts of the city.

The scene inside could feel ghostly, such as in the early morning with few stalls open for the few commuters passing through. The symbolic power of the landmark remained. You saw this when state officials had Governor Gavin Newsom announce initiatives to rev up California's tourism industry in June 2021, fifteen months after the travel sector "had the sledgehammer taken to it" (Newsom's words) by the orders to shelter in place at the beginning of the pandemic. The press conference took place not in Sacramento, but in a setting Newsom knew well from his days as San Francisco's mayor—the Ferry Building's nave, his podium strategically situated behind that tile mosaic of the state seal.

Optics count.

Once again, the Union Depot and Ferry House was employed to convey a larger message. Not of modernity, as at the St. Louis World's Fair, or as the endangered symbol of the shared civic landscape in the decades after World War II, but as an implicit reminder of past troubles overcome. Yet in a city and society that feels increasingly fragile, the saga of the Ferry Building in the twenty-first century was no longer a feel-good tale that only determined cynics could discount. Real life has a way of dislodging narratives. Or at the very least, reminding us never to take the future for granted.

PART IV

THE UNKNOWN

FOURTEEN

WHEN THE FERRY PLAZA FARMERS MARKET IS IN FULL SATURDAY swing, one way to dodge the determined foodies and casual browsers is to retreat to the plaza just thirty steps south of the Ferry Building. It sits atop three tiers of dark-veined granite, accessible by two flights of nine stairs or a ramp that ascends along the water to a trio of ferry gates that, like the plaza, were completed in 2021.

On weekdays the large plaza is quiet, perhaps with a few stragglers lounging in the wooden benches along its edge. Not so on Saturdays: Foodwise employees arrive before dawn to lug out tables and chairs for the patrons who will want to sit and enjoy their pastries and coffee, or that porchetta sandwich for which they endured the long line at Roli Roti. Once refreshed, the sustained consumers can return to the locally sourced scene below.

The granite rises with robust force. The plaza itself seems stunted, as if the Port and the operator of the ferry gates, the Water Emergency Transportation Authority, had set out to create a vantage point but settled on a plateau. In fact, the chosen height hints at what someday might be the norm—the elevation where San Francisco's constructed shoreline will need to be to serve as a protective buffer between the natural bay and the developed city. Here, more than anyplace on today's Embarcadero, you confront the existential predicament facing the Ferry Building, nearby piers, and resurrected waterfronts in other coastal American cities: sea level rise.

• • •

According to projections that were modeled by climate scientists in 2018 for the California Ocean Protection Council, a branch of state government, San Francisco Bay faces a 66 percent likelihood that average daily tides will rise forty inches by 2100, with roughly half of the increase during the next fifty years and the pace accelerating after that. There's a 5 percent chance that the levels climb an additional foot. The same report includes an extreme but peer-reviewed scenario where the projected increase soars to ninety-three inches during that same period—making grim numbers profoundly worse.

So-called king tides already arrive monthly during the winter, a natural occurrence related to the moon's gravitational pull that can send waves washing past Pier 14 into the Embarcadero's protected bike lane. Behind Pier 5, water swells up and over the edge of the public walkway. For now, that occasional splash of excitement is less fearsome than fun—but if current forecasts are anywhere near accurate, future generations will face a double bind. The threat isn't just that tides might creep upward as temperatures increase. It's that the extreme rainfall patterns we already experience will grow more intense, those destructive storms that in recent years have introduced terms like *atmospheric rivers* and *bomb cyclones* into conversations about the weather. For instance, if daily tides are a foot higher in 2050 than they are now—the "likely" projection—a major storm could surge thirty-six inches beyond where it would register today.

In the case of the Embarcadero, the hypothetical one-foot rise coupled with an "intense storm"—the sort that in the past might occur every five years—would send bay waters rushing toward the roadway in a dozen locations if the storm hit when winds were brisk and the tide was high. Kick the downpour's fervor to the scale of the bomb cyclone that hit the Bay Area in October 2021—a day-long deluge that was the equivalent of what scientists call a twenty-five-year storm—and the Embarcadero could be closed for nearly a mile between Folsom Street and Pier 9. Water spilling across the roadway could flow down into the BART and Muni subway beneath Market Street, potentially paralyzing both systems.

Studies of how sea level rise might alter the Bay Area date back to at least 1990, when the Pacific Institute, an environmental think tank, issued a report warning "the value of property threatened by sea level rise in San Francisco Bay is extremely high because of past development." The threat gradually percolated into public consciousness, and in 2011 the Bay Conservation and Development Commission mandated that all bayside development proposals take sea-level-rise projections into account. In a nutshell, the commission requires that any project which is intended to last beyond 2050 must be designed to be adaptable to the tides anticipated in 2100.

This explains the new plaza's location. The elevated zone is calibrated to meet the high end of anticipated water levels through at least 2070: the bay edge along the walk includes a solid concrete rim (or "bull rail," if you're the nautical type) that goes up another twelve inches. In building the plaza, the Port and the Water Emergency Transportation Authority are pursuing a design strategy known as adaptation, the idea that waterfronts can be fine-tuned with an eye to what we'll face in coming decades. The catch, of course, is that "fixing" one stretch of a shoreline does nothing to protect what remains exposed on either side. The new plaza and the elevated ferry gates might rebuff the surging tides to come, but the landmark next door would be more vulnerable than ever. The Ferry Building has ridden out many perils since opening day in 1898, from earthquakes and the onslaught of automobiles to political tumult, misguided renovations, and the wear and tear of urban life. Now it faces the implacable though seemingly far-off threat of rising waters, as if nature was determined to restore the marshes and tidal flats that long-dead San Franciscans covered and forgot.

The addition of the granite plaza is an indicator of the danger facing the icon to its north. And it's not as if our hefty landmark with that vaulted concrete foundation can be jacked up out of harm's way.

Or can it?

. . .

Steven Reel headed west from Philadelphia in 1992 to earn a structural engineering degree at Stanford University because, he says now, "structural engineering means 'earthquakes' at Stanford, and earthquakes make structural engineering a lot more interesting." The Bay Area was a good place to live, and local governments were investing heavily in seismic upgrades after Loma Prieta. With his degree in hand, Reel stayed put. He got married, he and his wife had a child, and they moved to Marin after deciding their infant son deserved more space than what was offered by the closet in their snug San Francisco condo.

In 2010, Reel successfully applied for a job at the Port of San Francisco and, to his surprise, grew intrigued by the historic aspects of making an urban shoreline function in the here and now: "I'd start studying old engineering drawings for projects and then go down the rabbit hole," recalls Reel, an easygoing bureaucrat with a beard that approached Rasputin-like proportions during the pandemic (he since has trimmed it back). He also began to notice regional planners stressing sea level rise in meetings.

"There were no hard and fast rules yet, but they wanted you to think about it," Reel said, explaining that among local regulators, "it was starting to become a *thing*."

His first project at the port was Brannan Street Wharf, where two ramshackle piers midway between the Bay Bridge and the ballpark were torn out and replaced by a four hundred-foot-long triangular green. The response to climate concerns involved a slight upward incline from the Embarcadero promenade and a concrete lip along the edge (the same move since used for the plaza near the Ferry Building). There was another natural threat to consider—the possibility that an earthquake on the scale of 1906 could strike again. Would the Ferry Building and the seawall hold, as before? Or would the three-mile-long agglomeration of boulders and concrete give way after all this time? Reel found himself with a new job title—manager of the seawall program—and responsibilities that included a $450,000 study with consultants being told to diagnose the barrier's health and prescribe possible remedies, from quick fixes in fragile spots to long-term shoring up as needed.

The findings, released in April 2016, answered some questions and posed a host of others.

A section of the seawall beneath the
Embarcadero promenade. *John King.*

The good news is that even with a cataclysmic earthquake,
or a Loma Prieta-scaled temblor with an epicenter near San
Francisco, "complete failure of the seawall is unlikely." The
rocks and boulders that form a dike beneath the concrete
wouldn't scatter like marbles. The Financial District wouldn't
be sucked into the bay toward Oakland.

But the combination of sandy fill atop soft mud, behind an
aged barrier with thousands of potentially moving parts of
varying size, is a dangerous combination. The fill was "subject
to liquefaction," the report confirmed, making it likely that
the seawall could slump and lurch outward, weakened by both
the pressure from liquefied fill and the seismic roiling of bay
mud below.

That turbulence, in turn, could rupture utility lines beneath
the Embarcadero. Finger piers could be severed from their bulkheads. Tracks for those popular, recently added streetcars could
be pulled apart.

"A repeat of the 1906 earthquake is predicted to cause as

much as $1b in damage and $1.3b in disruption costs," the report declared. Better to strengthen the entire three-mile seawall before a disaster struck—though the cost estimates to do this were "on the order of $2 to $3 billion." The consultants also emphasized that even with an upgraded seawall, the slow-moving threat posed by sea level rise "will necessitate intervention . . . over the next 100 years." Figure that in, and the combined price tag approached $5 billion.

The release of the report coincided with Mayor Ed Lee's selection of a new executive director for the Port, Elaine Forbes, a city native with a thoroughly San Franciscan lineage. One of her grandfathers was a retired longshoreman; her mother raised Elaine for several years in a Haight-Ashbury commune before moving to Marin, and Forbes now lives in the Castro with her wife. The Port director's earliest memories of the Embarcadero were visiting Pier 39, the Nantucket-scaled collection of souvenir shops and casual restaurants that opened in 1978—"there was so much live programming there back then"—and a place for which she still feels affection: "We don't want everything to be rarefied. Pier 39 may not be highbrow, but you can go there and have a fun experience. It's great for kids, and it's very diverse."

Forbes earned a master's in community and economic development at UCLA and held budget-related posts in several city departments before joining the Port in 2010 as deputy director for finance. Then she was named director, and Reel handed over the consulting team's report with its $5 billion price tag.

"I knew it was coming, so it wasn't a complete surprise, but it was scary," Forbes recalls. "That's a big huge problem to tackle."

To their credit, city officials didn't slip the report onto a shelf and hope nobody would notice. The following year's budget included $10 million to continue seawall research, money used to seed a ten-year contract with a team of twenty-one consultants to determine how to move from engineering studies to actual construction—and crafting a civic landscape that would be "as compelling as it is now, or more so," in the words of the team's landscape architect. The city approached voters with a $425 million bond in 2018 to fund the first round of projects; smartly, the campaign emphasized seismic concerns—lightening the ominous message with such creative touches as a neighborhood brewpub's limited release sour beer dubbed "Seawall's Sea Puppy." The maker went so far as to feature Reel at a happy hour event, "Meet the Engineer," an event the guest star amiably concedes was not well attended.

The bond passed with 83 percent support. "The earthquake message resonates," Reel says. "Without it, I don't think all this would have moved forward as it did."

Since then there's been another geotechnical study of the Embarcadero, one that included drilling 215 feet below the surface of the filled land inside the seawall. Late in 2021 came the first tentative steps, with the selection of twenty-three "early projects" that would go into conceptual design so they'd be eligible for federal or state funding when opportunities arose.

It makes sense to tackle the easiest fixes early, given the seismic threats posed to the Bay Area by the San Andreas and other faults. Breaking a daunting future into manageable parts also allows the Port and City Hall to shift attention from the more eye-popping aspects of climate adaptation—such as how portions of the Embarcadero might need to be raised as much as seven feet to prepare for 2100's more extreme projected water levels. With each step forward, the scale of the task becomes more stark.

Which leads us back to the Ferry Building.

As so often has been the case during the landmark's history, far more is at stake than one particular structure. If the Ferry Building in its heyday represented San Francisco's prominence within the region and beyond, in the twenty-first century it embodies how urban waterfronts can be reinvented without sacrificing their past identities. At the same time, the building remains essentially the same as it was in 1898—a heavy structure of concrete and steel that covers two acres and rises from a foundation atop bundled piles of tree trunks.

The assumption for the past twenty-five years has been that the landmark's impressive performance in 1906 and 1989 should ensure similar resilience when the next big earthquake hits. But the most recent geotechnical exam revealed a weak link: the section of the seawall behind the Ferry Building. Unlike the thick pyramids of boulders topped by concrete that define the rest of the seawall, the section that anchors the Ferry Building foundation is a solid concrete barrier that rests in a trench filled with liquefiable sand rather than the rubble that underlies almost everything else.

That detail places "the 125-year-old Ferry Building Seawall, building substructure, and surrounding piers at risk of damage in large earthquakes," according to the most recent Port update. This isn't just a concern for architecture buffs. San Francisco's disaster relief plans treat the outdoor spaces around the landmark as crucial spots for retreat and regrouping. In a worst-case scenario where the Bay Bridge is knocked out of commission, as was the case in 1989, reliable access to a functioning ferry system will be crucial for evacuating people from the downtown scene safely.

Assuming the bridge stays intact—the entire eastern span has been rebuilt since one section snapped in 1989—the Ferry Building has a role to play in recovery. The new plaza can serve as a staging area for bringing medical aid and supplies into the city over the water. Regular people who need to connect with family and friends know there won't be confusion if someone says "let's find each other at the Ferry Building." Forbes distills the issue this way: "It's a building that people love, and a building that's a workhorse in disaster response."

Where the goal with other projects in the initial batch is to begin construction—or at least draw up plans and secure funding—by the end of 2024, the Ferry Building to-do list starts with an "advanced engineering analysis" to grapple with what steps to take. The short-term ones might be as simple as injecting grout into the sand to lessen the likelihood of the seawall being destabilized. Beyond that, solutions are likely to be at a scale beyond what A. Page Brown or anyone of his era could have contemplated. One scenario is to erect an entirely new seawall around the edge of the Ferry Building's foundation, in essence creating a basement beneath it (which, on the bright side, makes tasks like replacing utility pipes amid the catacombs a lot easier). If you're doing that, it's only one more step—albeit sure to be costly and complex—to raise the entire building by several feet and resolve the challenge of sea level rise for another lifetime or two.

"Oh man, another big gulp," is how Forbes describes her reaction on hearing that Port staff wanted the initial projects to include an eighteen-month feasibility analysis of elevating the Ferry Building beyond harm's way. But the structure isn't just another of the piers that have come and gone over the last

170 years. "With the Ferry Building, the one thing I know about it is that it has to be saved   it has such a strong identification with the city," Forbes says. "So I talked myself into okaying this big expenditure."

. . .

The particularities of the Ferry Building aside, the dilemma facing San Francisco because of climate change resembles those of other urban waterfronts along America's coasts.

New Orleans and Miami are obvious examples. The former grows more vulnerable as the Mississippi Delta landforms that buffered it erode more each year. The latter is endangered not only because coastal neighborhoods hover near sea level but also due to the underlying layer of porous limestone that can allow high tides to bubble up through drains (a phenomenon known as nuisance flooding). New York City was devastated by Hurricane Sandy in 2012, which briefly returned Manhattan's shoreline to what it was in the 1600s.

But the city most analogous to San Francisco is Boston, 2,700 miles to the east.

No other large American metropolis was reshaped so thoroughly by filling in shallow water. The Shawmut Peninsula bears scant resemblance to the natural promontory that was, and extensive fill along the edges of Charlestown and East Boston turned those neighborhoods' shorelines into hectic shipping zones. This also was the case in South Boston, which flanks the historic heart of the city: by 1900, the marshes of the once-spacious bay between the two areas had been reduced to a channel bordered by a curved seawall, with warehouses and rail yards covering the imported soil behind it.

That area, originally known as Fort Point, today is called the Seaport District—where the scatter of surviving brick warehouses is joined by a waterfront promenade and stubby modern towers clad largely in glass. Not until 2014 did studies reveal that a combination of high tides and a storm surge could send the channel's waters flooding into the streets beyond it.

"We created a lot of real estate, and it's all vulnerable," says Richard McGuinness, Boston's deputy director for Climate Change and Environmental Planning. "There's not much wiggle room."

We're strolling on Fort Point Channel's stretch of Harborwalk, a public access path that wends along forty-three miles of Boston's shoreline, crossing multiple bridges along the way. Here, the promenade narrows and runs directly atop the seawall—a defining line more obvious than the Embarcadero's because no finger piers extend beyond the barrier's stacked granite blocks. In one case, where the structural wall of a 1902 warehouse straddles the seawall, an open-air corridor was cut through the edge of the building's lowest floor to allow public access—a tight passage of brick columns and planked woodwork that's atmospheric evidence of the thin line between nature and city.

As we walk, McGuinness pauses to explain how the green slope of a park that replaced a parking lot next to one of the channel's bridges is designed to rebuff waters that might rush over the seawall during storms. Three blocks to the west, a long grassy berm between two buildings will angle up eight feet to form a low hillside with tiered seating—and shield a planned park behind it that will adorn several acres of former industrial land. He's also honest about the weak links. The existing park's protective slope opens to allow a pathway to the Harborwalk. But if a storm approaches and someone forgets to deploy the storm barriers that are stored discreetly out of sight, waves crashing above the seawall would be funneled down the path as forcefully as if it was a culvert.

The Hub tasted such extreme weather in March 2018, when king tides coincided with one of the region's fabled nor'easters to send water cascading over Fort Point Channel's seawall. The surge was so powerful that cars in the adjacent low-lying blocks were submerged; a dumpster floated freely down one flooded street. If daily tides mount as projected, and storms continue to grow more fierce, the combination won't be pretty.

"By 2070 this whole area is under water" if nothing is done, McGuinness said candidly. "It's apocalyptic."

. . .

New York had its own taste of the apocalypse in 2012 with Hurricane Sandy.

The storm that descended on the city that October coincided with the month's high tides, unleashing storm surges of nearly fourteen feet across Lower Manhattan and waves that raced past concrete barriers intended to repel high waters. The death toll was grievous—forty-four people killed—and Sandy caused an estimated $19 billion in damages. It also showed the perils when a dense city rises directly next to the water, with some of its most valuable property located on what had been marshes in 1625, the year Dutch settlers established the settlement of New Amsterdam. Transit tunnels were flooded, shutting the subways for several days. Flood waters lingered inland until the storm and its eighty-mph winds receded. Power outages plunged as many as two million residents into darkness, some of them for weeks.

The federal response to the disaster included President Barack Obama's appointment of a task force intended "to improve the region's resilience, health, and prosperity by building for the future." This translated seven months later to Rebuild by Design, an unusual federal initiative that looked to teams of designers and engineers to conceive interventions that could accommodate against natural forces while showing an imaginative sensitivity to the existing realities and needs of a place.

One project that emerged with Washington's blessing (and partial funding) is Living Breakwaters, off the south shore of Staten Island, where two dozen people died as homes were pummeled by the hurricane's force. Conceived by SCAPE Landscape Architecture—which has its office near the tip of Lower Manhattan, midway between the East and Hudson Rivers—the design employs contemporary engineering to defuse tidal forces by simulating nature.

To do this, nine breakwaters of varying widths are being constructed 800 to 1,800 feet offshore. The structures will have stone cores encased in concrete fashioned with niches and crevices to allow reef-like living habitats to emerge. To speed the process along, the breakwaters are being seeded with oyster shells and baby oysters in the hope that the manufactured breakwaters provide ecological benefits as well as a buffer to lessen the flooding from Sandy-like storms.

That project is now underway. By the spring of 2023 seven breakwaters were complete or taking form, complete with artificial tide pools made of concrete.

Another Rebuild by Design project that's being implemented offers a cautionary tale—showing how real-world constraints often take precedence over ambitious visions for coexisting with nature, even if those visions look sexy and cool.

This project began life as "Big U," from a team headed by Bjarke Ingels Group, a Danish firm with a flair for self-promotion that includes Ingels's penchant for coining phrases like "sustainable hedonism" to describe his work. In New York, Ingels and his team proposed a ten-mile protective ribbon that

241

would run along the shoreline from West 57th Street, where the island's topography protects inland neighborhoods, around the tip of Lower Manhattan and back north along the East River and FDR Drive to East 42nd Street.

BIG's conceptual proposal was nothing if not ambitious, a flood control project "endowed with new social, aesthetic, economic and environmental assets." This included nods to the "diverse characters" of the different neighborhoods—like the suggestion that Chelsea could be protected in part by "a sculptural flood wall modeled on Richard Serra's work."

After Ingels's team was selected, the scale was pulled back to focus on a particularly vulnerable stretch of the East River along FDR Drive, where the team had conceived a procession of people-friendly protections, including storm barriers that would flip into place from the undersides of the elevated freeway and be covered in murals by local artists to "create an inviting ceiling when not in use." East River Park itself would be redone to sponge up excess water during storms. Then the city's own engineers reviewed the updated plan, and the bubble burst. The art-cloaked flip barriers became immense standard-variety locks. The resilient landscape envisioned along FDR Drive will be a park elevated eight to nine feet above pre-project levels. Along Stuyvesant Cove, a ten-block succession of floodwalls and floodgates is being installed to protect everything from neighborhood parks to an electrical plant knocked out of commission by Hurricane Sandy. Redone parks along the river will still have such amenities as playgrounds and tennis courts, and the new elevated paths will offer great views. But the primary job is to ward off natural forces. If that means altering the familiar landscape, so be it.

The changes infuriated a coalition of East Village artists and literati who held vigils and brandished signs with slogans like "No Ecocide on the Lower East Side." A more supportive constituency? The public housing residents just inland, next to the expressway, who remembered too well the havoc wreaked by Sandy. Construction crews began clearing out the existing 1930s-era park late in 2021, not long after work started on Living Breakwaters, and a movable floodwall to protect another park was completed the next summer.

"All these questions become local and messy, but there's a realization in the community that something needs to happen," says Daniel Zarrilli. Before leaving City Hall in 2021 to join Columbia University as a resiliency adviser, Zarrilli worked on climate-related issues for mayors Michael Bloomberg and Bill de Blasio. "Events will continue to shock us, and that forces us to confront them in a different way."

New York City now has budgeted $20 billion for adaptation, encompassing projects in all five boroughs. Zarrilli looks back on Hurricane Sandy as the prod to actually *do* things, similar to how Loma Prieta's memory has spurred San Francisco to invest in shoreline improvements that prepare for future earthquakes and, simultaneously, protect against sea level rise.

"Before Sandy we had a rich robust process to understand the threat—an academic understanding—but until it was shoved in our face we hadn't done anything," he explains. "The fact is, we're now implementing the biggest flood protection project in the country."

The current list of projects includes one that would remake the Lower Manhattan shoreline from the island's tip north to the Brooklyn Bridge —a proposed sequence of undulating parks and promenades on new landfill extending as much as two hundred feet beyond the current shoreline. The new realm would climb an average of seventeen feet above today's levels to withstand the most dire conditions that are forecast for

2100. Whether or not it gains traction is an open question. But the $5- to 7-billion price tag, plus the fifteen- to twenty-year timeframe, underscores the enormity that cities face in protecting tower-studded, economically vital areas far into the future.

Two city agencies released the conceptual proposal in December 2021, drawing on work by a team of design and engineering firms that includes SCAPE. "Sometimes, there may be no practical alternatives to going into the water," said Pippa Brashear, SCAPE's Resilience Principal. Providing community benefits is and should be a priority—but "when there's a certain level of urban density, you're going to do whatever it takes."

. . .

The vulnerabilities of Lower Manhattan and Boston's Fort Point are akin to the Embarcadero: In densely developed cities, there's little room for retreat. When there is space to maneuver, by contrast, cities can prepare for sea level rise with imagination and grace.

San Francisco has a test case in a surprise location—Treasure Island, the four-hundred-acre oval that hosted the Golden Gate International Exposition in 1939 and was created by building a rim of boulders on the shoals off Yerba Buena and then filling it with twenty million cubic feet of bay sand. After the fair closed in 1940, the US Navy took the island and turned it into a base, not returning it to the city until 1997. The question became what to do next. It's a spectacular location. It's also an artificial island in earthquake country, buffeted by afternoon winds. As for reaching the mainland, the task of accelerating into Bay Bridge traffic from a comically short onramp is not for the faint of heart.

Discreet defense: A rendering of Cityside Park, planned for Treasure Island. *CMG Landscape Architecture.*

That question is now being answered: construction began in earnest in 2022 on a stand-alone district that is planned to have eight thousand apartments and condominiums in buildings as tall as four hundred feet. Development will be concentrated in the southwest quarter of the island, a short walk to a new ferry terminal that offers a straight shot to the Ferry Building. The idea is to get people out of their cars, which is also part of the argument for so much housing in such a seemingly precarious location—you need a large population to attract grocery stores, which also are planned, and to have enough riders to help subsidize ferry service.

The most far-sighted aspect of Treasure Island's new incarnation is the waterfront park facing west, toward downtown San Francisco. The twenty-four-acre space will reach three hundred feet from the shore into the island, designed in distinct sections with a range of attractions but climbing gently as it moves east. The slope will mask how the buildings and streets of the island will be 3.5 feet higher than the ground level before redevelopment began (the outer rim of boulders will also be raised); the perimeter will be increased to heights above what's projected with thirty six inches of sea level rise and an extreme storm.

The park is a transition zone, in other words: if tides rise more quickly than forecast, or you extend climate range projections out beyond 2100, there's space to reshape the park in ways that discreetly add new heights and protection, yet don't have a levee-like feel.

"When parks are 50 years old, they need to get updated anyway," notes Kevin Conger of the landscape architecture firm CMG, which is leading the design of the island's parks and open spaces. "In the meantime, we'll have created a park where people want to be."

This blurring of the line between natural and constructed terrains also plays out along the north edge of the island. It's the part most exposed to strong tidal waves, and the longest distance to the ferry terminal. This is a later stage of development, but initial plans call for designing the 103 acres as more of a bayside habitat, so that as sea levels rise, the naturalized areas will transition to tidal marshes.

"Most likely, we're fine to the end of the century" in terms of living with rising tides, says Dilip Trivedi, a partner at the engineering firm Moffatt & Nichol, which is part of Treasure Island's design team. "Worst case, at least 50 years."

That said, he has no second thoughts about facilitating the erection of a new neighborhood fully exposed to the possible impacts of climate change. For him, the task is to make Treasure Island a place that is safe—but also feels like it belongs.

"It's not prudent to just try and hold back the waters," Trivedi says. "You have to build something resilient and work with the forces that you face."

. . .

Unlike Treasure Island, the Embarcadero and its seawall are tightly constrained. They're in the same bind as their counterparts in New York and Boston, but in a location that's far more central to the city's character—how it is defined both up close and from afar.

Yes, San Francisco's shoreline is an artificial construct drawn on a map by an engineer for the Board of State Harbor Commissioners in 1876. No matter. Too much exists behind it, too many buildings that house too many people who live and work and play without contemplating the fragility of the terrain they traverse. Nor would San Francisco voters be thrilled if their elected officials decided to write off the revived post-freeway Embarcadero because of higher water levels that may arrive . . . someday.

Which doesn't mean every surviving structure is sacrosanct, at least not to the Port.

"We'll keep them for as long as we can, but in some cases it's tricky," Elaine Forbes says of the finger piers, which are on the National Register of Historic Places. The dilemma is that the overall cost of remaking the Embarcadero—whatever that eventually means—will likely be so great that the piers reaching beyond it won't be a top priority. If developers take on most of the expense for Port-approved renovations, great. But voters banned hotels in 1990, and the state's Bay Plan from 1968 bans housing. Two potentially lucrative revenue options are off the table.

"My breaking point in making decisions as executive director would be, would it make sense to save these if the public is the only source of funds?" Forbes explains. "For many of our finger piers, the answer might be 'no.'"

Nor is there a magic bullet, that single act of herculean infrastructure that would remove the specter of sea level rise

once and for all. Dreamers do conjure them up—Boston studied the idea of a four-mile barrier that would extend across the
mouth of Boston Harbor, only to have academic experts con-
clude in 2018 that the project would cost at least $11 billion
and might not even work ("It does not make sense for decades,
if not ever, to consider a harbor-wide barrier system," the
author of the analysis told the *Boston Globe*).

A similar idea—a barrier across the Golden Gate with locks
that could open or close as needed—was raised in the Bay Area
in 2021, with the mayor of San Jose telling a group of regional
officials, "There's one location where we (all) are exposed to
sea level rise, and that is at the Golden Gate." So far, no public agency has shown a willingness to analyze whether it is
feasible—much less wise—to tinker with the hydrology of a
narrow channel that four hundred *billion* gallons of water
churn through on a typical day.

Realistically, adaptation planning in San Francisco and
other waterfront cities will involve a variety of responses at a
variety of scales. Treasure Island is one scenario. That batch
of "early projects" along the Embarcadero is another. The
situation facing the Ferry Building, as at so many times in its
history, is unique unto itself. This time around, the task is to
remake a bustling civic icon so that life seemingly goes on as
before. If anyone has challenged the need to invest what likely
will be hundreds of millions of dollars to save a 125-year-old
structure, the argument has gained no traction.

"The price would have to be really, really high before anything would think twice" about whether the Ferry Building's salvation is more trouble than it's worth, Reel says. He
describes how during the public discussions on what to do
about the Embarcadero, attendees would be asked to list pri-
orities. *What are you concerned about? What do you love?*

In the latter category, Reel recalls, "the Ferry Building kept getting named. People want to see it forever."

This still leaves an array of unanswered questions. How to decide how big of an engineering gamble to take. Whether to raise the structure, as implausible as that sounds, or build a new seawall to the east that would destroy the immediacy of the connection to the water. And what becomes of the tenants inside the building, especially the locally based merchants, if the building once again becomes a construction zone. "This is going to be the most difficult part of the (waterfront) discussion," Reel speculates. "I don't see any way around it. But perhaps that challenge can be the catalyst for a larger discussion about what we want the Embarcadero to be."

In a much different context, one San Franciscan offered a fatalistic take on what the future might hold: Lawrence Ferlinghetti.

Four years before his death in 2021, still living in North Beach, Ferlinghetti sat down in a neighborhood café to talk with a *Washington Post* writer about the beat era, the ninety-seven-year-old poet's life, and his enduring love for the city that he embraced long ago. At one point, the writer asked Ferlinghetti about what might happen after he was gone.

"It's all going to be underwater in 100 years or maybe even 50," Ferlinghetti said with a half-smiled shrug. "The Embarcadero is one of the greatest esplanades in the world. On the weekends, thousands of people strut up and down like it's the Ramblas in Barcelona. But it'll all be underwater."

FIFTEEN

IT'S SPRING 2022, AND JOHANA MORENO IS BENT TIGHT OVER THE Great Seal of the State of California in the Ferry Building's skylit nave. She's wearing a mask, tuning out everything in the grand space except for the cracked stone tiles that she's fastidiously replacing, one by one by one.

Moreno begins by removing the tiles and grouting and patches from damaged areas, whether the cause was structural movement beneath them, or somebody wheeling a too-heavy delivery cart across them, or the inevitable decay that comes with the passing of time. This is relatively simple, chipping out the material and laying down a smooth bed of mortar on which the new tiles will rest. The hard part is making Minerva and the prospector and that wooden ship near the Golden Gate look almost as good as they did back when the unknown artisans from Braidi & Pasquali were paid $800 to add a bit of class to the floor of a passenger concourse.

You can't go online and order replacements for nineteenth-century mosaic tiles: even if Moreno and coworker Erik Sandell knew what quarries supplied the kaleidoscope of marble and serpentine in hues from pure white to dusky green, the result wouldn't be the same. Present-day tiles tend to be thinner, not quite as large, more likely to shatter under the chisel of even the most skilled laborer. So Sandell might rummage for close-enough replacements from buckets of tiles salvaged from when the concourse floor was cut open in 2001. Or Moreno might make her own—blending putty dough with mineral pigments for strength and then adding dyes until she finds the right shade. She rolls the mix into something that looks like it came out of a square tube; Sandell takes the hardened concoction home and slices individual squares to the needed width, using the band saw in the workshop he tucked into the garage of a house in Marin he shares with several roommates. He polishes them with a buffer and brings the batch to work the next day so Moreno can summon up the past.

"We joke that I take it apart and she puts it together," Sandell says, referring to the pair's approach on projects they do for their employer, ARG Conservation Services.

For Moreno, who studied and taught conservation at the Universidad Externado de Colombia in her native country before moving to San Francisco in 2013 ("a love story," is her response to my question about what led her north), the payoff is the encounter with easily overlooked masterpieces from prior generations.

"People who don't work on these can't appreciate the (original) skill," Moreno says. "It's mind-blowing when you go down on your knees and look into the eye of the artist. The deeper I go, the more I appreciate the mastery. It's very humbling."

Sandell joined ARG five years after Moreno, fresh from earning a historic preservation degree at Columbia University in New York. He first thought of conservation as a career

Johana Moreno (bottom) and Erik Sandell restoring the California state seal, 2022. *John King.*

when seeing artisans at work in Rome, where Sandell was studying abroad. That intersection of artifact and context is what he loves about the Ferry Building's mosaic.

"It's such a beautiful piece of artwork, but also such a visible location," he said over coffee a few months later. "And the state seal! It blends so many historic symbols, and really ties you into the greater story of the whole Embarcadero."

This restoration effort by Moreno and Sandell is nowhere near as extensive as the work done prior to the Ferry Building's return, when the floor underwent major surgery and repairs. But twenty years brings wear all its own—structural movements and cracks are inevitable in a building that's longer than two football fields, resting on wooden piles driven deep into mud in a region riven by earthquake fault lines.

The 2022 freshening of the seal, during a pandemic that

thinned out visitors and office workers, throws a light on the underlying reality of a singular landmark, the waterfront that it defines, and a city like San Francisco: their stories never come to an end.

. . .

The thread that runs through all facets of the history of the Ferry Building is the structure's iconicity, to use an academic term. Purely as a work of architecture, it checks the boxes of what makes an icon. It has a memorable simplicity and a recognizable silhouette. The symmetry is compelling. It tested the engineering limits of its time with that massive concrete foundation, which is why the San Francisco chapter of the American Society of Civic Engineers in 1989 named it a "pioneering structure." There's another, more fundamental aspect to what sets an icon apart from other buildings: the Ferry Building has a civic component. At every stage of San Francisco history in the past 125 years, people have singled it out as their idea of what the city is. Or what the city was. Or what the city ought to be.

I wouldn't be so presumptuous as to suggest that this structure conceived in 1893 in the office of an architect with wealthy patrons is the single building that represents all 815,000 residents of today's San Francisco, or the 7.6 million people who live in the region. Better to see the Ferry Building as one in a constellation of local architectural stars—the Golden Gate Bridge and the Transamerica Pyramid but also Coit Tower, the fluted concrete shaft atop Telegraph Hill that opened in 1934 and was designed by Arthur Brown Jr. (no relation to A. Page Brown but also no slouch, being the architect of San Francisco City Hall). Sutro Tower, the 977-foot communication tower from 1973 that bundles three gigantic prongs of

steel into an ungainly yet arresting extension of the city's third
highest peak, has become a cult favorite.

For many people, their defining city landmark might not be
a lone building at all. Neighborhoods conjure up strong positive associations, such as the Castro for gay men attracted by
its reputation as a uniquely welcoming district, or the Haight
for psychedelic nostalgics who still revere the Grateful Dead.
Fog isn't a physical thing—try to hold it in your hand—but for
many people it's the natural element that sets San Francisco
apart from other cities.

. . .

This perceptual collage applies to all large American cities
in the twenty-first century. Is New York best defined by the
Empire State Building, the Statue of Liberty, the High Line or
the World Trade Center—and if the latter, the Twin Towers
felled on 9/11 or the 1,776-foot-tall successor that opened in
2014 and is touted as "a new civic icon for the country" by the
firm that designed it? Is Chicago the Water Tower from 1869,
Wrigley Field from 1914, the tapered power of 1969's John
Hancock Center or Aqua, architect Jeanne Gang's eighty-six-
story concrete slab from 2009 that rises one block from Millennium Park with a still-startling form that looks as though it has
been shaped by the wind? In splayed-out cities like Los Angeles
or Miami, where downtown is one neighborhood among many,
do unifying works of architecture exist?

Whatever the verdict, the Ferry Building is the rare structural icon that has played a multitude of roles during its
life. That's not the case with the Golden Gate Bridge, which
opened to traffic in 1937 and from then on has been a fog-
shrouded seductress. The Transamerica Pyramid went from
architectural pariah to a public favorite in only a handful of

years. The Sutro Tower has never had that much to say. With the Ferry Building, there have been profound shifts of meaning as the city and the region evolved.

That reality fascinates Anthea Hartig, director of the National Museum of American History at the Smithsonian Institution. Before that, she worked in San Francisco as regional director of the National Trust for Historic Preservation and then the executive director of the California Historical Society.

"You can read the coming of age of San Francisco in the Ferry Building," Hartig says. "We see it as so quaint today, but it offered a tremendously complicated interface with the bay and the city. So many meanings can be layered into it." Not just the obvious ones—a transportation hub, a waterfront landmark—but also "the exemplification of the insensitivity of urban renewal and freeways" that led to thirty years of physical isolation.

Another layer applies when the Embarcadero is added to the mix. The bumpy evolution from industrial waterfront to a corridor of consumption, a terrain where longshoremen have been replaced by vendors of garlic fries and Ghirardelli sundaes during Giants baseball games at Oracle Park. The wholesale produce market made way for towers in the 1960s, but growers sell organic seasonal produce outside the Ferry Building three days each week. The Exploratorium's exhibit designers conjure up interactive science wonders on a pier where, for decades, cotton was piled high in a shed.

"How a place is used by different forces and different communities is really vivid here," Hartig says, referring to the Ferry Building and the waterfront around it.

Keba Konte knows this well—the Red Bay Coffee owner who as a pre-teen would be rousted out of bed by his father and be driven to the Embarcadero for crab fishing after packing lunch (boiled egg, a candy bar, and a banana). Who as a student at San Francisco State University made extra money by taking tourists around Fisherman's Wharf in a pedicab and serving clam chowder in sourdough bowls at Alioto's, a longtime restaurant on the wharf.

He was born in Haight-Ashbury before moving with his mother to Ingleside, then a working-class neighborhood in the southern part of San Francisco that was popular with Black families. His mother was a portrait photographer with her darkroom in the basement; fascinated by "the magic," Keba studied art and photography at San Francisco State University before exploring a succession of passions that included rap journalism and Pan-Africanism and, in 2006, helping to open a coffee shop in Berkeley.

That led to Red Bay, which started in 2014 and is predominantly a roastery. The Ferry Building cafe came about because of the pandemic: Peet's, the chain founded in Berkeley that was one of the first two businesses to open at the Ferry Building in 2003, closed several of its San Francisco outposts in 2020. That left a hole to fill—coffee is a must on damp bay mornings—and Michele Meany thought of Konte.

He remembers his visit as a prospective tenant in October 2020: "It was dead, even on a Saturday, nothing was happening." But he didn't blink before signing the lease: "Any other time, this would have been a dream we couldn't possibly afford."

• • •

What is that dream, the old/new waterfront of northeast San Francisco? There's no single answer, just as there's no single answer for what this or any city represents. There never has been, especially not now.

From the right, conservative critics lump the Embarcadero in with the rest of San Francisco as "American Dystopia"; financial pundit Jim Kramer in 2022 described on air how he and his wife saw one man on the Embarcadero attack another with a hammer and declared, "I do not let staff go outside (there), even in daytime." There was much worse violence in 2015, when Kathryn "Kate" Steinle, a thirty-two-year-old woman from the East Bay, was shot dead while walking with her father on Pier 14. The killer was an undocumented immigrant and five-time deportee who had been released from the San Francisco County Jail three months earlier. The tragedy flared into a national sensation seized on by Donald Trump as he launched his ultimately successful campaign for the White House, and when a jury found the killer not guilty of murder *or* manslaughter—he claimed the gun went off accidentally after he found it on the pier—the verdict played into the hands of people who characterize San Francisco as, yes, a lawless dystopia.

On the left, naysayers distill it to a precious enclave of the bourgeoisie, or a beachhead for the tech world that critics say is corroding San Francisco's free-thinking soul. Almost a caricature of this view can be seen in the two tenants that now occupy the space left behind in the Ferry Building by Coblentz, Patch, Duffy & Bass when the firm moved back to the Financial District in 2014. One level is leased by Niantic, the software firm best known for the onetime mobile phenomenon Pokémon Go. The upper level is home to Shack15, described loosely by "operations director" Tobias Johansson as a coworking space with a membership that is "50% start-up entrepreneurs and 98% tech."

When Johansson and I toured the space in the summer of 2022, the allure was easy to see: The partitions underneath the peaked skylight had been removed to open the space to views from all directions ("minimal is the key"). Besides the comfortable spacious seating, a bar-like central counter served as a members' cafe in the morning and a lounge at night.

"We're fostering the new generation of entrepreneurs," said Johansson, who moved to the Bay Area in 2005 when his employer, Meltwater, relocated from Norway to San Francisco. The company describes itself in news releases as a firm that "provides social and media intelligence," and founder Jørn Lyseggen conceived of Shack15 as a string of small coworking cafes in the South Bay. When he saw the Ferry Building space, the idea of a laid-back Silicon Valley beachhead went *pffft*.

"It was an 'If we build it, they will come' kind of thing," Johansson explained.

The jury on that is still out; Shack15 opened in January 2020, just in time for COVID to shut things down, on and off, for the next two years. But the day of our visit, a fair number of people were settled in with their laptops. More and more events are held nightly, tapping into the arts world as well as business. And if Johansson has the tech lingo down pat— "We're here to support the founders' journeys," he said at one point—his love of the setting shines through: "When I come into the building early in the morning, and can smell Acme baking its bread . . . . This is a magical place."

To reduce urban settings to cartoon images—dystopia! Tech town!—ignores the complexity of the cultures that have staked their own small claims to the waterfront terrain. Consider Pier 7, a five-minute walk north of the Ferry Building past the Bloomberg office. It opened in 1990 as the first public space created during the Embarcadero's transformation, turning an asphalt parking lot on aged piles into a pedestrian zone with wooden planks beneath your feet and faux-Victorian railings and lampposts.

Few tourists find their way out to the end, except hardy ones stretching their legs to shoot photos of each other in a setting you won't find at home. The people on hand tend to be fishing—mostly Asian men, but also some Blacks and some Whites.

There's a different culture where the pier touches ground: skateboarders, a throwback to the 1990s when the Embarcadero was a skating magnet for its variety of spaces shaped by processional stairs and low retaining walls—the type of design features often employed by designers to evoke an urbane ambiance, rarely with much success.

The day I pause to watch, the most expressive skateboarder is Israel, no last name offered, who moved from Austin five years ago. He works two jobs to pay rent, jobs that he chose based on the flexibility of the hours, and navigates the city's skating landscape as often as he can. Among his regular stops is the miniature plaza at the entrance to Pier 7, a clearing defined by three raised concrete pads that extend toward the street at progressively longer lengths.

"There's no beauty in it, just the obstacle in itself," shrugs Israel, who figures he touches down at Pier 7 three times a month. "Different platforms, different heights, different ways to be creative." The Port in the past has tried to undermine the appropriation—topping the platforms with wood at one point, and periodically adding metal knobs that are intended to be deterrents and soon disappear ("de-nobbed")—but people like Israel keep coming back.

"All up and down the Embarcadero there are so many obstacles . . . It's cool to find something not meant to be skated,"

Israel says before adding a comment that might have come
from Anthea Hartig, or Chris Meany, or Keba Konte, each in
a much different context. "It's got a history you want to pay
homage to . . . It's an iconic spot."

• • •

Another way to gauge the cultural relevance of today's Ferry
Building, and whether it reflects the contemporary city around
it, is by comparing it to other icons resurrected in the late twentieth century with an eye to popular appeal.

Take Faneuil Hall Marketplace in Boston, which started
the festival marketplace trend with its blend of historic architecture augmented by jugglers and pushcarts, where developer
James Rouse on opening day in August 1976 welcomed curious visitors to "a new kind of retailing with small merchants
and small shops selling food and other items." By the time
that repackaged agora turned twenty, comparable to the Ferry
Building in 2022, the "new kind of retailing" included a Dis-
ney Store and a shop selling Christmas decorations year-round.

"We warned in the beginning tourism would corrode," Jane
Thompson, the wife and business partner of Rouse's architect,
Benjamin Thompson, sadly told the *Boston Globe* in 1996,
"and it's come true."

Ben Thompson died in 2002. Jane Thompson followed fourteen years later. We can only guess what they would have said
about the current incarnation of Faneuil Hall, where a large
space near the central building's domed rotunda for much of
2022 held "Dino Safari: A Walk thru Adventure!" with ani-
matronic dinosaurs doing battle, an interactive earthquake,
and $18 tickets for the thirty-minute tour. Disney is long gone;
so is the replica of the TV sitcom bar *Cheers* that closed in
2020 (the show itself, inspired by a saloon on Beacon Hill,

ran from 1982 to 1993). The sheltered kiosks that line the central market building are overwhelmed by standard tourist tchotchke fare, from T-shirts to shot glasses.

At Ghirardelli Square, forerunner to Faneuil Hall Marketplace, the 2008 remake was no match for the recession that arrived on its heels. By 2013, the retail spaces were 50 percent vacant, and yet another developer had stepped in. Things are much better now, with branches of several popular local eateries, but you can't escape the feeling you're in a calorific Ghirardelli bazaar. The original ice cream and chocolate shop below the clock tower has added an express branch on the ground floor facing the bay, and a major new "chocolate experience" that replaced Cellar360 with a numbing expanse of sweet gifts and a dining room where the hot fudge sundaes are served with a bay view.

So when wary locals and repeat visitors grumble that the Ferry Building isn't what it used to be, they're right. Neither is anyplace else, including those other remade landmarks expected at once to straddle present and past, delivering both urban authenticity and a robust bottom line. While making it all seem like it was preordained.

• • •

Ultimately, there is no single Ferry Building.

That has always been the case, which is why it has survived.

If the structure that opened in 1898 had "only" been the world's second-busiest transportation depot, or the tallest building on the waterfront, or a place to show guests from out of town, it would have become another old building that architecture buffs adore and the rest of us don't think much about. Another structure that had its moment, and then the moment was gone.

The Ferry Building in context, 2021. *Courtesy of Noah Berger.*

What makes the Ferry Building and similar landmarks into icons, however you define that nebulous word, is that they stay lodged in public consciousness, taking on new personas as the worlds around them change. They always have something to contribute to the discussion of what makes a city vital at *this* point in time.

That's why New York's Chrysler Building is iconic, for instance. Newer towers have joined it near Grand Central Station, most recently the ninety-three-story One Vanderbilt Avenue with its computer-generated contortion of angular vertical jabs. Far from being upstaged, the Chrysler looks better than ever. Architect William Van Alen's exuberant telescoping shaft from 1930 with its art deco flair and stainless steel crown argues ever more eloquently for the virtues of craftsmanship and nuanced spirit at skyline scale.

But the urgent discussions about urban America in the second decade of the twenty-first century revolve around questions more pressing than high-rise aesthetics: the hammerblow of COVID-19 in 2020 revived the old fears that the nation's big cities are on the brink.

It's not that companies are moving to the suburbs, but that many employees would rather work from home than go to the office, a shift that threatens to undermine everything from downtown retail to transit systems and the business tax revenues that fund social services. The current mood is reminiscent of that San Francisco waterfront plan from 1943 that began by acknowledging fears that "new standards of living and other social forces are destroying (the city's) reasons for existence." This is part of why San Francisco is a favored target of conservative pundits: the extremes are so extreme. The contrast between posh mansions with stunning views and the visual squalor of people camping on the streets, many of them consumed by drugs and mental illness, is too stark.

The contradictions exist. They're also part of the story. If there's a silver lining to the pain and stress and stasis of the past few years, perhaps it will be that the upheaval allowed San Francisco and other overheated centers to start inching back toward being something other than arenas of the very rich and very poor.

Cities like San Francisco will endure. They'll bewitch immigrants and young people and rootless dreamers drawn to places where they can light their own peculiar spark. The Embarcadero and other urban waterfronts will be reengineered in response to sea level rise, if only to help protect the city that grew up within its artificial shore. And the San Francisco icon that by its presence will continue to signal what's at stake—reminding us where we are, playing a role we can't begin to fathom—will be the Union Depot and Ferry House that rose before any one of us was born.

AFTERWORD

The wide spot in the Embarcadero Promenade near Pier 14 was packed that Thursday morning, and not with joggers or selfie-snapping tourists bewitched by the open bay. Picture instead a bustling crowd of political luminaries up to and including Representative Nancy Pelosi, on hand for the kind of gathering that elected officials like best: celebrating a win with big dollars attached. As in a precedent-setting federal plan to protect San Francisco's bay shoreline from the inexorable onslaught of sea level rise.

"Our future depends on taking action now," said Pelosi, the Speaker emerita who had been introduced by the Port of San Francisco's executive director, Elaine Forbes, as "a national treasure." California's lieutenant governor, Eleni Kounalakis, proclaimed that the strategy proposed for San Francisco "will have ripple effects on waterfronts across California and the rest of the country for generations to come." But the real star of the show—"the big humma-humma here today," Pelosi enthused—was the one individual who stepped to the podium in full military uniform: Col. James J. Handura, commander of the South Pacific Division of the US Army Corps of Engineers.

The corps isn't an obvious object of Bay Area affection, given the mammoth department's mixed record in terms of its role in reshaping the American landscape and environment since being founded in 1802. It played a central role fashioning the network of floodwalls and channels and shipping locks around New Orleans that failed so spectacularly during Hurricane Katrina. As recently as 2021, the corps proposed guarding Miami against hurricanes and storm surges by girdling the shoreline with a six-mile-long seawall as tall as 20 feet (it abandoned the plan a year later because of local opposition).

The plan for San Francisco released on January 26 is massive, as befits the corps, with a twenty-year scope and an estimated $13.5 billion budget to prepare the bay shoreline for the future. But the goal isn't simply to repel nature by force: The authors describe it as "the first (Army Corps) study in the nation where sea level rise is the primary driver of projected coastal and combined flood risk." In other words, the plan is to physically adapt the waterfront, incrementally, with an eye to projected worst-case scenarios for extreme weather and seal level rise through 2100—but also continue to monitor how climate change affects the coastal conditions beyond that. In short, the premise of the Army Corps plan is that hydraulic engineering isn't enough. Facing the future means accepting that sea level rise is coming, though we won't know the pace or extent for decades to come.

"It's not only a step forward for San Francisco, it's a step forward for the Corps of Engineers," Handura said. "What we're doing in the bay will be a model for other (urban) projects."

Among the officials watching from the sidelines that day was Brian Harper, civil works director of the corps' Oklahoma-based Regional Planning and Environmental Center. Nodding at some comments, smiling at others, the bureaucrat in direct charge of the work later seconded Handura's optimism that the approach envisioned for San Francisco can be applied to other urban regions nationwide.

"Something like this is replicable elsewhere," Harper said of the corps' desire not to impose absolute solutions, but to accept the uncertainties of climate change. "We're designing for the unknown. It's a different way of handling the relationship between the federal government and cities."

It also validates the work done by the Port since that ominous 2016 study on the Embarcadero seawall's vulnerability to earthquakes and sea level rise. Beyond the morale boost, the Army Corps' determination that there's a national need to protect San Francisco's bay shoreline means 65 percent of the project's cost will be paid by the federal government if Congress gives the project a green light. Which still leaves the city on the hook for roughly $4.7 billion, but that's a lot less than $13.5 billion.

Two months of public outreach followed, from walking tours to data-studded presentations to neighborhood groups, resulting in more than 150 detailed sets of comments from various individuals and interest groups, including four regional agencies. Three months after that came a heartening signal: "In June came the effort's validation: Army Corps leadership gave the official okay to turn the draft study into a full and final plan that will include responses to these critiques." Top brass also signaled that it likes how things are going, with a formal statement from the Army Corps' chief of planning, Eric Bush, that called the San Francisco effort "one of the most consequential and important studies we have underway, and it is amongst the most innovative work."

The completed document is to be released in the summer of 2025, and presented to Congress as part of the Army Corps' proposed budget for the following year. Assuming the initial request for funding is approved, subsequent rounds of funding are routine.

If all this happens, the Ferry Building will never be the same.

The draft plan confirms what the Port had been suggesting for years: the best way to "fix" the central Embarcadero is to rebuild the seawall and increase its height from three to seven feet, depending on the location. The Ferry Building is in the middle of everything, so that means raising it in place—probably by constructing a concrete dam of sorts about the perimeter, turning the foundation into a dry basement, and then slowly jacking the 660-foot-long structure above long-term sea level rise projections and reinforcing its seismic stability.

No more low-tide journeys for repair crews into the catacomb-like arches!

Sound complicated? It is. Even the draft plan's environmental impact report concedes that such large-scale construction "may cause adverse effects . . . including material alteration, structural instability, and loss of integrity of design and setting through physical damage."

There's a limit to what we know about the structural implications of the plan: while it calls for actions as bold as lifting a 126-year-old urban landmark attached to thick concrete, design work won't begin unless Congress gives the plan the green light. But the prospect of closing the Ferry Building for years of upheaval was enough to alarm one very interested party: Hudson Pacific Properties, with its master lease that runs until 2067 and its 50-plus tenants ranging from Google and Shack15 down to Far West Fungi.

"While we appreciate and respect the realities of climate change, we have to be sensitive about how we approach the building," is how one Hudson Pacific executive described his employer's concerns to me last spring. The firm's language in its written response to the draft plan was more direct: "While the Draft Plan discusses risks posed to the Ferry Building by sea level rise and seismic activity, it does not fully consider the risks or challenges entailed by the proposed solution."

Though Hudson Pacific is only one voice in the 150-plus crowd of commenters, nobody else focused so intently on how all this might affect Arthur Page Brown's serenely majestic masterpiece. Would the

Colusa sandstone crack if the building is jacked up? How will the clock tower be kept from toppling over? Can you really alter the one-of-a-kind foundation with its vaulted arches resting on tree trunks that have been submerged in bay mud for 130 years?

And then there's the larger impact of such a project—the need, in all likelihood, to close off the central portion of the Embarcadero while the blocks at the foot of Market Street are remade, and one of the city's most iconic buildings is transformed.

"Mitigating flood and seismic risks are important . . . (but) it is impossible to weigh the risks posed against the cost of shutting down one of San Francisco's greatest treasures, quite possibly for many years," declares the letter from Hudson Pacific, concluding grimly that "this Plan, intended to save the waterfront, could instead cause its early demise if not undertaken in a more cautious and incremental fashion."

Such a warning, hyperbolic though it may be, tapped into an undeniable truth: the Ferry Building is one of the few bright spots in downtown San Francisco's stubbornly slow recovery from the economic repercussions of COVID-19.

Charles Phan announced in May of 2024 that Slanted Door would not reopen in the landmark, but two months later the space was snapped up by a pair of local restaurateurs with a Michelin star. Nearly every other retail spot was filled—and just as in 2003, not by national chains. They're purveyors such as Lunette, a casual corner space devoted to Cambodian street food that opened in June of 2024. The owner is Nite Yun, who was born in a refugee camp in Thailand, immigrated with her parents to California's Central Valley at the age of two, moved to San Francisco after high school, and then took courses on how to open a restaurant at La Cocina, a nonprofit business incubator in the Mission district that specializes in giving immigrant women and women of color the tools to try and launch their own food business.

This is how cities evolve and prosper in today's urban world—drawing strength not just from global economic trends or technological innovations but also the intriguing currents of culture and life that bubble up from below. If the result isn't cheap in a city like San Francisco, (most dishes at Lunette are $21, including one called "student noodles" that will never be mistaken for Top Ramen), that's part of the current scene as well.

The question ahead is when, and how, work along the Embarcadero will begin: when the seawall will be rebuilt and how to fulfill Forbes's assurance back in January that "the waterfront of the future has to be at least as majestic as the waterfront of today."

Anyone familiar with how the review process for large-scale construction projects can drag on in San Francisco and California has a right to wonder if last January's grand promises of unstoppable momentum will come to pass. But Brian Harper, the Army Corps official whose department is the one taxed with moving things forward, seems unruffled by the task.

"You have opposing views," Harper said nonchalantly a few months after all the comments rolled in, saying the final draft will answer many of the questions that have been raised. "The intersection of all those groups creates complexity."

However things play out, Harper and his crew grappling with the multipronged threat of sea level rise and earthquakes and extreme weather will continue to fly from the Army Corps' Oklahoma office to the West Coast, and the building that in some ways is more symbolically relevant to San Francisco's future than ever.

"The Ferry Building is one of my favorite destinations—I love it. I love the location, the vendors, everything," Harper said, his smile palpable over the phone. "We understand it's an important hub. It's also a great building."

ACKNOWLEDGMENTS

Crafting the acknowledgments for this book is difficult because so many people helped out, and so selflessly, at each point along the way. Architecture buffs, transit advocates, people involved in the current scene and people who remember when *that freeway* was there—they're all drawn to the Ferry Building and the Embarcadero, and what the waterfront says about the city they love.

The genesis of *Portal* dates back to 2013, when I helped organize "Unbuilt San Francisco," a multi-venue exhibition at the California Historical Society, the College of Environmental Design at UC Berkeley, the public policy think-tank SPUR, the San Francisco Public Library, and the San Francisco chapter of the American Institute of Architects. Surveying roads not taken made me think harder about how we got where we are—and I wouldn't have ventured in that direction without the prodding of people such as Waverly Lowell, now curator emeritus of the Environmental Design Archives at Cal; Anthea Hartig, then the executive director of the California Historical Society but now director of the Smithsonian Institution's National Museum of American History; Thomas Carey of the SFPL's

History Center and Allison Arieff, who has moved on from SPUR to become an editor at the MIT Technology Review. Thank you all.

Having an idea is one thing. Launching a book-length manuscript is another. That's why I appreciate Donald Lamm, the onetime chairman of W. W. Norton who offered to coach me on the strange world of book proposals when I mentioned my idea for *Portal* over lunch one day. After making my proposal into something coherent, Don asked if I'd mind if he sent it to Norton. Truly, without him this book would not exist. Nor can I overstate the role of Tom Mayer, the Norton editor who pushed hard for a better and more thorough manuscript while understanding the importance of doling out praise and criticism as the need arose.

Another crucial form of assistance came from people who generously took time to read portions of the manuscript—starting with Cynthia Butler, whose smart eye improved every chapter that she read. Madeline King, Steven Reel, Maureen Hardy, Andrew Wolfram and Alan Kren all made the final text more precise and accurate than it otherwise would have been.

Librarians are the most pleasantly helpful people I know, and a pleasure of *Portal* is how it allowed me to work with so many who went beyond the call of duty again and again. This is particularly true of Frances Kaplan at the California Historical Society, and Susan Goldstein and her crack crew at the SFPL History Center. I also thank such helpful souls as Betsy Frederick-Rothwell, curator of the Environmental Design Archives; and reference librarian Jason Stratman at the Missouri Historical Society, who excavated information on the 1904 World Fair's San Francisco Building that probably hadn't been inquired about since, you guessed it, 1904. The Prelinger Library is an only-in-San Francisco world unto itself, a gift to civic life from Megan and Rick Prelinger. (Not a librarian but an archivist of his own passions: Glenn Koch, whose collection of San Francisco memorabilia is a wonder, and whose generosity in sharing it is a delight.)

The people I've interviewed along the way constitute another form of research, and a thoroughly pleasant one—from former mayor Art Agnos making time for me over two lunches to Jane Connors, the general manager of the Ferry Building who led me up rickety stairs on a tour of the clock tower, a glorified storage attic if ever there was one. Plus all the participants in the restoration who take such pride in what emerged from the grinding process: Chris and Michele Meany and Richard Springwater on the development side, Hans Baldauf and Cathy Simon and Jay Turnbull on the architectural one. The Port of San Francisco's staff has gone beyond the call of service in tackling various details and arcana while trying to prepare an urban waterfront for come what may.

Beyond this, in no particular order except alphabetical, I thank Alec Bash, Pippa Brashear, John Briscoe, Noah Berger, John Blanchard, Michael Corbett, Boris Delepine, Sue Conley, Jonathan Cordero, Jonathan D'Agostin, Christine Farren, Erica Fisher, Elaine Forbes, Rod Freebairn-Smith, Drew Gordon, James Haas Dan Hodapp, Jeanne Gang, Ian Garrone, Tobias Johansson, Keba Konte, Woody LaBounty, Rick Laubscher, David Lei, Olle Lundberg, Brie Mazurek, Richard McGuinness, Carl Nolte, Ross Merrill, Anita Monga, Johana Moreno, Diane Oshima, Mark Paez, Elaine Petrocelli, Olia Rosenblatt, Jasper Rubin, Erik Sandell, Peggy Smith, Daniel Solomon, Will Travis, Gena Wirth, Bobby Winston, and Daniel Zarrilli. And yes, I apologize to all of you that I missed.

Amid the research, there also was my day job as the urban design critic of the *San Francisco Chronicle*—the rare newspaper that still appreciates the importance of conveying why the built terrain around us matters. Publisher Bill Nagel and editor Emilio Garcia-Ruiz allowed me to take a leave to get the book rolling; they also went the extra mile by providing access to the *Chronicle*'s irreplaceable photo archive, which Peter Hartlaub and Anna Sarpieri then mined for precious ore. Rob Morast let his most scattered writer ramble at length about Ferry Building arcana; the early enthusiasm of my late editor Mark Lundgren makes me miss him all the more.

More than anything, I'm grateful to Cynthia Butler for all that she has done to make it possible for me to write this book—her wise reading and rare insight, and her loving willingness to sacrifice any semblance of a predictable life through the relentless cycles of research and writing and chasing odd tangents. Thank you.

A NOTE ON SOURCES

Portal is rooted in the rich history of one specific place. Fortunately, it's a place filled with people who love San Francisco despite its flaws and have the technical chops to compile information about the city's past and take it online in accessible ways. The best example is *FoundSF.org*, a self-described "participatory website" curated by Chris Carlsson and LisaRuth Elliott with a progressive bent; without it I'd still be trying to track down information on topics as disparate as the ecology of Yerba Buena Cove, post-1848 land claims and the Freeway Revolt. More narrowly, the Market Street Railway's website *streetcar.org* is a treasure trove on how people have navigated the city terrain. Nor would it have been possible to recount the controversies of distant generations without the online archives of so many newspapers and magazines—particularly the *San Francisco Chronicle*, which dates back to 1865, and the *San Francisco Examiner* that launched two years before that.

PART I: HEYDAY

The best accounts of the Bay Area's emergence are found in two very different books. *San Francisco: the Bay and Its Cities* is a flavorfully detailed guide crafted by writers in the federal government's Work Projects Administration and published in 1940, just as the region was about to be transformed by World War II; many details are outdated, but not such observations as "What is supremely important to San Franciscans is that they be let alone to think and act as they please." There's an entirely different tone to Mel Scott's *The San Francisco Bay Area: A Metropolis in Perspective*—more narrowly focused on the physical evolution of cities and counties and the infrastructure binding them, but narrated with accessible care. One is infused with literate pleasure; the other emphasizes geographic context. They're both invaluable.

There's no shortage of books about San Francisco's waterfront, from the freewheeling days of the Barbary Coast onward. Two were of particular value to *Portal*: Nancy Olmsted's *The Ferry Building: Witness to a Century of Change, 1898–1998*, and Michael Corbett's *Port City: The History and Transformation of the Port of San Francisco, 1848–2010*. For an earlier version of the origin story, *The Port of San Francisco* by Edward Morphy from 1923 remains an engaging resource in terms of how today's shoreline came to be (spoiler alert: there's a lot of weirdness along the way).

The biennial reports of the Board of State Harbor Commissioners, which appeared from 1865 until 1940, offer an episodic tale of how the state agency that ran the Port continually navigated new challenges, with varying degrees of success. If your obsession isn't the waterfront so much as the commuter vessels that arrived and departed, dip into *San Francisco Bay Ferryboats* from 1967 by George Harlan—a loving tribute written before the slow but steady resurgence of waterfront transit began.

In writing about the Ferry Building's architect, I was helped immeasurably by Kevin Starr's chapter on "Arthur Page Brown and the Dream of San Francisco," in his book *Inventing the Dream: California through the Progressive Era*—part of a seven-volume cultural history of the state. But the mother lode of information on the short-lived architect is a two-volume scrapbook kept by his family that now resides at the California Historical Society; it's so thorough it even contains the article where Brown told the *San Francisco Call*, "I keep a scrapbook and paste all the articles in it for the coming generation to read." Thank you, sir.

From the shelf of books on San Francisco's near-destruction in 1906, I particularly enjoyed Charles Keeler's *San Francisco through Earthquake and Fire* for its adrenaline-fueled exuberance. For a more analytical study of what went wrong and why, the last word in the structural aspects is Stephen Tobriner's *Bracing for Disaster: Earthquake-Resistant Architecture and Engineering in San Francisco, 1838–1933*. More approachable, and equally important, *San Francisco Chinatown: A Guide to Its History and Its Architecture* by Philip Choy spells out how the theatrical look of post-earthquake Chinatown very much was an act of cultural self-preservation.

The guidebooks and postcard collections of the era are tucked into thoroughly entertaining folders at the California Historical Society and the San Francisco History Center at the San Francisco Public Library. A more accessible survey of such ephemera is *San Francisco Golden Age Postcards & Memorabilia* from 2001, by Glenn Koch. It includes a postcard showing the cameo appearance of the Ferry Building at the 1904 World's Fair, a strange sight indeed.

The rise of the automobile in American cities is recounted, not approvingly, in Peter Norton's *Fighting Traffic: The Dawn of the Motor Age in the American City*, while Robert Fogelson's *Downtown: Its Rise and Fall, 1880–1950* does a smart job at showing the cumulative impact of decades of short-sighted decision making by the nation's large cities. The mindset of the early auto age is also on stark display in an official document: Miller McClintock's *Report on San Francisco Citywide Traffic Survey* from 1937, in which a city of more than six hundred thousand people is reduced to a diagram for efficient movement of four-wheeled vehicles. For how the bridges that connect San Francisco to Alameda County came to be, an insightful recent account is Stephen Mikesell's *A Tale of Two Bridges: The San Francisco-Oakland Bay Bridges of 1936 and 1913.* The most thorough collection of articles on the campaigns to replace the ferries with bridges is at the California Historical Society—a mammoth set of scrapbooks beginning in 1921 that were kept by Ted Huggins, a Standard Oil Co. publicist. The San Francisco History Center has three cartons of material related to the city's open competition for a Bay Bridge design in 1926 and 1927.

The saga of the waterfront strike of 1934 that closed ports along the West Coast is covered in a thoughtful chapter of *Endangered Dreams: The Great Depression in California*, another volume in Kevin Starr's state history. The most comprehensive account is David F. Selvin's *A Terrible Anger: The 1934 Waterfront and General Strikes in San Francisco*, published in 1996.

This section ends with the odd vision of San Francisco as it might have been conceived by Le Corbusier, though the culprit was US Steel. Except for an online handful of newspaper articles from the time, perhaps all that remains is a thin folder of publicity material that resides in the SFPL History Center.

PART II: RELIC

The best account of the Port of San Francisco's decline after World War II, including the ill-advised development proposals along the way, is Jasper Rubin's *A Negotiated Landscape: The Transformation of San Francisco's Waterfront Since 1950*; fortunately, Rubin leavens the bureaucratic tail chasing with moments of wry observational humor. Regarding the various plans he writes about, the craziest journey into the realm of hyperbolic make-believe is *San Francisco World Trade Center: Prospectus*; I'm surprised it hasn't been digitized by the invaluable Internet Archive (archive.org), where so many dusty-but-insightful past reports can be found—such as the 1947 plan that laid the groundwork for the Embarcadero Freeway, *A Report to the City Planning Commission on a Transportation Plan for San Francisco* (https://archive.org/details/reporttocityplan1948dele).

Chris Carlsson recounted the history of the Freeway Revolt at FoundSF, complete with the lyrics to Malvina Reynolds' "Cement Octopus" and a link to her recording of the song. The successful opposition to the Panhandle Freeway was the subject of an excellent piece in 2015 by Griffin Estes at the local news site Hoodline, (https://hoodline.com/2015/03/panhandle-freeway-revolt/).

To grasp the fervor of San Francisco's anti-growth crusaders in the 1960s and early 1970s, I recommend that you track down *The Ultimate Highrise: San Francisco's Mad Rush toward the Sky*, a collection of pieces assembled by the *Bay Guardian* alternative weekly in 1971. The apocalyptic warnings haven't stood the test of time, but there's an excellent account of the battles over Ferry Port Plaza and the US Steel high-rise by Richard Reinhardt. Another intriguing perspective on that era is *Making City Planning Work* by Allan Jacobs, the city's planning director from 1967 to 1973; it's a memoir of sorts, with a chapter on the Transamerica Pyramid—a building he vehemently opposed.

A real-time sense of San Francisco's combative journey, I have argued, comes through the estimated sixteen thousand daily columns written by Herb Caen between 1936 and his death in 1997. Portions have been assembled in a dozen collections, but that format doesn't convey the wickedly deft way Caen put every word to use in his short items; the essay columns, including some that I quote, often show his maudlin rather than masterful side. The two best collections? The *San Francisco Book* from 1948 conveys the dilemmas facing the city after World War II. *One Man's San Francisco* offers vivid and broad-minded insight into how long-time residents grappled with the cultural upheaval of the 1960s.

The most detailed architectural study of the subject of *Portal* is Charles Hall Page & Associates' *Union Depot and Ferry House, San Francisco: Design Guidelines for Restoration and Adaptive Use of the Ferry Building,* from 1978. *San Francisco's Central Place, Reestablished,* was published five years later by I. M. Pei & Partners, now Pei Cobb Freed & Partners—a handsome booklet laying out what proved to be the final installment in the saga of Ferry Building makeovers that never came to be.

PART III: REBIRTH

The archives of the Ferry Plaza Farmers Market are voluminous, and easily accessible online, offering a detailed if boosterish account of how a Saturday market could become entwined with a city's waterfront identity; a good place to start, not surprisingly, is https:// foodwise.org/about/history-of-foodwise. The non-profit's paper folders include several of the articles I drew from regarding the rapturous early response to the resurrection of the Ferry Building.

Case studies abound of that restoration. Architect Cathy Simon looked back at the project in her book from 2022, *Occupation: Boundary.* The Urban Land Institute's 2015 analysis focuses on the success through a business lens. The odd mating dance between the building's developers and the sustainable food community was detailed entertainingly at the time—"The interior space is designed to be as far away from a suburban food court as a Cinnabon is from

a Frog Hollow Farm peach tart"—in "Ferry Tales Can Come True,"
by Kim Severson in the April 23, 2003, *San Francisco Chronicle*; it
serves as a tasty bookend to Paolo Lucchesi's reflective piece almost
fifteen years later, "Does the Ferry Building Still Reflect Local Food
Culture?" (*San Francisco Chronicle*, March 10, 2018).

In terms of the revived Embarcadero, the most detailed account
of the recent metamorphosis—including admissions of what went
wrong—is the Port's *Waterfront Land Use Plan 1997–2014 Review*.
This was a sequel of sorts to 1997's *Port of San Francisco Waterfront Land Use Plan*—a document showing how in the right circumstances, methodical planning done in a spirit of collaboration can
uplift countless lives.

PART IV: THE UNKNOWN

The sobering and definitive study of the projected long-term impact
of sea level rise along San Francisco Bay—at least for now—is *Adapting to Rising Tides: Bay Area* from the Bay Conservation and Development Commission. The commission posted the roughly seven
hundred pages of nine counties' worth of data just weeks after the
full arrival of COVID in March 2020, but it lives on at https://www
.adaptingtorisingtides.org/project/art-bay-area/.

The Port of San Francisco's equivalent came six months later,
Multi-Hazard Risk Assessment for the Embarcadero, a report that
required eighty-two pages for the executive summary alone. A good
distillation of the information, including maps and a video aimed at
the general public as well as regularly updated links to ongoing work,
is at https://sfport.com/wrp/mhra.

For the situation facing Boston, Anthony Flint's "Boston Takes
on Climate Change" in the Spring 2021 issue of *Planning Magazine*
offers an excellent overview; there's no deeper dive into the arti-
ficiality of urban shorelines than *Gaining Ground: A History of*

Landmaking in Boston by Nancy Seasholes. The concepts behind SCAPE Landscape Architecture's "living breakwaters" are explored in an August 2021 *New Yorker* profile of SCAPE founder Kate Orff by Eric Klinenberg —"The seas are rising. Could oysters protect us?" at https://www.newyorker.com/magazine/2021/08/09/the-seas-are-rising-could-oysters-protect-us. The contorted balancing act along Manhattan's East River is captured by Keith Gessen in "The Destroy-It-to-Save-It Plan for East River Park: New York's first climate adaptation battle is here," in the May 10, 2021 *New York Magazine* (https://www.curbed.com/2021/05/east-river-park-nyc.html).

BIBLIOGRAPHY

NEWSPAPERS

Daily Evening Bulletin (San Francisco)
San Francisco Call
San Francisco Chronicle
San Francisco Examiner
Wave (San Francisco)

BOOKS AND ARTICLES

"25 of the World's Best Food Markets." *Food & Wine.* Updated June 16, 2017. https://www.foodandwine.com/travel/25-of-the-worlds-best-food-markets.

"About the Harborwalk." Boston Harbor Now. Accessed October 9, 2022. https://www.bostonharbornow.org/what-we-do/explore/harborwalk/about-the-harborwalk/.

Ackley, Laura A. *San Francisco's Jewel City: The Panama-Pacific International Exposition of 1915.* Berkeley, CA: Heyday, 2014.

"Alice Waters." California Museum. Accessed October 9, 2022. https://www.californiamuseum.org/inductee/alice-waters.

"Allianz and Hudson Pacific Properties Form Joint Venture to Acquire Iconic Ferry Building in San Francisco." October 9, 2018. Allianz. https://www.allianz-realestate.com/en/newsroom/press-releases/09-10-18-allianz-and-hudson-pacific-properties-form-jv-to-acquire-ferry-building.

"Anniversary of the Mount St. Helens Eruption." Earthsky.org. May 18, 2021. https://earthsky.org/earth/this-date-in-science-cataclysmic-eruption-at-mount-st-helens/.

"Arthur Page Brown (Architect)." Pacific Coast Architecture Database. Accessed October 9, 2022. https://pcad.lib.washington.edu/person/1396/.

"Background—Overview." Lower Manhattan Coastal Resiliency. n.d. https://www1.nyc.gov/site/lmcr/background/background.page.

Bean, Lowell John. *The Ohlone Past and Present: Native Americans of the San Francisco Bay Region*. Menlo Park, CA: Ballena Press, 1994.

Beebe, Lucius, and Charles Clegg. *Cable Car Carnival*. Oakland, CA: G. Hardy, 1951.

"Berkeley Landmarks: Charles Keeler House & Studio." Berkeley Architectural Heritage Association. n.d. http://berkeleyheritage.com/berkeley_landmarks/keeler_house.html.

Bialick, Aaron. "How Friedel Klussmann Saved the Cable Cars 70 Years Ago." San Francisco Municipal Transportation Agency. January 26, 2017. https://www.sfmta.com/blog/how-friedel-klussmann-saved-cable-cars-70-years-ago#:~:text=In%20response%2C%20Friedel%20Klussmann%20founded.

Brekke, Dan. "Boomtown, 1870s: 'the Chinese Must Go!'" KQED. February 12, 2015. https://www.kqed.org/news/10429550/boomtown-history-2b.

Brown, Arthur Page. "Architecture of California," *San Francisco Chronicle*, December 20, 1894

Brugmann, Bruce B., and Greggar Sletteland. *The Ultimate Highrise; San Francisco's Mad Rush toward the Sky.* San Francisco Bay Guardian, 1971.

Buel, James W. *Louisiana and the Fair: An Exposition of the World, Its People and Their Achievements.* St. Louis, MO: World's Progress Publishing, 1904.

"Cable Cars: How Cable Cars Work." Cable Car Museum. Accessed October 9, 2022. http://www.cablecarmuseum.org/mechanical.html.

Caen, Herb, with illustrations by Howard Brodie. *Baghdad by the Bay.* Garden City, NY: Doubleday, 1949.

Caen, Herb. *One Man's San Francisco.* Garden City, NY: Doubleday, 1976.

Caen, Herb. "Shove It Up Your Skyline," *San Francisco Chronicle Sunday Punch*, October 25, 1970.

Caen, Herb, with photographs by Max Yavno. *The San Francisco Book.* Boston: Houghton Mifflin, 1948.

Cannell, Michael. I. M. Pei, *Mandarin of Modernism.* New York: Carol Southern, 1995.

Carlsson, Chris. "The Freeway Revolt: Historical Essay." FoundSF. n.d. https://www.foundsf.org/index.php?title=The_Freeway_Revolt.

Choy, Philip P. *San Francisco Chinatown: A guide to Its History and Its Architecture.* San Francisco: City Lights, 2012.

"Chronology of 1942 San Francisco War Events." Museum of the City of San Francisco. Accessed October 9, 2022. http://www.sfmuseum.org/war/42.html.

Chu, Alice. "From Redevelopment to Reconciliation: Housing Mistrust in San Francisco." Edited by Larry Dang. Medium. June

2, 2018. https://larrydang.medium.com/from-redevelopment
-to-redemption-history-of-housing-mistrust-in-san-francisco
-da9f3b10d0d4.

Cook, Anne, Karl Kilstrom, and Diane Oshima. *Port of San Francisco Waterfront Land Use Plan: Republished Version.* San Francisco: Port of San Francisco, 1999.

Corbett, Michael R. *Building California: Technology and the Landscape.* Salt Lake City: William Stout (published on behalf of the California Historical Society), 1998.

Corbett, Michael R. *Port City: The History and Transformation of the Port of San Francisco, 1848–2010.* San Francisco: San Francisco Architectural Heritage, 2010.

Davies, Andrea Rees. *Saving San Francisco: Relief and Recovery after the 1906 Disaster.* Philadelphia, PA: Temple University Press, 2012.

Delgado, James P. *Gold Rush Port: The Maritime Archaeology of San Francisco's Waterfront.* Berkeley: University of California Press, 2009.

Demarest, Michael. "He Digs Downtown." *Time*, August 24, 1981.

DeMars, Vernon. "The Embarcadero Freeway vs. the Ferry Building Park: Selected Correspondence and News Clippings from August 1955 to December 1957." Fran Violich Collection, Environmental Design Archives, University of California, Berkeley, 1985.

"Design & Construction Stats." Golden Gate Bridge. Accessed October 9, 2022. https://www.goldengate.org/bridge/history
-research/statistics-data/design-construction-stats/#maintower.

Eliel, Paul. *The Waterfront and General Strikes, San Francisco, 1934.* San Francisco: Hooper Printing, 1934.

Estes, Griffin. "The Panhandle Freeway and the Revolt That Saved the Park." *Hoodline.* March 29, 2015. https://hoodline
.com/2015/03/panhandle-freeway-revolt/.

Evers Hitz, Anne. *San Francisco's Ferry Building.* Charleston, SC: Arcadia, 2017.

Ferlinghetti, Lawrence. "The Poetic City That Was." *San Francisco Chronicle.* January 14, 2001. https://www.sfchronicle.com/ books/article/The-Poetic-City-That-Was-2965336.php.

"The Ferry Building." Urban Land Institute Case Studies. December 17, 2015. https://casestudies.uli.org/the-ferry-building-5/.

Flint, Anthony. "Boston Takes on Climate Change." *Planning Magazine,* Spring 2021. https://www.planning.org/ planning/2021/spring/boston-takes-on-climate-change/.

Flint, Anthony. *Wrestling with Moses: How Jane Jacobs Took on New York's Master Builder and Transformed the American City.* New York: Random House, 2009.

Fogelson, Robert M. *Downtown: Its Rise and Fall, 1880–1950.* New Haven, CT: Yale University Press, 2001.

"Food Halls of America." Cushman & Wakefield. 2016. https:// www.retailstrategies.com/wp-content/uploads/2016/12/CW -Retail-Food-Halls-Report-web.pdf.

"Foodwise: Education. Farmers Markets. Community." Foodwise. Accessed October 9, 2022. https://foodwise.org/#about.

Ford, Robert S. *Red Trains in the East Bay: The History of the Southern Pacific Transbay Train and Ferry System.* Glendale, CA: Interurbans, 1977.

Frieden, Bernard J., and Lynne B. Sagalyn. *Downtown, Inc.: How America Rebuilds Cities.* Cambridge, MA: MIT Press, 1989.

"Geographic Index, 1900–1974." Curt Teich Co. Records, Record Group 3, box 2, folder 27. Midwest MS Teich Co., Newberry Library, Chicago.

Gilfoyle, Timothy J. *Millennium Park: Creating a Chicago Landmark.* Chicago: University of Chicago Press, 2006.

Givens, J. D. (James David). *San Francisco in Ruins: A Pictorial History of Eight Score Photo-Views of the Earthquake Effects,*

Flames' Havoc, Ruins Everywhere, Relief Camps. Denver, CO: Smith-Brooks, 1906.

Gleick, Peter H., and Edwin P. Maurer. "Assessing the Costs of Adapting to Sea-Level Rise: A Case Study of San Francisco Bay." Oakland, CA: Pacific Institute for Studies in Development, Environment, and Security, (1990) 2004.

Hallidie, Andrew Smith. *The Invention of the Cable Railway System.* San Francisco: n.p., 1885.

Harlan, George H. *San Francisco Bay Ferryboats.* Berkeley, CA: Howell-North, 1967.

"History of Foodwise." Foodwise. Accessed October 10, 2022. https://foodwise.org/about/history-of-foodwise/.

"History of Golden Gate Park." San Francisco Recreation and Parks. n.d. https://sfrecpark.org/1119/History-of-Golden-Gate-Park.

"History of the California National Guard during the 1894 Railroad Strike." Works Progress Administration, 1940. Digitized February 10, 2015, by the History Office, Camp San Luis Obispo, CA. https://www.militarymuseum.org/1894%20Railroad%20Strike.pdf.

Hoover, Herbert. *The Memoirs of Herbert Hoover*, vol. 3, *The Great Depression, 1929–1941.* New York: Macmillan, 1951.

Hoover, Herbert. "Public Papers of the Presidents of the United States." Washington, DC: United States Government Printing Office, 1929. Accessed October 9, 2022. https://hoover.archives.gov/sites/default/files/research/ebooks/b2v1_full.pdf.

"Island History." Treasure Island Museum. Accessed December 14, 2022. https://www.treasureislandmuseum.org/island-history.

Jacobs, Allan B. *Making City Planning Work.* Chicago: American Society of Planning Officials, 1980.

Kahn, Edgar Myron. "Andrew Smith Hallidie." *California Historical Society Quarterly* 19, no. 2 (1940). https://www.sfmuseum.org/bio/hallidie.html.

Keeler, Charles. *San Francisco and Thereabout*. San Francisco: California Promotion Committee, 1902.

Keeler, Charles. *San Francisco through Earthquake and Fire*. San Francisco: P. Elder, 1906.

Keeling, Brock. "Theft, Human Feces, Sponge Baths: Ferry Building Furious over Occupy SF Crimes." SFist, November 11, 2011. https://sfist.com/2011/11/11/ferry_building_sends_letter_to_city/.

Kennedy, David M. *Freedom from Fear: The American People in Depression and War, 1929–1945*. New York: Oxford University Press, 1999.

Kentfield, Calvin. "San Francisco: The Waterfront." *Holiday Magazine*, Vol. 29, no. 4 (April 1961).

King, John. "The Ferry Building, San Francisco." *Architectural Record*, November 2004.

King, John. "Unbuilt San Francisco." *The Urbanist*, September–October 2013. https://www.spur.org/publications/urbanist-article/2013-08-28/unbuilt-san-francisco.

Koch, Glenn D. *San Francisco Golden Age Postcards & Memorabilia, 1900–1940*. Sausalito, CA: Windgate Press, 2001.

Koetitz, F. A. "The Tower of the Union Ferry Depot, San Francisco." *American Builders Review* 6, no. 1, January 1907.

Krieger, Alex, David A. Cobb, Amy Turner, David C. Bosse, James Carroll, Barbara McCorkle, Nancy S. Seasholes, Sam Bass Warner, and Anni Mckin. *Mapping Boston*. Edited by Alex Krieger, David A. Cobb, and Amy Turner. Cambridge, MA: MIT Press, 1999.

Lange, Alexandra. *Meet Me by the Fountain: An Inside History of the Mall*. New York: Bloomsbury, 2022.

Laubscher, Rick. "Coming to Town." Market Street Railway. April 24, 2022. https://www.streetcar.org/coming-to-town/.

Laubscher, Rick. "Market Street Subway Dreams." Market Street Railway. December 9, 2021. https://www.streetcar.org/market -street-subway-dreams/.

Lesy, Michael. *Looking Backward: A Photographic Portrait of the World at the Beginning of the Twentieth Century.* 1st edition. New York: W. W. Norton, 2017.

"Library Guides: Central Railroad of New Jersey Terminal." New Jersey City University Libraries. Accessed October 9, 2022. https://njcu.libguides.com/centralrailroad.

Lipsky, Florence, and Cynthia Schoch. *San Francisco, la grille sur les collines* [San Francisco: The Grid Meets the Hills]. Marseilles: Parenthèses, 1999.

Lowe, David. *Lost Chicago.* Boston: Houghton Mifflin, 1975.

Lucchesi, Paolo. "Does the Ferry Building still reflect the Bay Area's Food Culture?" *San Francisco Chronicle*, March 9, 2018. https://www.sfchronicle.com/restaurants/article/Does-the-Ferry -Building-still-reflect-the-Bay-12741553.php.

Macomber, Ben. *The Jewel City: Its Planning and Achievement; Its Architecture, Sculpture, Symbolism, and Music; Its Gardens, Palaces, and Exhibits.* San Francisco: J. H. Williams, 1915.

Magnin, Cyril, and Cynthia Robins. *Call Me Cyril.* New York: McGraw-Hill, 1981.

Magnuson, Ed. "Earthquake." *Time*, October 30, 1989.

Mall, Scott. "FreightWaves Classics: Port of Philadelphia Has Served Region for 300+ Years." FreightWaves. July 30, 2021. https://www.freightwaves.com/news/freightwaves-classics-port -of-philadelphia-has-served-region-for-300-years.

"March 27, 1923—Chicago River . . . A Parking Garage?" Connecting the Windy City. March 27, 2019. http://www .connectingthewindycity.com/2019/03/march-27-1923-chicago -river-parking.html.

Maslin, Marshall, ed. *San Francisco and Bay Cities: A Camera Tour in Color.* San Franciscoi The Printing Corporation, 1938.

Meeks, Carroll L. V. (Carroll Louis Vanderslice). *The Railroad Station: An Architectural History.* New Haven, CT: Yale University Press, 1975.

Mikesell, Stephen D. *A Tale of Two Bridges: The San Francisco-Oakland Bay Bridges of 1936 and 2013.* Reno: University of Nevada Press, 2017.

Morphy, Edward. *The Port of San Francisco.* Sacramento: California State Printing Office, 1923.

Norton, Peter D. *Fighting Traffic: The Dawn of the Motor Age in the American City.* Cambridge, MA: MIT Press, 2008.

O'Connor, Charles James, Francis H. McLean, Helen Swett Artieda, James M. Motley, Jessica B. Peixotto, Mary Roberts Coolidge, James M. (James Marvin) Motley, and Jessica B. (Jessica Blanche) Peixotto. *San Francisco Relief Survey; The Organization and Methods of Relief Used after the Earthquake and Fire of April 18, 1906.* New York: Survey Associates, 1913.

O'Connor, Thomas H. *Building a New Boston: Politics and Urban Renewal, 1950–1970.* Boston: Northeastern University Press, 1993.

Oda, Meredith. *The Gateway to the Pacific: Japanese Americans and the Remaking of San Francisco.* Chicago: The University of Chicago Press, 2018.

Olmsted, Nancy. *The Ferry Building: Witness to a Century of Change, 1898–1998.* Berkeley, CA: Heyday Books, in conjunction with the Port of San Francisco, 1998.

Olmsted, Nancy. *Vanished Waters: A History of San Francisco's Mission Bay.* 2nd ed., rev. and expanded. San Francisco, CA: Mission Creek Conservancy, 2010.

"One World Trade Center." Skidmore, Owings & Merrill. n.d. https://www.som.com/projects/one-world-trade-center/.

"Our Story." Slanted Door Group. Accessed October 9, 2022. https://slanted door group.com/about.

Pilkey, Orrin H., Linda Pilkey-Jarvis, and Keith C. Pilkey. *Retreat from a Rising Sea: Hard Choices in an Age of Climate Change.* New York: Columbia University Press, 2016.

Plyer, Allison. "Facts for Features: Katrina Impact." The Data Center. August 26, 2016. https://www.datacenter research.org/data-resources/katrina/facts-for-impact/.

Polk, Willis, and Richard W. Longstreth. *A Matter of Taste: Willis Polk's Writings on Architecture in the Wave.* San Francisco: Book Club of California, 1979.

Porter, Julia Gorman, and Gabrielle S. Morris. "Julia Gorman Porter, Dedicated Democrat and City Planner, 1941–1975: An Interview." Berkeley, CA: Regional Oral History Office, Bancroft Library, University of California, 1977.

"Proposition M and the Downtown Growth Battle." San Francisco Bay Area Planning and Urban Research Association. November 23, 2008. https://www.spur.org/publications/urbanist-article/1999-07-01/proposition-m-and-downtown-growth-battle#:~:text=In%20November%20of%201986%2C%20San.

Purdy, Helen Throop. *San Francisco: As It Was, as It Is, and How to See It.* San Francisco: Paul Elder, 1912.

Restoration & Adaptive Use, the Ferry Building, Port of San Francisco: A Proposal from Continental Development Corporation. San Francisco: The Corporation, 1979.

Robinson, James P. *Report upon the Condition and Requirements of the City Front of San Francisco Made to the San Francisco Dock and Wharf Co., January 25, 1859.* Sacramento, CA: H. S. Crocker, 1859.

Rothstein, Richard. *The Color of Law: A Forgotten History of How Our Government Segregated America.* New York: Liveright, 2017.

Rubin, M. Jasper. *A Negotiated Landscape: The Transformation of San Francisco's Waterfront Since 1950.* Chicago: Center for American Places at Columbia College Chicago, 2011.

San Francisco: The Bay and Its Cities. American Guide Series. New York: Hastings, 1940.

San Francisco and Its Environs. San Francisco: California Promotion Committee, 1903.

San Francisco, the Metropolis of the West. San Francisco: Western Press, 1910.

The San Francisco-Oakland Bay Bridge. Pittsburgh, PA: United States Steel, 1936.

San Francisco's Central Place, Reestablished. San Francisco: I. M. Pei & Partners, 1984.

Saxton, Alexander. *The Indispensable Enemy: Labor and the Anti-Chinese Movement in California.* Berkeley: University of California Press, 1975.

Scott, Mel. *The San Francisco Bay Area: A Metropolis in Perspective.* 2nd edition. Berkeley: University of California Press, 1985.

Seasholes, Nancy S. *Gaining Ground: A History of Landmaking in Boston.* Cambridge, MA: MIT Press, 2003.

Selvin, David F. *A Terrible Anger: The 1934 Waterfront and General Strikes in San Francisco.* Detroit, MI: Wayne State University Press, 1996.

Severson, Kim. "Ferry Tales Can Come True / Farmers' Market Returns Home to Inaugurate Ferry Building Food Plaza." *San Francisco Chronicle*, April 23, 2003. https://www.sfchronicle.com/food/article/Ferry-tales-can-come-true-Farmers-market-2653663.php.

"Slow Food and Carlo Petrini." eGullet Society for Culinary Arts & Letters. May 14, 2007. https://forums.egullet.org/topic/102640-slow-food-and-carlo-petrini/?hl=petrini.

Soat, John. "The Dot-Com Crash: 15 Years Later." *Forbes.* Octo-

ber 13, 2015. https://www.forbes.com/sites/oracle/2015/04/13/
the-dot-com-crash-15-years-later/?sh=7c8ffc8a5354.

"State Seal of California." State of California Capitol Museum.
Accessed October 9, 2022. https://capitolmuseum.ca.gov/state
-symbols/seal/.

Stott, Rory. "Spotlight: Carlo Scarpa." ArchDaily. June 2, 2019.
https://www.archdaily.com/638534/spotlight-carlo-scarpa.

Spitzer, Tadeusz B. World Trade Center in San Francisco. San
Francisco: Board of State Harbor Commissioners for San Francisco Harbor, 1947.

Stahl, Jeremy. "The Exploitation of 'Beautiful Kate': How
Trump and His Conservative Allies Twisted the Facts of a
Deadly San Francisco Shooting to Stoke America's Xeno-
phobia." Slate, August 10, 2017. https://slate.com/news-and
-politics/2017/08/the-death-of-kate-steinle-and-the-rise-of
-donald-trump.html.

Starr, Kevin. Endangered Dreams: The Great Depression in California. New York: Oxford University Press, 1996.

Starr, Kevin. Inventing the Dream: California through the Progressive Era. New York: Oxford University Press, 1985.

Steele, James. William Pereira. Los Angeles: University of Southern
California, Architectural Guild Press, 2002.

Sugrue, Thomas. "Miller McClintock," Scribner's Magazine,
December 1937.

Sula, Mike. "Carlo Said He's Sorry." Chicago Reader (blogs), May
23, 2007. https://chicagoreader.com/blogs/carlo-said-hes-sorry/.

Talbot, David. Season of the Witch: Enchantment, Terror, and
Deliverance in the City of Love. New York: Free Press, 2012.

Teaford, Jon C. The Rough Road to Renaissance: Urban Revital-
ization in America, 1940–1985. Baltimore: Johns Hopkins University Press, 1990.

Tobriner, Stephen. Bracing for Disaster: Earthquake-Resistant

Architecture and Engineering in San Francisco, 1838–1933. Berkeley, CA: Bancroft Library, University of California, 2006.

Todd, Frank Morton. *The Chamber of Commerce Handbook for San Francisco, Historical and Descriptive; a Guide for Visitors* . . . . San Francisco: San Francisco Chamber of Commerce, 1914.

Traveler's Guide to San Francisco. San Francisco: California Guide Book Company, 1928.

Travis, Will, and Martin Meeker. "Will 'Trav' Travis: Leading Environmental Regulator for the Public Interest." Interview by Martin Meeker. Berkeley, CA: Oral History Center, Bancroft Library, 2015.

Uhlig, Carl. "The Foundation of the Union Depot and Ferry House of San Francisco." *America Builders Review* 4, no. 3 (September 1906): 259.

Valencia, Milton J. "The next Big Dig? UMass Study Warns Boston Harbor Barrier Not Worth Cost or Effort." *Boston Globe,* May 29, 2018. https://www.bostonglobe.com/metro/2018/05/29/the-next-big-dig-umass-study-warns-boston-harbor-barrier-not-worth-cost-effort/BdEjVDgNNucNM8gP1tlZ4O/story.html.

Van Malderen, L. (Luc). *American Architecture: A Vintage Postcard Collection.* Mulgrave, Australia: Images, 2000.

Von Hoffman, Nicholas. "Who's In Charge Here?: San Franciscans Are Fighting to Hold On to Their City, but They Are Losing." *Holiday* , Vol. 47 no. 3 (March 1970).

Watkins, Carleton E., Eadweard Muybridge, I. W. Taber, Balfe D. Johnson, and I. W. (Isaiah West) Taber. *San Francisco Views, 1850–1915.* Sausalito, CA: Windgate Press, 1993.

Weiss, Jeff. "Driving the Beat Road." *Washington Post,* June 30, 2017. https://www.washingtonpost.com/graphics/2017/lifestyle/the-beat-generation/.

Whitehill, Walter Muir, and Lawrence W. Kennedy. *Boston: A*

Topographical History. 3rd edition. Cambridge, MA: Belknap Press of Harvard University Press, 2000.

Wilkerson, Isabel. *The Warmth of Other Suns: The Epic Story of America's Great Migration.* New York: Random House, 2010.

Wilson, Ralph. "History of Potrero Point Shipyards and Industry." Pier 70 San Francisco. Accessed October 8, 2022. http://pier70sf.org/history/p70_history.html.

REPORTS, PLANS, AND GOVERNMENT DOCUMENTS

"Adapting to Rising Tides." ART Program, San Francisco Bay Conservation and Development Commission. Accessed October 12, 2022. https://www.adaptingtorisingtides.org/project/art-bay-area/.

Bartholomew, Harland. *The San Francisco Bay Region: A Statement Concerning the Nature and Importance of a Plan for Future Growth.* San Francisco: Regional Plan Association, 1925.

Ciampi, Mario J. *Downtown San Francisco: General Plan Proposals: An Excerpt from the Report Downtown San Francisco.* San Francisco: Department of City Planning, 1963.

Downtown Plan: Monitoring Report 1985–2009. San Francisco: San Francisco Planning Department, 2011.

"Embarcadero Early Projects." Port of San Francisco. Accessed October 9, 2022. https://sfport.com/wrp/embarcadero-early-projects.

"Executive Order—Establishing the Hurricane Sandy Rebuilding Task Force." Washington, DC: Obama White House Archives, December 7, 2012. https://obamawhitehouse.archives.gov/the-press-office/2012/12/07/executive-order-establishing-hurricane-sandy-rebuilding-task-force.

The Fort Point Channel Landmark District: Boston Landmarks

Commission Study Report Petition #201. Amended December 9, 2008. https://www.boston.gov/sites/default/files/embed/f/fort -point-study-report.pdf.

The Great 1906 San Francisco Earthquake. United States Geological Survey, 2019. https://earthquake.usgs.gov/earthquakes/ events/1906calif/18april/.

"A History of BART: The Project Begins." Bay Area Rapid Transit. n.d. https://www.bart.gov/about/history/history2.

Hossfeld, Dan, Dana Brechwald, Clesi Bennett, Shannon Fiala, and Amber Leavitt. *San Francisco Bay Plan: Climate Change Policy Guidance.* San Francisco Bay Conservation and Development Commission, July 2021. https://www.bcdc.ca.gov/bpacc/ San-Francisco-Bay-Plan-Climate-Change-Policy-Guidance.pdf.

"The Impacts of Climate Change." Chapter 4 in *The Financial District and Seaport Climate Resilience Master Plan.* December 29, 2021. https://fidiseaportclimate.nyc/wp-content/uploads/ 2023/02/FiDi-Seaport-Climate-Resilience-Master-Plan_Chapter -4.pdf.

"Living Breakwaters Project Background and Design." Governor's Office of Storm Recovery. n.d. https://stormrecovery.ny.gov/ living-breakwaters-project-background-and-design.

The Loma Prieta, California, Earthquake of October 17, 1989, Highway Systems v. B. Denver, CO: US Government Printing Office, 1998.

McClintock, Miller. *Report on San Francisco Citywide Traffic Survey: W.P.A. Project 6108-5863.* San Francisco: Pisani, 1937. Uploaded to Internet Archive November 30, 2015. https://archive.org/details/reportonsanfranc1937mccl/page/n3/ mode/2up.

Multi-Hazard Risk Assessment: Northern Waterfront and Embarcadero Seawall Summary Report. Port of San Francisco Waterfront Resilience Program, August 2020. https://sfport.com/

files/2021-11/Multi-Hazard%20Risk%20Assessment%20 Executive%20Summary.pdf.

Northern Waterfront: A Report. San Francisco: Department of City Planning, 1969.

Port of San Francisco Waterfront Land Use Plan: 1997–2014 Review. San Francisco: Port of San Francisco, 2015.

The Progressive Port of San Francisco: Preferred Pacific Gateway of General Cargo and Special Commodities. San Francisco: Board of State Harbor Commissioners, 1953.

Reel, Steven. "Informational Presentation: Earthquake Vulnerability Study of the Northern Waterfront Seawall Progress Update." Presented at San Francisco Port Commission Meeting, October 13, 2015. https://www.onesanfrancisco.org/sites/default/files/2017-05/Agenda%20Item%207%20-%20PRT%20Sea%20Wall%20Update%20Presentation.pdf.

A Report to the City Planning Commission on a Transportation Plan for San Francisco. San Francisco, CA: De Leuw, Cather, 1948. Uploaded to Internet Archive April 12, 2016. https://archive.org/details/reporttocityplan1948dele.

San Francisco Subway: Double Traffic Paved Vehicular Driveway below Tidewater Level: Planned and Constructed by California Harbor Commission in 1924. Pamphlet. Sacramento: California State Printing Office, 1925.

San Francisco World Trade Center: Prospectus. San Francisco: San Francisco World Trade Authority, 1951.

Scott, Mel. *New City: San Francisco Redeveloped.* San Francisco: San Francisco City Planning Commission, 1947.

Scott, Mel. *Western Addition District: An Exploration of the Possibilities of Replanning and Rebuilding One of San Francisco's Largest Blighted Districts under the California Community Redevelopment Act of 1945.* San Francisco: San Francisco City Planning Commission, 1947.

Shoreline Development: A Portion of the Master Plan of San Francisco: Preliminary Report. San Francisco: San Francisco City Planning Commission, 1943.

State of California Sea-Level Rise Guidance: 2018 Update. California Natural Resources Agency, Ocean Protection Council. http://www.opc.ca.gov/webmaster/ftp/pdf/agenda_items/20180314/Item3_Exhibit-A_OPC_SLR_Guidance-rd3.pdf.

Union Depot and Ferry House, San Francisco: Design Guidelines for Restoration and Adaptive Use of the Ferry Building. San Francisco: Charles Hall Page, 1978.

United States Bureau of Foreign and Domestic Commerce and United States Bureau of the Census. "1890, Thirteenth Number," in *Statistical Abstract of the United States, 1890.* https://fraser.stlouisfed.org/title/statistical-abstract-united-states-66/1890-521396.

What to Do about the Waterfront: A Report to the Citizens Waterfront Committee. San Francisco: Livingston and Blayney, 1971.

FILM, VIDEO, ETC.

"1989 Loma Prieta World Series Earthquake Coverage (ABC & CNN)." YouTube video, 2:49:27. Accessed April 27, 2022. https://www.youtube.com/watch?v=Oz3z9b-W2ok.

Anthony Bourdain: No Reservations. Season 5, episode 15, "San Francisco." Aired August 10, 2009.

"A Trip down Market Street Before the Fire, (4K scan, 2018-10-11)." Prelinger Archives. https://archive.org/details/MarketStreet19064KScan20181016.

"Building the Bay Bridge: On Film from the Prelinger Archives." Oakland Museum of California. YouTube video, 24:29. Accessed October 9, 2022. https://www.youtube.com/watch?v=bPeUwA4YtRg.

"Ferry Plaza Farmers Market Ribbon Cutting Ceremony, April 26, 2003." Foodwise. YouTube video, 2:16. Accessed October 11, 2022. https://www.youtube.com/watch?v=NlA3ravEPhA.

"Herb Caen Day." YouTube video, 49:31. Accessed October 9, 2022. https://www.youtube.com/watch?v=A7IKfqI4594.

"Mabel and Fatty Viewing the World's Fair at San Francisco, Cal." Library of Congress Motion Picture, Broadcasting and Recorded Sound Division, video, 19:06. https://www.loc.gov/item/00694430.

"Maltese Falcon, the (1931) (Movie Clip) Her Name's Wonderly." Turner Classic Movies, 3:09. Accessed October 9, 2022. https://www.tcm.com/video/1312460/maltese-falcon-the-1931-movie-clip-her-names-wonderly.

Reynolds, Malvina. "Cement Octopus." Omni Recording Corporation. Released December 16, 2007. YouTube video, 2:56. https://www.youtube.com/watch?v=dKqZmYE-yI8.

Somebody Feed Phil. Season 4, episode 10, "San Francisco." Aired October 30, 2020.

INDEX